Dean 2016
(April Fool's Day
present!)

Pulsation

Pulsation

*From Wilhem Reich to
Neurodynamic Psychotherapy*

Seán Haldane

PARMENIDES

Printed and Bound in Great Britain by
TJ International Ltd, Padstow, Cornwall

Cover design by Bite Design, Cork

ISBN: 978-0-9574669-2-0 (Paperback)
978-0-9574669-3-7 (E-Book)

CONTENTS

Atmospheric pulse waves. Pulse waves over the
ocean. Hearing pulse waves. Rainbows and clouds.
Atmospheric 'rain'. Apparent oscillation of the moon.
Atmospheric oscillation, not pulsation. The aurora
borealis. The auroral sub-storm. The magnetosphere.
Cosmic superimposition. The auroral streams.
Auroral pulse waves.

ACKNOWLEDGMENTS

My journey in the understanding of pulsation has been complex. I can only list those who have taught me or helped me out at various stages, in approximately chronological order across 40 years:

Adolph Smith, biophysicist; Jean Ambrosi, psychoanalyst; Marie-Christiane Beaudoux, psychologist; Jack Marvin, psychologist; Jack Kornfield, psychologist; Myron Sharaf, psychologist; Léo Dubord, psychotherapist; Richard Farson, psychologist; Ghislaine Lanteigne, sociologist; Bernd Laska, philosopher; Jerome Eden, weather engineer; Michael Rothenberg, paediatric psychiatrist; Martin Seymour-Smith, poet and polymath; David Henry, psychotherapist; Andrew Silver, film-maker; Kay Collis, psychologist; Derek Carroll, physician; Gerd Bergerson, textile designer; David Stove, philosopher; Jaak Panksepp, neuroscientist; Nigel Parker, osteopath; Julian Barbour, physicist; Frank Röhricht, psychiatrist; Stuart Brody, psychologist; Mathias Grote and James Strick, historians of science.

I especially acknowledge the plain-speaking help I received in the later stages of writing this book from my old friend Daniel Schiff, psychologist, and from James DeMeo, geo-physicist, who have both laid themselves on the line in carrying forward Wilhelm Reich's controversial work. And the conclusions of this book owe much to my collaboration over the past 10 years with my friend and colleague Jose Ignacio Xavier, neuro-psychiatrist.

I also want to thank my patients/clients in psychotherapy and in neuropsychology who cannot be named but from whom I have learned much about human pulsation.

INTRODUCTION

This book collects essays and notes written over a long period, between 1977 and 2013, as I returned in different contexts to this book's core subject, pulsation. The work of Wilhelm Reich has been essential in my study of pulsation, since he first made it definitive of life, and my initial training as a psychotherapist was in Reich's methods. My thinking since 1985 or so when I undertook a deliberate re-evaluation of Reich's work has been based in my own view of pulsation.

In another book, *Time / No Time*, I explore the paradox of time and timelessness in poetry and physics. I suggest that our sense of time in a timeless universe is intrinsic to our experience as pulsating organisms in a universe of pulse-waves. (Several pages in Chapter 3 of this book which discuss the distinction of 'unequal phase' pulsation from 'equal phase' pulse-waves are common to both books.) My theme is the everyday presence of pulsation as evidence of life in a universe which is mainly un-alive.

A focus on pulsation can, and I think should, guide any psychotherapy. But more specifically, with a neuropsychiatrist colleague José Ignacio Xavier I have in recent years formulated an approach to 'neurodynamic psychotherapy' such as was first proposed by the grandfather of neuropsychology, Alexander Luria, in 1925 but never realised. This is partly a pulsation therapy. It takes into account current 'affective neuroscience' as well as the work of Reich and his successors in 'orgone therapy', and our own work.

The neuropsychologist Jaak Panksepp in *Affective Neuroscience* and *The Archeology of the Emotions* has brought neuroscience forward from its original emphasis, by Luria and others, on the brain, to a science of the neural network of the whole body. We are not just brains on sticks. The neural network, and for that matter the 'volume transmission' throughout the body of what Candace Pert has called the 'molecules of the emotions', involve not only the Central Nervous System of voluntary action and control, but the Autonomic Nervous System of involuntary action and reaction, in a dynamic system. Modern neuroscience is a science of the body as much as the brain. Neurodynamic Psychotherapy is inevitably 'body-oriented'. And since dynamics itself has in modern physics been established as intrinsically relational – that is a dynamics of interaction in the here and now rather than of historical cause and effect – Neurodynamic Psychotherapy is relational too.

I am sceptical about any model of psychotherapy in which one person is the therapist and the other the patient (or client, or customer). There are brilliant and sensitive psychotherapists, but they are rare, and still more rare are those among them who know how to work with pulsation and the 'character armour' (to use Reich's term) that impedes it. Since the 1980s when I wrote *Emotional First Aid* and *Couple Dynamics* I have favoured a Do It Yourself / DIY approach in which a person can be his or her own therapist, or people in couples can work therapeutically with each other. But this is difficult to put in practice without some guidance, and the human need remains to confide with a specialist (whether, as originally, a shaman or priest, or more recently a psychotherapist) when stuck in an emotional impasse or feeling unable to live fully. A 'supported DIY' therapy for healthy people with a clinical specialist in private practice is feasible. And at the level of public 'mental health' services, at least in the NHS in the UK, there is now a movement towards 'body-oriented psychotherapy' in groups and individually which includes what are in effect Reichian and neurodynamic methods. Unfortunately this knowledge is rare in physical medicine, where an understanding of pulsation and blocks to it may be vital across a wide range of chronic conditions – what Reich called the 'biopathies', meaning illnesses where the person's whole life has in a sense become ill, and biological pulsation is impeded.

Here is a 'thought experiment':

Imagine you are looking out onto a field. Two spherical objects come drifting down through the air and hover above the ground. UFOs? Cosmic jellyfish? They are identical in size and in colour.

The one on the left is repeatedly expanding in size then contracting by about a third, in a steady rhythm of equal phases: 10 seconds to expand, 10 seconds to contract.

The one on the right is also repeatedly expanding in size then contracting by about a third, in a steady rhythm of unequal phases: 5 seconds to expand, 10 seconds to contract.

Which one of them looks alive?

If you look at a baby or a cat sleeping, you can see the pulsation of the breathing as an unequal phase expansion and contraction – shorter in-breath and longer out-breath. If you see a jellyfish in an aquarium pulsating as it moves along, you can note the same unequal phase. It's right in front of you! And in you: just pause for a minute and pay attention to your breathing.

This book aims to place pulsation where it belongs, as definitive of life. Understanding our human pulsation has huge implications in understanding issues of health and illness, pleasure and pain, happiness and despair. But understanding how pulsation functions in the context of a non-pulsating universe, and how its presence distinguishes the living from the non-living, also has huge implications in understanding nature at large. I would like to think that this book belongs with what used to be called 'natural history'. It proposes a distinction between pulsation in the living, and 'pulse waves' in the non-living.

This book will discuss Reich's theory of 'life energy', which he called 'orgone energy' – insofar as it is related to pulsation – and offer reasons for rejecting it, while respecting possible evidence of biological and atmospheric 'fields' which suggests that even if the 'orgone' is not life energy, and not life itself, it describes what used to be called the 'aether' in physics and which may, after all, exist as the 'cosmic ocean' of the universe. I support Reich's theory of the function of the orgasm, but I believe this is better expressed in terms of pulsation than in terms of the discharge of 'life energy' or of mechanical tension – what Reich, unnervingly at least to me, called 'sex economy'. Reich thought of calling his body-oriented psychotherapy 'orgasm therapy', but backed off – understandably, since it implied that the therapist might be giving the patient an orgasm. But even in the anything-goes world of 21st century sexuality (so far), in which every variety of sexual activity is open to experiment and discussion, there is a curious lack of focus on orgasm itself. Could it be that what Reich defined as 'orgasm anxiety' still exists?

I am not a biologist, I am a naïve observer – with my own eyes, occasionally supplemented by microscopes or telescopes or binoculars. My observations of people in the context of psychotherapy or in neuropsychology clinics are less naïve – and perhaps not naïve enough, in that I have had to work within accepted clinical frameworks. I can offer no authoritative analysis in biochemistry or biophysics, although I can in psychology and neuroscience. Insofar as I am capable of thinking for myself, this is not rooted in any academic discipline, but in my personal experience.

In the first chapters of this book the distinction between equal phase oscillation (non-life) and unequal phase pulsation (life) is explored on the microscopic level of observations of protozoa, on the macroscopic level of the aurora borealis, and on the human and animal levels somewhere in between. Pulsation cannot be defined without a discussion of what is *not* pulsation – what I distinguish as 'pulse-waves' whether in solutions containing pulsating micro-organisms, in the atmosphere surrounding us pulsating humans, or the cosmic ocean.

In later chapters the book turns to human pulsation, especially as experienced or blocked in orgasm, and to neurodynamic psychotherapy. I set out a framework for this therapy, and provide instructions for do-it-yourself work, for individuals and couples.

Note: I invite the reader to feel free to read the chapters of this book in any order. For readers who are interested mainly in neurodynamic psychotherapy, chapters 1, 3, 7 and 8 will be of most interest. For readers interested mainly in the biophysics of pulsation, then chapters 2 to 6 will be of most interest.

However the biophysics and the neurodynamic psychotherapy are related, in that an exploration of pulsation is common to both. We are the fish, as it were, in the cosmic ocean. We are alive, our environment is not. But we need to know where, as well as how, we live.

1

HUMAN PULSATION

The first scientist to identify pulsation as a basic life function was the psychiatrist Wilhelm Reich. My psychology PhD dissertation, *Human Pulsation*, 1977, focused on Reich's theory that the opposing branches of the Autonomic Nervous System mediated alternating expansion and contraction of the organism in relation to the world. But neither Reich nor I had realised that pulsation in a living organism is not merely alternating expansion/contraction, as in the oscillation of a pendulum, of the earth's atmosphere, or of energetic pulses in electromagnetic fields or sound waves. These are all 'equal phase' (sine waves). In the living organism, pulsation, as in the propulsive movement of a jellyfish, the beating of a heart, or breathing in and out, is 'unequal phase': an expansion is followed by a slower contraction.

Reich had identified expansion/contraction in the universe at large as pulsation, and this led him into a vision of the entire cosmos pulsating with 'orgone energy.' But the universe does not pulsate. Only living organisms do. Nevertheless there is a relation between the non-living pulse waves of the universe at large and the living pulsation of organisms: in organisms the pulse waves are enclosed in a membrane whose resistance to the universal pulse waves forms pulsation. Reich approached this in a distinction between 'closed orgone' and 'open orgone', but still assumed universal pulsation.

Reich's huge claims for 'orgone energy' and his terminology, arrived at in a period when he was adapting to English after forty years of German, can be off-putting for the modern reader. His 'orgone accumulators', following a parody of them by Woody Allen as 'the orgasmotron' in a 1970s film, *The Sleeper*, are usually a subject of ridicule. The faithful publisher of most of Reich's books, Farrar Straus & Giroux, in 2011 surprisingly published the journalist Christopher Turner's *Adventures in the Orgasmotron* which offers a character assassination of Reich and an extended jeer at his work about which Turner, although he does a good job with social-historical details, shows next to no knowledge. It is hard to break out of a vicious circle where Reich is derided as crazy and where scientists and clinicians who are interested in his work tend to become defensive or secretive and disinclined to subject his theories even to constructive criticism. His psychiatric followers in the USA, the 'orgonomists', tend to circle their wagons (in two main factions) and to issue statements which reflect an official line. Nevertheless they and their non-medical associate the geophysicist James DeMeo continue to replicate some of Reich's biophysical work, and there are a few capable and dedicated 'orgonomic therapists'.

The French writer Michel Leiris in *La Littérature comme Tauromachie* compares the writer to a bullfighter who in getting as close as possible to the bull has to run not only the risk of getting injured or killed, but the deadly risk of being ridiculed if he has to make a dash for it or commits a pratfall. The fear of ridicule is a powerful incentive to keep our heads down and avoid any dangerous truth.

Outside the Anglo-American world, however, there seems to be less fear of ridicule. In 2005 I gave a paper on Neurodynamic Psychotherapy at the annual conference of the German Society for Psychosomatic Medicine where Reich's ideas were very much evident, and there is a particularly lively Reichian and 'post-Reichian' clinical scene in Brazil. Reich's work still has a long way to run.

I reject Reich's theory of 'cosmic orgone energy' since it offers no distinction between life and non-life. However there are many unexplained field phenomena in living organisms and the atmosphere, and I discuss some of them in this book. Above all I am grateful to Reich for identifying pulsation as the basic life function. An understanding of this function opens new ways to work with human health and illness, and to discover the relation of us humans with the world. I agree with the philosopher Robert Corrington that Reich was above all a great naturalist. Since reading his books and having trained in and practised his methods of therapy, I think I see *nature* more clearly.

In the long run, I think, Reich's observations will prove more durable than his theories. In this way he is like Darwin. Darwin's theory of natural selection has recently come in for a terrible pasting at the hands of logical philosophers. The theory simply does not stand up since it relies on *post hoc* conjectural chains of cause and effect, not on the statement of workable natural laws. Darwin's big error was to equate natural selection with the artificial selection of stock-breeding, which requires interventions by a planning mind (the stock- breeder's) which are not available in wild nature. David Stove's *Darwinian Fairytales* and Jerry Fodor's and Massimo Piattelli-Palmarini's *What Darwin Got Wrong* do conclusive demolition jobs on Darwin's theory and on the teleological burbling of such putative successors as Richard Dawkins. (The teleology – ascribing 'purpose' to everything from genes and bacteria upwards – stands in for the mind of the stock-breeder). Stove died before Fodor and Piattel-Palmarini's book came out, and his approach was very different, but these two books form a pincer movement on the flaws in 'natural selection' and I doubt whether anyone who has carefully read both books can continue to believe in it. Furthermore recent research in genetics (see Spector's *Identically Different*) has done another demolition job on natural selection by demonstrating that genes only operate if permitted to do so by 'epigenetic' factors influenced by the environment, and these epigenetic factors can in turn be inherited. This research threatens a return of the dreaded Lamarckian 'inheritance of acquired characteristics' – a heresy in the religion of evolutionism.

All the same, Darwin's bold assertion that we are 'descended from the apes', as the horrified Victorians put it, changed the world. Actually the fossil evidence was already there, but Darwin had the guts (and he suffered from a probably psychosomatic gut illness) to state his conclusions. His writings as a historical narrative of evolution are irreplaceable, and his observations (some of them, such as in his work with barnacles and plants, overshadowed by his natural selection theory) will be invaluable into the foreseeable future. It takes courage to *observe* outside the box of one's contemporaries. Both Darwin's and Reich's diaries express the anguish of the observer of things nobody else wants to see.

Given Reich's scandalous reputation, it may seem absurd to compare him with Darwin. And his theory of 'orgone energy' not only needs modification, as does natural selection, it does not, in my view, hold up. However I don't reject Reich's *observations*. Like Darwin he made them courageously and alone. They are replicable. And they can inform a research programme for years to come.

This study of pulsation would be impossible without frequent reference to Reich, as well as to other scientists, philosophers and, dare I say it, poets.

And since I owe my subject to Reich, I am going to start this book with a brief autobiographical history of my involvement with his work.

I first came across references to Reich in 1969 in the novels and essays of Norman Mailer whose focus on total orgasm as a sign of freedom and independence chimed in with my own rather rebellious attitude. This had never been a political rebellion, since growing up in Northern Ireland with its unsolvable conflicts, then going to Oxford during the Cuban missile crisis which was met with hysterical demonstrations for nuclear disarmament, had disillusioned me with any kind of politics. For me independence was linked to my experience of an intensely physical sexual relationship in my teens against the background of hypocritically Puritan but violent Belfast, with a girl of German Jewish origin most of whose family had been killed in the concentration camps. I had been brought up with what Reich would have called a 'sex positive' attitude. My mother came from an Anglo-European family of humanists, she was an agnostic, and she was always ready, although never stickily, to talk to me openly about love and sex if I asked. I had been born in Sussex during the war and I did not meet my father until he came back from the army when I was 2 ½. Until then I lived in a benign matriarchy: my mother (who was aged 19 when I was born), my unconventional painter grandmother, and my gentle grandfather who taught me boys' things like playing cricket with a miniature bat he had made for me. My mother had read Margaret Mead's *Coming of Age in Samoa*, so I was allowed to run naked in the sun. Like many other war babies during a shortage of food, I was breast-fed for a year. When my father arrived he was at first something of a nervous wreck ('shell-shock') and a disciplinarian, having commanded hundreds of soldiers, and my idyll was interrupted for the first time by authority, especially when we went to live in Northern Ireland close to his much more conventional family. I suppose this set a pattern in me of feeling securely loved and at the same time threatened by and rebelling against any constriction. But eventually my father reverted to his normal cheerful attitude of 'live and let live.' Although he occasionally went to church he thought for himself and he never forced religion on his family. When I was 18 and my girlfriend's father came to him indignantly complaining about our relationship, my father politely told him that I was old enough to look after my own life. I also realised at about that time, from the poems that sprung out of the relationship, that I was, unavoidably, a poet – although I was shy of calling myself one.

I studied English at Oxford. It was then heavily linguistic and historical, and luckily avoided mention of any literature after 1900: 'value judgments' were disparaged, so we did not have to waste our time arguing about what writers we liked or disliked, we were just expected to know everything possible about the language they used and their historical circumstances. Values were expressed outside the curriculum, and Robert Graves who was then Professor of Poetry (a five year post for distinguished outsiders) discussed them vigorously. When I met him, he gave me his blessing, as it were, in a crucial and very open conversation about poetry. He was, with Hardy, one of the great love poets in English of the 20th century, and I lost some of my instinctive shyness about the celebration of sexual love in my poems.

By the time I came across Reich's work I was aged 26 and after a few turbulent years in America and Europe I was living with my second wife, her daughter, and our baby daughter, on a farm in Ladysmith, Quebec. I was teaching English reluctantly, part time, at Carleton University in Ottawa, 50 miles away mainly via dirt roads. We were doing 'back-to-the-land' farming (we had a huge vegetable garden, we kept chickens and ducks, we tapped maples, I felled trees, planted new ones, and sold lumber, I mowed fields and ran cattle on them) and we had started a small poetry publishers, The Ladysmith Press. Our love relationship was, at the time, intense. When I turned to Reich's *Character Analysis* and *The Function of the Orgasm* I found it easy to accept their views. Reich's description of the orgasm pulsation broadly matched my own experience, but I realised that I tended to control my breathing by tightening my abdominal muscles just before the moment of climax. I was able to stop doing this, once I was aware of it, and to 'surrender', as Reich put it, to the 'orgasm reflex', a repeated convulsion of the whole body with the out-breaths at climax. My sensations intensified and at last I felt strong emotion along with the sensations. (They must have been slightly detached from each other). I had always, I suppose because of my 'sex positive' upbringing and the extreme excitement and intensity of my first sexual relationships, been able to rejoice in what Reich called the 'streaming' sensations in sex, which can cause anxiety in some people and are suppressed by the 'character armour' anchored in their musculature, or by cutting contact as excitement mounts. Without much critical analysis I accepted easily enough Reich's idea that the 'streamings' were the flow of life energy in the body, although I disliked his term for this energy, 'orgone', which made me think of hormones. It was an example of a major problem with Reich, which for then I was able to side-line since I could read *Character Analysis* in German: the problem being that most of Reich's work is translated into English where it sounds unnatural and ponderous compared to the German.

Similarly, the English speaking world is condemned to a version of Freud derived from Ernest Jones's absurd pseudo-scholastic translations of Freud's down to earth *Es* (*It*), *Ich* (*I* or, in effect, *Self*) and *Ueber-Ich* (*Over-I* or *Over-Self*) into the *Id, Ego,* and *Superego.* When Reich came to America in 1937 he felt scorched by his experiences in Europe where colleagues had let him down, and his relationships even with supporters became formal. I suppose no-one dared to sit him down and say 'Look, Willy, your terminology sounds un-English, and we don't like acronyms except for names of organisations. Furthermore your translator isn't a native English speaker. A "plague" is something external, like a plague of mosquitoes, or when it's internal it usually kills you: the word can't be used for a chronic condition.' So Reich's followers were saddled with OR (orgone) DOR (deadly orgone), ORANUR (orgone in contact with nuclear radiation), EP (emotional plague), and eventually such monstrosities as HIG (hooligan in government) which even the (genuinely) loyal 'orgonomists' leave on one side. But they seldom question Reich's basic terms as translated into English by Theodore Wolfe. As Graves wrote in a poem: 'Little children, parasites, and God may flatter me with complete agreement.' Reich did not deserve such agreement from his followers, but towards the end of his life, under much persecution, he abused them if they disagreed. (Bernard Grad, a professor of biology at McGill University, Montreal, who worked with Reich at this time remembered being accused of having 'emotional plague' if he dared to argue.)

For a while my Reichian reading (though not the acronyms!) influenced my poems – e.g. in a sequence called 'The Ocean Everywhere' – to the extent that an astute friend said they were becoming didactic: I was putting across a message. I also discussed Reich briefly in a short book of essays, *What Poetry Is*. But something was going wrong. First in my marriage (but I am not going to discuss this here), then in my working life. I had stopped teaching at Carleton in 1970. Luckily I had been able to avoid teaching poetry there (I didn't believe in teaching poetry), but English 101 with the ignorant but patronising students was a farce. ('A very perceptive analysis', a student politician once remarked condescendingly in one of my classes.) And the place was rife with a new Canadian nationalism, meaning that teachers from the UK or especially the US, were given a hard time, and this nationalism was also creating something called 'Canlit' ('Canadian Literature') which meant the Ladysmith Press, which published poets we liked irrespective of nationality, was being squeezed out by other presses which took government grants for publishing Canadians. We didn't take grants, on principle, and just about broke even. My poems, also, were becoming more rare and somewhat prosaic – drying up, in fact. Always restless, I began to feel impatient with poetry for the fact that I was dependent on waiting for it to occur, with what I now saw as a kind of Keatsian passivity. I wanted to *do*! I was liking the world and people around me less and less and I wanted to change them! I began to think of studying medicine then training to become a Reichian psychiatrist. Then a bookseller in Montreal who had read *What Poetry Is* said there were some 'Reichians' in Montreal, and put me onto a Professor of Physics at Sir George Williams University (now Concordia) called Adolph Smith.

Adolph had been born in Lower East side New York in 1928 – a few years before Hitler gave 'Adolph' a bad name. Adolph's Jewish immigrant parents had not yet heard of Hitler… In Montreal he had been in therapy with a French psychoanalyst, Jean Ambrosi, who had been trained by Jacques Lacan in France but since coming to Montreal had trained in Gestalt therapy and 'Bioenergetics', an athletic form of Reichian therapy (it used pre-set exercises and 'stress positions') devised by a gym teacher turned psychiatrist, Alexander Lowen, who had trained in Reich's 'orgonomic therapy' then moved on. Everyone moved on in the 1970s, from one thing to another. The orgonomists were centred in New York, were all psychiatrists and were not open to training non-medical therapists. I now realised that a broadly Reichian training could be obtained from various sources, and that I could become a semi-regulated 'psychotherapist' or possibly a regulated clinical psychologist.

Adolph had completed therapy in New York with one of Reich's most orthodox colleagues, Chester Raphael. (But they were all orthodox and it was clear from their *Journal of Orgonomy* that they tolerated not the tiniest disagreement with Reich's findings, although given Reich's fate their embattled 'with us or against us' stance was comprehensible.) Adolph assured me that Ambrosi's Reichian 'body-work' (a phrase that always makes me think of car repair workshops) was not very different from Raphael's and more sensitive since he brought in other methods. I began weekly therapy with Ambrosi, in French, and although his methods were indeed eclectic (linguistic analysis from Lacan, 'owning your projections' from Perls's Gestalt therapy, bioenergetic exercises, hypnotism), he was a very sensitive worker with the breathing, expression of emotions, and the systematic working through the 'segments' of 'body armour' until spontaneous pulsation occurred. And he did not back off from sexual issues. Interestingly, he thought that since I was obviously at ease with the Reichian work, I shouldn't be afraid of using my brains on good old fashioned psychoanalysis. But I didn't buy into this, having a prejudice against Freud since reading his ridiculous attempt at anthropology in *Totem and Taboo* from my father's bookshelves. Furthermore my deepest experiences in therapy with Ambrosi were through the 'body-work'. In this, the patient lies on his or her back on a mat and is encouraged to intensify the breathing and any emotional expression that may occur. The therapist may listen and talk, but also intervenes through touch, pressing on or manipulating the body to enable the letting go of muscular 'blocks' to full breathing and spontaneous movement. In particular, Ambrosi helped me work through a degree of 'eye blocking': I found it hard to feel or express fear or anxiety through my eyes. Imaginatively (but I think I had mentioned I was afraid of fire), he decided to light a candle on a shelf in a darkened room and have me breathe in fully while opening my eyes wide and looking at the candle. I flipped into a terrified re-living of an incident when I was aged about two (I later checked the details with my mother). In our ancient country house during the war we had no flush lavatories, only a chemical lavatory in a room with no electricity. My mother would take me in there, setting a candle on a wall shelf. On one occasion as she bent down to wipe my bottom her golden hair caught alight in the flame of the candle. She shrieked and beat the flames out. There was a strong smell of burning hair. I relived all this – an example of the kind of memory which seems locked into the body and which is often released in Reichian therapy. (In fact it is not locked into the body but the brain: 'muscle memory' is a two way street in which stimulation of the brain can cause muscular sensation and vice versa: brain and body are all part of the 'neural network.') This reliving is a sort of exorcism, but it can help open a person up. The way I looked at the world changed somewhat: the muscles around my eyes were more mobile There had, I realised, been a dead area of my cheeks below my eyes, giving a slightly sad expression which now disappeared. I felt my gaze was more focused.

When I breathed out fully in therapy my body would convulse in the pulsations of the 'orgasm reflex', but this does not mean I had an orgasm in the therapy, although I occasionally felt an undirected sexual excitement, along with 'streamings.' Luckily my 'armour' against the reflex was minimal. The orgasm reflex – in the presence of contact (i.e. the person is aware of the therapist's presence and not cutting off) – is the 'test' that the therapy is working. No wonder Reich's methods cause anxiety – even talk of them. In the usual jungle-drums process, by the time the orgasm reflex is explained along a chain of a few people it has become clear that Reichian therapists give people orgasms...

This being the 1970s, individual therapy every week was accompanied by monthly or fortnightly group sessions. As in almost all therapy groups I ever attended (or ran in my later work) most participants were 'therapists' of all stripes – psychologists, medical doctors, clinical social workers, counsellors. There was much public expression of emotion, many new relationships were formed (and consummated off-stage, as it were), and there was a lot of discussion of how one perpetuated society's oppression by oppressing oneself. Personal liberation would become social/political liberation. (Given the context, this involved the political independence of Quebec, but as mentioned earlier, my growing up in Belfast had immunised me against political activism. I put up with mildly racist teasing about being a 'tête carrée' – a 'square head', meaning an English-speaking Canadian).

Although Ambrosi used Reich's methods, he had formulated a strong critique of all emotionally cathartic therapy as exorcism. He thought it was easy enough to cast out a devil through emotional abreaction – but the devil would come back next day. (He eventually spelled this out in a book, *L'analyse psycho-énergétique* in which there is a description of how he performed just such a temporary exorcism on a Corsican villager.).

During my two years of working with Ambrosi I did an 'internship' at a psychotherapy centre 'Associates for Human Resources', AHR, in Boston. There I worked with various other psychotherapists. I had also started a private practice part time in 'counselling' in Ottawa, so I had 'clients' to discuss. I wrote a paper on a frightening spontaneous exorcism of a client, and curiously the AHR faculty member who was most helpful and sensitive in understanding it was not a Reichian at all, but a Buddhist therapist, Jack Kornfield, who went on to become one of the founders of modern 'Mindfulness' therapies (now popular even in the British NHS). Kornfield was doing an external doctorate in psychology at Saybrook Institute (then Humanistic Psychology Institute, and later to become Saybrook University) in San Franciso, and he put me onto this. Between 1974 and 1977 I shuttled back and forth to San Francisco and worked under 'field faculty' in various settings, including the Child Study Centre of Ottawa University (to learn about childhood development) and its nursing faculty (to learn anatomy and physiology), to complete my dissertation on *Human Pulsation.* My main supervisor was Richard Farson, at Saybrook, a hard-nosed but unconventional psychologist who with Carl Rogers had co-founded Western Behavioural Sciences Institute in San Diego. He was something of a rebel and wrote a book, *Birthrights,* on children's liberation, but he eventually became an organisational psychologist and witty promoter of paradox. Farson had no particular respect for Reich's work and his insistence on psychological rigour was invaluable, although it required re-writing my dissertation twice. My other supervisors were Adolph Smith to help with the biophysics and physiology, and Myron Sharaf, a professor of psychology and psychiatry at Tuft's university in Boston who had studied with Reich and eventually wrote his biography, *Fury on Earth.* (My external examiner was Michael Kahn, a social psychologist at the University of Southern California).

During most of this period I travelled down to Boston one weekend a month to do seminars on orgonomy with Sharaf and to discuss my dissertation. The practical side of the seminars was in the usual 1970s therapy groups, as with Ambrosi's – about a dozen people in their bathing suits or underwear subjecting each other to various bodily therapy sessions under Sharaf's supervision. (Even now I sometimes pick up a journal article by some distinguished and respectable psychiatrist or psychologist and my mind flashes back to Boston in 1975 or so and the person in their underwear shaking their fists at the ceiling or calling for Mommy). This free-for-all would have had Reich turning in his grave, and in fact Sharaf's ambivalence towards Reich was all too evident. He liked to quote Jung to the effect that the therapist was 'the wounded wounder', and there was always a sense of wallowing in pain and struggle in his work. He was a brilliant expounder of Reich's ideas while undermining them at every turn.

Sharaf's ambivalence was understandable. His first wife, Grethe Hoff, had at one point left him for Reich. In the madness of Reich's later years, as revealed in the later publication of his journals, his love for Grethe shines out as the last bastion of sanity and love.

Although having worked with Sharaf I can claim the magic laying on of hands that is so often treated with reverence in psychoanalytic circles – 'I worked with Myron, and he worked with Reich' – and although he was supportive of me in his own way (i.e. he understood and undermined me at the same time, as with Reich), I cannot say I was deeply affected by him, as I was by my work with Ambrosi (who had his own faults of Corsican rhodomontade). Not that I am eager to claim another magic laying on of hands from Lacan via Ambrosi…

Sharaf, the wounded wounder, emphasised his flaws in a rather masochistic way – although, confirming Reich's concept of masochism as containing sadism, this emphasis was used to provoke others to reveal *their* flaws. As Reich wrote, masochism is 'suffering used as a weapon.' Obviously, I found myself thinking, Reich had not cured Myron. Perhaps this was another source of Myron's ambivalence. Actually Reich in his later years wrote that it was impossible to straighten a tree that had grown crooked. He knew his own therapy had its limits, and even in his early 'Sexpol' work in Germany had focused on prevention of the 'character armour' forming, before it was too late. But his therapy aroused expectations. How about 'orgastic potency' as a goal?

I had seen Dusan Makewejew's film on Reich, *W.R. Mysteries of the Organism,* in the Black Cat pornographic cinema in Hull, Quebec (across the river from Puritan Ontario where the film was banned.) Sharaf appears in it, showing an orgone accumulator to his son. 'Fuck freely', a woman's voice intones to a background of slides ostensibly (but not) from Reich's Sexpol movement in 1930s Germany. Reich had prophesied gloomily that misinterpretation of his work would lead to 'an epidemic of free fucking'. To my mind, having grown up in Belfast where sex was a secret vice, peeping Toms were rampant as young people attempted to find privacy in alleyways or in the hills around the town, and the place seethed with an almost tribal fear and hatred exploited by politicians, Sexpol was one of Reich's greatest achievements. 'Make love, not war! would be an oversimplified slogan of the 1970s, but before this in my second serious love relationship my girlfriend was from a Catholic background, the other side of the socio-political barriers from me, and we found there were no psychological or emotional barriers between us at all, although our angry and Puritanical 'communities' hated each other. Reich had hoped that providing contraception and sexual encouragement and advice to young people would stop them getting sucked into fascism. (His book *The Mass Psychology of Fascism* is still valid in 2013, allowing for changes in context).

As for the orgone accumulator (known in yet another acronym as an ORAC) I had been doing some experiments with one I had constructed, making its walls out of layers of sheet metal and fibre glass, in a barn in a gloomy November. After a few days of building it, even before I put the walls together, I felt a warm glow in my face and had developed a suntan. There was 'something in it'. For a year or so Adolph visited regularly from Montreal and we replicated some of Reich's experiments.

Adolph was another person who had not been 'cured' by orgonomic therapy – or not totally. His breathing was often obstructed by chronic asthma. But he was one of the most sparkling and alive people I had met. A New York Jew, he had triumphantly married a blonde blue-eyed German nurse and they had sons whom they were bringing up 'free', along A S Neill's Summerhill School principles. (Neill was one of only a few friends of Reich who had been able to speak to him fearlessly). Adolph had done a PhD in the biophysics of electromagnetism so as to ascertain whether it was identical with the orgone. It wasn't. But Adolph was no more certain than I – and a lot less certain than Reich – about what orgone actually was. As a true experimentalist, he was a sceptic – even about the work of his colleague Bernard Grad who had lost his position as a biology professor at McGill (although he retained tenure) for experimenting with mice in accumulators. Adolph and I found it hard to replicate the famous T-To experiment which Reich had demonstrated to Einstein who seemed at first impressed but who cut contact with Reich. In T-To a thermometer suspended above an accumulator box shows almost 1 degree C higher temperature than a thermometer above a dummy control box. This defies the second law of thermodynamics. Given temperature variation in a room, the experiment is difficult to control, and by the 1970s various attempts at replication had been inconclusive, even those by orgonomists. Their own worst enemies, some of them rejected double-blind controlled experiments because these don't allow for the character structure of the observer. (Years after the period I am describing, the T-To experiment was carried out more convincingly). Adolph and I did consistently find that our own and others' body temperatures rose by about 0.5 C after a period sitting in the accumulator. 'Suggestion', perhaps. If 'suggestion' produces the thousands of unexpected results in parapsychological and other non-mechanistic research, it is a powerful force indeed. But in fact, as acknowledged even by the most orthodox proponents of scientific method, consistency of observations among different observers is a valid scientific tool.

Reich himself had emphasised that orgone is a *slow* force – unlike electricity. We could demonstrate nothing dramatic about the accumulator. On the other hand, we and most people who sat in it for half an hour or so did feel vagotonic effects (sensations of warmth, relaxation, and sometimes tingling). One woman walking through the room where the accumulator stood (it looked like a cupboard), not knowing what it was, idly stuck her hand in as she went by and withdrew it abruptly exclaiming, 'I got an electric shock!' (She had not touched the accumulator wall, which might have produced a mild shock from static electricity, but there appears to be a relation between static electricity and the field effects Reich ascribed to orgone.)

The most original experiment Adolph and I did with the accumulator was to put a pot of geraniums in it for some hours each day, with a control pot of geraniums kept in the same corner of the room but without the accumulator sessions. We photographed each group with infra-red film which accentuated the evidence that the accumulator group grew somewhat more vigorously. (I have lost our notes, so all I can report is from memory).

Perhaps Reich's most dramatic work was with 'cloud-busters', racks of hollow pipes grounded in running water, directed at the sky to draw off (or in a later theory to shoot) 'energy' in stuck weather such as droughts, and to cause rain. Adolph and I improvised a cloud-buster from some old basement jack poles of tubular steel and grounded them in the River Quyon, at that point a creek meandering across my fields. The weather was sweltering, and eventually it showered, then cleared to a sparkling blue sky with white puffy clouds and a light breeze. No way of proving we had caused it. But I have a Super-8 movie, a few minutes long, showing clouds actually rotating in the sky above the pipes. Do clouds sometimes naturally rotate in this way? I think not. But establishing cause/effect in weather modification is made difficult by rapidly changing conditions. A simple example is the idea, promoted by a mystic called Ivan Saunderson, that if a person stares for a few minutes at a small cumulus cloud, the cloud will dissolve. True. But all small cumulus clouds dissolve after a few minutes, whether stared at or not: they are transitory phenomena.

I bought myself a high resolution microscope and trained myself to use it. I replicated some of Reich's 'bion experiments' in which life seems to emerge as vesicles, then protozoa, from decaying vegetable matter which has been sterilised by boiling under pressure (autoclavation). This is conventionally assumed to be due to 'spores', but how do these survive autoclavation? And whatever their origin, protozoa pulsate.

Adolph and I had, if nothing else, sharpened our powers of observation of nature. As Reich himself noted, seeing and feeling the orgone required practice, a sort of adaptation. This was not self-hypnosis, however. If you open your eyes to seeing light around people you may eventually begin to see it: you are not hurrying along in the everyday whirl. But although Adolph and I were both 'Reichians', and acknowledged that Reich had not been fabricating his data, much of which we could replicate, and we both deduced that there was 'something in' the orgone theory, we remained sceptical enough not to accept it as Reich had proposed it. There were undoubtedly energetic atmospheric and human 'fields' which Reich's devices intensified, but we questioned the idea these were due to a specific 'life energy'.

Our scepticism was added to in conversations with Bernd Laska, who visited us from Germany. He was publishing a Reichian magazine (*WR Blätter* or *WRB*) in which I had published an article on dowsing, another phenomenon which is dismissed by official science (as an 'ideomotor' phenomenon due to self-suggestion) but which is easily experienced: I had dowsed for a well on a hilltop in Quebec with a local dowser and the dowsing fork (cut from a nearby hazel bush) moved so sharply of its own accord as I walked over what turned out to be a vein of water 200 feet below (we drilled a well into it), that it twisted my elbows. Adolph and I had also written a joint article for *WRB* about evidence that the sexual experience of rats could change their endocrine system. There was no need for 'life energy' to explain this kind of biological event which was due to observable and measurable physiological changes (e.g. an increase in the male rats' testosterone levels when they were kept in the company of female rats – a phenomenon measured many years later in human beings).

Bernd was not very interested in Reich's physics but he had studied the Sexpol movement and Reich's socio-political work. (He once remarked grimly, about *The Mass Psychology of Fascism,* that in the last analysis Hitler had turned out to be a more effective social psychologist than Reich.) By that time, my marriage had broken up, and I was living in Ottawa with my new companion/wife and our baby daughter. My new wife was a sociologist, she had read much of Reich's work, and the four of us had discussions I still remember with a feeling of loss: I would say that we all had a respect for Reich's work, a fascination with it, and (except for my wife) a sense of gratitude for it. But none of us was a *follower.* Unfortunately I was to find that as I became a full time Reichian therapist, I was drawn into the 'for or against' position Reich himself had adopted (with some justification given his own life).

Some years later I corresponded briefly with Gerd Bergerson, whom I had known when a boy in Northern Ireland: she was a Norwegian textile designer who had a tweed workshop in the Mourne mountains, an attractive woman with red-brown hair who was flirtatious with my father, to my mother's irritation. The English occultist Colin Wilson had published a mainly inaccurate book about Reich in which he mentioned that Gerd Bergerson had been Reich's love before he left Norway in 1937. I wrote to her (she was then over 80) and she replied warmly, stating among other things: 'I could never have married Reich. He was a fanatic.'

By the time I got my PhD I was calling myself a Reichian therapist. I held back from pursuing registration ('licensing') as a clinical psychologist because I was working in Ontario which did not recognise non-residential doctorates (although mine ticked all the boxes in terms of areas covered), and because I did not want then to conform to the requirements of a professional association. I was based in a psychotherapy centre called 'Uvannik' – another typically 1970s entity – the word being Inuktituk (Inuit – 'Eskimo') for something like 'togetherness.' The various therapists based there fought and intrigued against each other for clients.

Towards the end of my time in Ottawa, while completing my PhD dissertation (for the third time), I did a study of my first 100 clients in therapy. I concluded that 20% made huge improvements, there was a middle 60% who had made some movement but not necessarily achieved any lasting change, and 20% had probably been harmed by the therapy. The trick was, I hoped, to identify through early assessment those who might be harmed.

In 1979 we moved to British Columbia – Vancouver at first, then Victoria. The West Coast was the place to be for psychotherapy of all sorts. In Vancouver I opened an elegant office and announced my arrival with a pamphlet about Reichian therapy to which I attached a short paper about how the therapy worked to enable a more full pulsation of the breathing, via emotional expression, and that one measure of this pulsation was what Reich had called the orgasm reflex. I had applied for a business licence, and was visited by two detectives from the Vancouver police who asked 'How do you give your patients orgasms?' Interestingly, they accepted my explanation about the therapy and I got my license. On the bright side, I had a rush of referrals from the University of BC (UBC) Sexual Dysfunction clinic of their hopeless or unappetising cases – for example a civil servant who was a coprophiliac. (These cases were as hopeless after my treatment as before). I also rapidly built up the usual caseload of psychiatrists and psychologists looking at first for new methods they could use – what Reich called 'picking the cherries from the pie' – in their more conventional practices, then settling in to do some work on themselves. I also began giving courses for UBC on another idea of Reich's, 'Emotional First Aid.'

I didn't want to pick the cherries from Reich's pie and only continue the safe side of his work, and I tend to go to the extremes of any activity, so I eventually entered into correspondence with Jerome Eden, a peripheral writer for the psychiatric *Journal of Orgonomy*, originally from New York but now based in Idaho where he engaged in cloud-busting and according to his books and newsletters waged a ceaseless one man battle against UFOs who were trying to take over the planet. The orgonomists helped finance him, and I suppose it added to their own sense of loyalty to Reich's ideas, but in fact they kept a safe distance, and Jerry, an ex-primary school teacher, had to scrounge a living supply-teaching and by playing his guitar in Idaho bars. I visited him and his wife Desiree several times. Jerry was partly an imitation Reich: stocky, dark, Jewish, uncompromising. He would repeat proudly that he had never known Reich but when he started cloud-busting Reich remarked to an orgonomist with whom Jerry was in therapy, 'This is someone who sticks his neck out.' Jerry was living in a part of Idaho known for its back-to-the land hippies and its Nazis and other right-wingers. He made some of his living rain-making. (Farmers were impressed enough by his results to pay him.) He felt he was a poet and he was close. Once, on a winter night, he pointed out to me that it was already 'snowing' in the room we were in: if I defocused my eyes I could see what appeared like slanted snowflakes in the air. We went outside. Sure enough, it was beginning to snow. Jerry quoted one of his own poems:

> Long before it rains it rains,
> It snows before it snows,
> Long before we die we die,
> And this the body knows.

He was super-sensitive to changes in air and atmosphere. I learned a lot from him about how to *see*. For him, cloud-busting was restoring 'atmospheric pulsation'. By which he meant a sparkle in the air, ripples in the sky, puffing clouds. He was also entirely dogmatic about Reich, taking every word for true, and about UFOs, believing every report of cattle maiming or abduction, supposedly by UFO people, as reported in the *National Enquirer* on sale in his local supermarket. In Reich's last terrible years before being imprisoned because a colleague had transported accumulators across state lines, and having all his books, including psychoanalytic and sociological studies, burned by the Food and Drug Adminstration in an '*auto da fè*' (he died in prison), he had engaged in a battle, using cloud-busters, against a UFO invasion. Jerry was continuing the battle. Reich had proposed that UFOs ran on orgone energy and (paradoxically) transformed it into deadly forms – as if the 'life energy' (orgone or OR transformed into 'deadly orgone energy' or DOR) were a form of petrol that produced pollution. All people concerned by the UFO threat should get together in a 'Planetary Professional Citizens Committee' or PPCC, in which they could exchange information about local atmospheric conditions and UFO interference. I was of course sceptical about UFOs, but with my previous wife in Quebec I had seen unexplained green lights moving oddly in the sky, and I was inclined to believe, as usual, that 'something' was happening. To support Jerry, I got together with a Swiss-American psychologist from California, Roland Frauchiger, who was also a friend of Jerry's, to set up a PPCC in the form of a typed journal (no computers then). But our weather reports respectively from Vancouver Island and California were too mild for Jerry: we were not reporting UFO sightings or effects. We both withdrew from the PPCC, and in my case from friendship with Jerry. I had gone too far. Since I owed so much to Reich, as I saw it, I had been willing to go all the way with his ideas. But I was now in a very embattled, if not paranoid, position. I broke up with my wife and was ready to cast my life to the winds. But suddenly, in this crisis, I began writing poems again. Apart from a brief spurt of poems when I had met my wife, poetry had gone dead for me. I had, I thought, abandoned it. But as an old friend in England, Martin Seymour-Smith, with whom I began a new correspondence at this time, wrote: 'You may have abandoned poetry, but it didn't abandon you.' Martin, as it happened, had written sympathetically but sceptically about Reich, among others, in a now unjustifiably neglected book, *Sex and Society*. Corresponding with him, and more crucially, re-uniting with my wife, put me back on track.

I began to wind down my psychotherapy practice. I wrote two published books, *Emotional First Aid* and *Couple Dynamics* in which I took what I could from Reichian therapy and gave it back to the ordinary person for him or herself to use. The intensity of doing Reichian therapy had been too much for me. The 'transference' issues were too strong. Reich himself had affairs with clients and ex-clients. I was sometimes tormented by the emotional closeness – often spurious – of the therapy. I also became too emotionally close to a few clinicians who did training therapies with me. As Reich wrote agonisingly at one point, 'isn't transference the same as love?' I found that in those cases where the therapy did work it was almost too moving for the therapist, me, and could lead to emotional entanglement. The most practical way to deal with this was to detach myself emotionally – but detachment is not the best thing for the therapy. I found that I was 'burned out'. The few colleagues I felt close to were living far away so there was limited peer support. And where the therapy did not work it was too disappointing and this could do harm. The therapy was not very effective in changing people, as my Ottawa study had showed, unless they were already on the way to change. There were, thankfully, that 20% or so whose emotional and sexual functioning, by their own estimates as well as mine, had become more open, but there were also that 20% who showed deterioration and whose lives became more miserable. So now I proposed, in *Emotional First Aid* (a phrase I owed to Reich who suggested that it would be useful with children) that people could help each other in emotional emergencies by understanding and encouraging a safe emotional expression. In *Couple Dynamics* I proposed a series of exercises that a couple could do together to move towards emotional openness and, yes, shared orgasm. Neither book was a great seller. Both were bought by counsellors and therapists, not the ordinary citizens I and my publishers were hopefully waiting for.

I studied Reich's works again, with a more critical eye than ever, subjecting them to whatever scientific analysis I was capable of. Some of this book derives from my notes at that time.

I finally realised that my research for *Human Pulsation*, and my work with Adolph were so physiologically and neurologically grounded that I was ready to become a neuropsychologist. Neuropsychology is not only about the brain and behaviour, it is about the body and mind. I decided to become an orthodox clinical psychologist/neuropsychologist, and studied for the North American post-doctoral licensing exams (the Examination for the Practice of Professional Psychology or EPPP) which I passed in

Vancouver in 1986. It must have wiped me out, since as I was walking back into the city centre from the examination site a 'hooker' called out to me from an alleyway, 'How would you like me to make you feel like a new man?' But I was already a new man. I became registered in British Columbia and in the Canadian Register of Professional Health Service Providers. I worked at the other end of Canada, in Prince Edward Island, for three years, learning more about community psychology and practical neuropsychology than ever since, then in BC again, then at the end of 1994 I moved back to England to work in the NHS, setting up memory clinics in deprived areas of East London.

I had re-grounded myself in poetry, in my wife and family, and in clinical neuropsychology. But I have never stopped seeing some of the things I saw in my Reichian years, and I still feel I have a debt to pay to Reich – Reich the naturalist.

Adolph, despairing of the rise of Quebec nationalism (which included anti-Semitism) in Montreal, moved to California to work for NASA on their exobiology project, exploring ways of detecting life in soil samples on Mars (and keeping the bions in mind).

In 1990 I was passing through Idaho, on a move from the East Coast back to BC. I stopped in Coeur d'Alene and rang Gerry's number. Desiree answered. 'Gerry's dead. He got skin cancer. He turned black all over. He kept fighting to the end.'

2

VITALISM AND LIFE ENERGY

Vitalism

By the end of the nineteenth century the scientific reduction of life to physical principles was complete. Twentieth century biophysics ('life physics') as explained in a typical textbook (T Hall), concludes that 'all things are composed of matter. The expression of the release and use of energy by living matter is the thing we call "life". And 'when this release and use of energy ceases we call it "death". The energy meant here is chemical, electrical, mechanical, radiant, and atomic. 'Energy can only be measured by its effects on matter.' This means all matter, not simply that matter we call living. 'Energy is independent of life. Life, however, is completely dependent on energy.' And the origin of this life, this particular kind of material structure which can metabolise energy, is in a chance combination of molecules in a primeval 'soup' bombarded billions of years ago by ultraviolet or cosmic rays (the theory of J B S Haldane and A Oparin). Under favourable circumstances this life has replicated itself, with minor changes and adaptations through 'natural selection' – the tautologous doctrine that what best survives, survives – but following the same genetic 'blueprints' until the present. The biophysical vocabulary is derived from mechanical technology: blueprints, programmes, mechanisms, replication, reproduction.

'Vitalism' was a late nineteenth century approach which attempted to read a purposive force into what already seemed a bleak mechanistic view. Georg Stahl, the discoverer of 'phlogiston', a theoretical precursor of oxygen, was an out and out animist. The embryologist Hans Driesch revived Aristotle's concept of 'entelechy' or purposiveness to explain the problem of how cell functions in the embryo are apparently determined not by genetic factors, but by position and pattern. In embryology and cell biology vitalistic ideas still occasionally emerge – to the peril of their protagonists. The 1937 Nobel prize winner Albert Szent-Gyorgyi remarked in the 1950s that for a modern biologist to be thought a vitalist is 'worse than being a Communist'

One of the most lucid exponents of the mechanistic approach, Jacques Monod, in *Chance and Necessity*, maintained that vitalism depends on the existence of still uncovered 'mysteries', but that as mechanistic research reduces the number of such mysteries, the field of vitalistic speculation is also reduced and must eventually disappear. This argument can seem convincing if science is seen as the dispassionate and fair-minded settling of problems. Karl Popper claimed that in science theories, not people, compete; and that whereas in tribal societies the originator of an unacceptable theory might be attacked and killed, now it is the theory that is attacked and modified. Perhaps the last person to be burnt at the stake by the Inquisition on account of a theory was Giordano Bruno. (His heresy was that he believed Jesus's physical presence on earth to have been an illusion, but at the same time he believed the universe was infinite and contained many worlds, in their turn containing living creatures.) Galileo recanted to avoid the same fate.

But now it is mechanistic science, not the church, that refuses to look at certain persistent 'vital' issues. One apologist for modern biology, Peter Medawar, blandly admitted that many theories of science are not refuted by their successors, they are merely 'left behind'.

> The substitution of the structural for the colloidal conception
> of 'the physical basis of life' was one of the great revolutions
> of modern biology; but it was a quiet revolution, for no one
> opposed it, and for that reason, I suppose, no one thought to
> read a funeral oration over protoplasm itself.

Colloids are a solution of microscopic particles and the biology Medawar was referring to studied them with a view to determining whether or not some colloids contained living particles, or were a stage of matter out of which life might emerge – as protoplasm. (See Chapter 4).

Medawar made a lot of capital out of attacking the already moribund vitalistic approach, reading its funeral oration with a certain animus derived from militant atheism. He was the Richard Dawkins of his day. He died of a heart attack *in a church* – which, as the poet Martin Seymour-

Smith wickedly pointed out, was something like when a French Cardinal died, in the same year, in a Marseilles brothel.

Many people when asked to define life would reply in such terms as: excitement, movement, action, feeling, emotion, attraction, or sexuality. They would be describing what *feels* alive. Or if asked to be more objective they would describe what *looks* alive and above all what *moves*: a turtle is alive, a rock is not.

But the sun and planets move – and rhythmically too. Are they alive? Lava moves from a volcano. Is it alive? Common sense denies this. The simplest of dialogues about life and non-life become discussions of *what kind of movement* is characteristic of life. The Greeks in the hylozoic ('matter-life') tradition believed that everything which moved, down to the smallest atom, was alive. God has been seen as the 'Primum Mobile', or Prime Mover. Kepler, like the hylozoists, equated all movement with life and saw even the planets as animated. Modern science denies the planets life and grudgingly allows it to organisms, with the criteria of demarcation being those specific movements called metabolism, irritability etc. – not discussed as movement but in terms of chemical analysis. The results of metabolic 'transport' for example, are analysed chemically and announced to be evidence of life. (This was the principle of the life-detecting devices on the American Viking landings on Mars). But the kind of movement which occurs in this transport is seldom discussed: even analysis of the pumping of lipids across membranes is swiftly reduced to a process of counting molecules. And if we are to believe Richard Dawkins, what we call life is simply the fulfilment of the Selfish Gene's mission to replicate itself, or for DNA to produce more DNA.

But chemistry is the cart, not the horse: science began with observations of movement. The biologist does not look for metabolism in a stone, he or she looks for it in something which initially he or she suspects is alive. The criteria for this suspicion are mysteriously not mentioned. It is as if the movement of life is too crude and obvious to merit scientific analysis. And the researcher often goes so rapidly to the rational debate of 'why' that observation itself is prematurely abandoned unless by the very persistent. The physicist Julian Barbour has remarked that Galileo 'stopped looking for *causes* of motion and instead, like the early astronomers, sought merely to *describe* actually observed motions. He no longer asked: *why* does the stone fall, but *how* does the stone fall?'

The quantum physicist Erwin Schroedinger's last book, *What is Life?* concluded:

> My body functions as a mechanism according to the laws of Nature... Yet I know that I am directing its motions... The only possible inference from these two facts is that I – I in the widest meaning of the word, that is to say, every conscious mind that has ever said or felt 'I' – I am the person, if any, who controls the 'motion of the atoms' according to the Laws of Nature... Consciousness is never experienced in the plural, only in the singular.

Animism

Mae-Wan Ho, in *The Rainbow and the Worm – the Physics of Organisms*, adds to this in defining the self as 'a domain of coherent space-time structure'. However she does not distinguish between life and non-life, even in a worm and a rainbow. In her study, even atoms and molecules are in a sense conscious. She is an animist.

The business of science is to resolve problems of demarcation, to make distinctions, to experiment with processes temporarily isolated from the whole. But if animism is the true position to take about the universe, it and we are all alive. In Thomas Hardy's poems, for example, trees struggle with each other for space like tortured people, and the hills and vales of Wessex become alive. But in science such all or nothing explanations lead to what Popper calls 'essentialism', in circular statements that everything *is*. In one side of Parmenides' vision in his *Peri Physeos / About Nature*, around 500 BC, everything is a material plenum. Over two thousand years later, Berkeley states that everything is *im*material – a huge thought in the mind of God. And one might respond rudely to both with: 'So what?' If *everything* is material or immaterial, or blue, or red, then there is nothing more to say. Once all is God, or as in some New Age thinking all is 'energy', the process of scientific enquiry – or indeed of any thought – must grind to a halt. The synthesis of modern physics and Eastern mysticism much touted in the 1960s and 1970s under the influence of Fritjof Capra's *The*

Tao of Physics merely allowed the mysticism to devour the physics. An anthropologist, Geoffrey Gorer, has remarked that for a tribal African it is self-evident that everything a Westerner considers to be solid and material is a manifestation of spirit. This concept would be welcome in mystical physics, or perhaps to Bishop Berkeley (although I suspect he would want to distinguish God from God's creation: Berkeley was not a pantheist.) It is pure animism. But it creates at least one obvious problem: what about death?

Logically, if everything in the universe is alive, we never die – we just transmute from one state into another. Even better if there is no time: we are simultaneously all the things we ever were or shall be. As Mae-Wan Ho puts it, after a brilliant logical argument (but it depends on David Bohm's interpretation of the quantum wave function as non-collapsible – which is very complicated indeed, and questionable):

> Just as the organism is ever-present to itself during its entire life history, and all other individualities are ever present to it, the universe is ever-present to itself in the universal duration where creation never ceases by the convocation of individual acts, now surfacing from the energy substrate, now condensing to new patterns, now submerging to re-emerge in another guise.

Got it?

Before accepting this 'conscious universe' argument (the ultimate extension of animism where all the individual 'souls' become one universal soul) I think there is the need for a much more concrete and simple discussion about life and non-life. It could be, after all, that the universe consists of living and non-living things, quite distinct from each other.

Life versus Death

The biologist Francois Jacob pointed out that the early definitions of life by vitalists opposed it always to death:

> For Bichat, life is 'the sum of the functions that oppose death';
> for Cuvier, 'the force that resists laws governing inanimate

bodies', for Goethe 'the productive force against action of external elements'; for Liebig, 'the motor force that neutralises the chemical forces, cohesion and affinity acting between molecules.'

Jacob cites an early encyclopedia definition of life as 'the opposite of death.' This is maintained in modern definitions. The Oxford English Dictionary defines life as: 'animated existence. Opposed to *death*.' American Heritage Dictionary: 'the property or quality manifested in functions such as metabolism, growth, response to stimulation, and reproduction, by which living organisms are distinguished from dead organisms or from inanimate matter.'

Monod pursued a distinction between a 'metaphysical vitalism' such as that of Bergson, and a 'scientific vitalism' such as that of Polanyi, which depends on the shrinking area of 'mysteries' unsolved by mechanistic science. Animism too can be pursued from a metaphysical or a scientific point of view. Monod considers Teilhard de Chardin to be similar to Bergson in taking off from an evolutionistic initial position, but becoming animistic in his ascription of life properties to the whole universe, from elementary particles through to galaxies: 'there is no *inert* matter, and therefore no essential distinction between matter and life.'

Monod surprisingly but aptly exposes the animistic basis of Marxist dialectical materialism: the whole universe is seen as material, including humanity, but its laws nevertheless inexorably fulfill an 'evolutionary project' for humanity, in which the 'animistic projection' can be recognized, even if in disguise. Monod could have added that the tyranny of materialism (with its iron laws of history' and such leaders as Stalin, the 'man of steel') can be as bad as the longer known tyrannies of religious idealism: each holds organic life in contempt. A group of poets (Riding, Graves, Kemp) wrote in 1937 of 'that materialism which is a refusal to be impressed by matter', and 'the savage attack on matter which has produced modern material comfort. An aeroplane is, for example, the result of a contempt for the physical universe.' The modern invention of nuclear warheads emphasizes their point. The science of materialism at its logical extreme is a science of the *destruction* of matter and of that natural organisation of matter called life.

Vitalism was at its most mystical where it tried, in a world in which reason had deposed God, to rehabilitate him in the form of an organising principle which operates purposively. If life is operating according to some purposeful plan, the plan might as well be called 'God.' But not all vitalism has been based on concepts of purpose. Henri Bergson, as Monod admits, rejected the idea of 'final causes.' But he replaced it with an 'élan vitale', a turbulent flux of time as humanly experienced. This time flux becomes the animating principle of the entire universe, and in the mush of Bergsonian 'intuition' there is no place for demarcation between what is alive and what is not. The distinction between 'lived time' and 'spatialized time' which is basic in Bergson's philosophy is not a distinction between life and death but between two ways of experiencing life. Reich claimed that 'life energy' resolved the conflict between mechanism and vitalism, but this is in fact a combination of the two sides into a form of mechanistic vitalism and also a complete animism: the 'life energy' is discerned everywhere. At the very end of his life this animism becomes apparent, and he writes not only of 'the cosmic ocean' (which may make sense – see Chapter 6) but of the 'cosmic life energy'. But we do not think of a real ocean as being itself alive. We see it as a medium, or a continuum, which contains living creatures. Why should the cosmic ocean be any different?

Life and Energy

The ancient Greek words *psyche, pneuma,* and *thymos,* for different aspects of the soul or mind, the Latin *spiritus* and *anima,* the Sanskrit *prana* and *atman,* and their cognates in other Indo European languages, including the English word *soul,* all originate in words for 'breath'. (For this and other etymologies referred to in this section, see C D Buck, 1949). This breath is often thought of as a divine force, originally breathed *into* us by a God or Gods. But leaving aside religious beliefs which are unlikely to have existed before the words themselves in their ancestral forms came into use, it appears that one simple observation underlies the various concepts which we now associate with the words: that human life is breath.

The English word *life* is rather a special case. With its relatives (e.g. *Leben*) in the Germanic languages it is related to words like *leave* and is thought originally to have expressed the idea of the body being *left* at death. In this stark and minimalist definition, *life* is simply *not death.* In Old English the word *lif* meant usually the (living) *body* (as in the modern

German for body, *Leib*). The word used for life in the sense of *alive* was *cwic* (now *quick*, as in the Anglican Church Creed, *the quick and the dead)* which is related to Greek *bios,* Latin *vita,* Irish *beo* and similar words in most Indo European languages, all of which express life as activity. Similarly the Russian *zhiv*: Pasternak's 'Dr Zhivago' could be rendered in English as 'Dr Lively'.

The word *energy* which has been adopted throughout the Indo-European languages is a more specialised concept, implying force applied to action. It derives from the Greek *energein,* to operate or effect, from *ergon,* activity. *Ergon* and *work* are both derived from the proto Indo-European **werg.* The root *org-* in such words as *orgasm, orgy,* and *organism* also derives from **werg.* Reich derived o*rgone* from this root, and since he had studied some Greek at school it is surprising that he invented such a tautology as *orgone energy.* He might as well have said *energy energy.* Nevertheless *orgone,* in Reich's theory, *works* in organisms and in the atmosphere.

The various *breath* concepts of the soul or mind express something more subjective, and more fundamental: the soul (or the psyche in Greek, the spirit in Latin and taken into English) is often thought even to survive death – even if only as a twittering shade in Hades. *Spirit* retains this survival connotation, as well as the connection with breath (*inspire* and *expire*).

Words reflect underlying realities. If words are not respected, confusion results. It is rife in the 'energy talk', a kind of chatter about 'the energy', that invades informal discussions among scientists and medical people who wish to synthesise science and mysticism (see, for example, *Scientific and Medical Network Journal* 1998). It is worth further sorting out the inter-relations of the words discussed above.

Life and *energy* as defined in Indo-European languages are both levels of movement – the first observable in the movement of the organism itself, the second in the movement of what the organism affects. (Although the concept in physics of a 'wavicle' of matter/energy seems at first schizophrenic, it is logical enough: energy cannot be separated from what produces it, they are linked in the same *motion*.)

The word cluster *psyche/spirit/soul/animate*, referring to *breath* is on another level, however. Although classical mythology came up with personified images for some of these words – for example the spirit as a ghost after death – they express inner, unobservable conditions. They are normally perceived subjectively, and are linked to the sense of *self*. They *move*, but are not observed to move: rather they are *felt* to move, as thought or *emotion* (literally what 'moves out', in being expressed, from the inner self). And as we *feel* the spirit/soul etc., it is a kind of emotion. My book *Emotional First Aid* was translated into German as *Erste Hilfe für die Seele. Erste Hilfe* is, literally, *First Aid. Seele*, for *emotion* is *soul*, but with undertones of mind and self. In neuropsychology one theory (A K Ommaya, 1992) suggests that 'consciousness is a type of emotion.'

Attempts to define 'life energy' and other 'energies' which 'mechanistic science' supposedly ignores usually founder in epistemological confusion. Perhaps the best way out of 'energy talk' is to consult a good etymological dictionary.

Over a hundred terms, from different societies, were claimed by Krippner and White in *Future Science* to describe what they call the 'X-energy' which they maintain produces such phenomena as telepathy and psychokinesis (PK). Polynesians refer to 'mana' which can be transmitted by contact and becomes immanent in objects handled by people. Mana approaches a physical concept of energy, as something which can be 'stored' in objects rather like electricity in a battery. The poet Robert Graves discussed the Moslem 'baraka' and the Bantu 'Muntu' as a 'grace' and a 'vital force' which may be taken on by objects in familiar use. And in the electronic age, words from technology are being co-opted to describe emotional states: 'she turned me on', 'he had good vibes', 'she really gave me a charge', 'I blew my circuits', 'I'm wired'. There is an intuition that when a person is depressed or elated, angry or sad, on form or out of sorts, 'something' is involved which includes more than the specific feeling or sensation. Even Charles Darwin, a rationalist if there ever was, in *The Expression of Emotion in Man and the Animals,* invoked Herbert Spencer's concept of 'nerve force' to explain the fact that emotion could be channelled (a facial expression of grief bringing on a rush of tears), reversed (the fear expression being the opposite of anger) and held back. Darwin's analysis anticipates the repression concepts of Freud and Reich.

The machine picture of the human organism becomes obviously

inadequate when emotion is discussed. We all know we are not machines. Reich, in *The Electrophysiology of Pleasure and Anxiety* suggested that the minute shifts in electrical potential or in chemical balance which occur as an emotion is felt are not adequate to explain the subjective excitation and vigorous expression of the emotion. He asked, crucially, 'What is sensation? How can matter experience itself?' But he ignored a great body of work already in existence which suggested that excitation could be readily explained through the functions of the nervous system – what we would now call the neural network.

In some forms of hypnotism (originally mesmerism) and faith healing, physiological changes are induced deliberately without a person even being touched (unless in the emotional sense). All 'suggestion' – whatever suggestion is. But suggestion can often be ruled out by the ignorance of the subject as to what effect is intended.

Intensive 'body-oriented' psychotherapy provides evidence of similar phenomena. As with Mesmerism, the passing of the hand over a person's body without touching can produce convulsive movements and emotional outbursts. The reader can experiment with this by lying down with the eyes closed and having a friend pass their hand along different parts of the body an inch or so above the skin, never touching, but allowing the hand to pause for a few minutes at a time above a few sensitive spots such as the forehead, the throat, between the navel and the ribs (over the autonomic plexus) and the genitals. You will probably be able to tell where your friend's hand is – with a sensation of what seems more than simply warmth or disturbance of the air.

This evidence supports the concept of some kind of life *field* in which contact at a distance is felt. But – and this must be emphasised – this is not necessarily evidence for some kind of *life energy*. Of course the word *energy*, along with 'vitality', 'vigour', 'liveliness' etc., expresses the subjective sense of containing the capacity for movement (work). But it is an imitation of physics to describe emotional excitation or tingling sensations as 'energy'. Indeed the word is usually only used in these senses by adepts of neo-Reichian or 'bioenergetic' therapy and those people to whom this concept has filtered through. Some adepts have become incapable of identifying their feelings by such ordinary words as 'excitement', 'tingling', 'warmth', 'anxiety', 'butterflies in the stomach', or 'shuddering'. Everything has become reduced to 'energy' ('I feel the energy'), as if the person was merely a battery, induction coil, or dynamo. With regard to human experience, at least, 'energy' is a reduction.

The psychologist Cyril Burt (whose work has been discredited, supposedly because of fake reports of test data, but recent findings suggest he was posthumously framed by a rival) remarked concerning the cognitive problem of 'wavicles' in physics:

> A psychologist may be permitted to suggest that the old distinction between matter and energy resulted from the way biological needs determined the evolution of our senses... When seeing light we should at the same time have felt the presence or impact of the photons; and mass and energy would from the outset have been regarded as merely different ways of perceiving the same thing.

Such a view conforms to the animism of modern physics: *everything* is energy/mass. At this point scientific investigation might as well end. But in practice, the energy-mass equation is dismantled in investigations of the interrelations of energy and mass, and they are treated as different states. Are life and non-life, then, merely different states of energy?

If the concept of energy is discarded for a moment, how can the phenomena described earlier be explained in the simplest way? At the least it can be proposed that they are phenomena of *life interacting with life*. There are, of course, human reactions to the intervention of non-life (such as a rock falling on a person who then screams) or of physical energies (e.g. an electric shock). Non-living agents (e.g. a warm bath) can certainly produce pain or pleasure for the living. But these can be easily enough explained in terms of the mechanics of the nervous system.

Apparent action at a distance between two people in the same room but not touching is impossible to explain mechanistically unless gross reductionism is employed. Thus: the energy field of the healer's hands passes into the energy field of the recipient's body, and moves this field (hence the emotional reactions, emotion being merely subjectively perceived movement of energy) or re-channels it. In such a view, emotions are reduced to physics and humans are seen as transducers or batteries. In turn this electrical view rests on mechanical hydraulics. Even Reich's anti-mechanistic theory of life energy becomes mechanistic once the movement of the proposed energy is discussed in physical terms. Admittedly, normal science does not accept that human beings can apply or receive biophysical energy in this way. But such a description is, nevertheless, an extension of normal physical principles.

It therefore becomes important, in a prospective science of 'life energy' to explore the interface between the living and the non-living. Neither the solely non-living (a power dam producing electricity) or the solely living (two people falling in love) can provide evidence for life energy – though each may be *described* as producing 'energy'. The ambition of researchers into life energy must be to demonstrate that the energy which they suppose is characteristic of life *also exists, although in another form or state, outside what is normally seen as alive.* Only in this way can they show how energy can flow into and out of the human organism. Again the model is taken from physics. It is no coincidence that the two most ardent exponents of a scientific view of life energy both lived at epochs when normal physics was making breakthroughs in the understanding of non-living energy: Mesmer at the time when Franklin and others were discovering the laws of electricity, and Reich at the time when Bohr and Einstein were discovering the laws of atomic energy. It is as if, in each case, a parallel advance in the understanding of the laws of life was described, in the metaphors currently used in the science of non-life, although only to be denigrated. Interestingly, a near-contemporary of Reich's, Fritz Mauthner, wrote at length and despairingly about the impossibility of escaping metaphor in any scientific or other discussion. Although Mauthner was popular in the German literature of the early 20th century, Reich shows no signs of having read his work – which might have instilled a useful sense of the limitations of language in scientific description.

Mesmer's tubs or 'baquets' containing bottles filled with iron filings were in their own way reminiscent of the voltaic batteries then being developed. Reich's 'accumulators', 'field meters', and 'cloud busters' are reminiscent of the atomic technology of reactor piles, Geiger counters, and radiation sources – though Reich, more sophisticated than Mesmer, was well aware of the parallels. He had first thought the accumulator effects were nuclear radiation, and for some years tended to refer to 'orgone radiation' or even 'solar radiation' rather than 'orgone energy'. Finally he believed a life-positive technology of 'orgone' to be the only salvation from the deadly technology of nuclear energy.

An easy view would be that Mesmer's and Reich's theories were merely imaginative extrapolations to the domain of human function, of the contemporary developments in physics. Thus each can be dismissed as parodying science, making up a pseudo-science. In the case of Reich, though, even if his theoretical framework does not completely hold up, his *observations* remain of great interest.

'Life Energy'

Reich described his years at medical school in Vienna just after the First World War as a time when he was influenced by the vitalists Driesch and Bergson, as well as by Freud. As a leader of a student seminar in sexology he became quickly drawn to psychoanalysis. Later, in 1952, during the boom years of psychoanalysis in North America, in an interview with a psychoanalyst, he was concerned to emphasise that his 'discovery of the orgone' was rooted in Freud's libido concept. His working career had been as a psychoanalyst and therapist, and retrospectively a certain legitimacy and continuity to his own discoveries could be provided in this acknowledgment of a debt to Freud. On the other hand, in *The Function of the Orgasm* he discusses the influence of the vitalists before that of the psychoanalysts, and it is likely that the former was primary, although he viewed it critically:

> I always had Driesch's concepts in mind when I thought of vitalism. My vague feeling of the irrational nature of his assumption proved to be true. He later found refuge among the spiritists…
>
> For some time I was taken for a 'crazy Bergsonian', because I agreed with him on principle, without, however, being able to state exactly where his theory left a gap. His *elan vital* was highly reminiscent of Driesch's 'entelechy'. There was no denying the principle of a creative power governing life; only it was not satisfactory as long as it was not tangible, as long as it could not be described or physically handled. For, rightly,

this was considered the supreme goal of natural science. The vitalists seemed to come closer to an understanding of the life principle than the mechanists who dissected life before trying to understand it.

The mechanistic part of Reich would have understood Bertrand Russell's savage attack on the vagueness and un-testability of Bergson's philosophy: Bergson is easily made mincemeat of by a rational critical analysis, even if for Bergsonians such a critique would be irrelevant because their philosophy is based on intuition rather than on rationalism. Bergsonianism as such could not have held the interest of someone so admittedly interested in mechanical processes as Reich, another of whose favourite philosophers was la Mettrie. Reich states flatly: 'in my medical studies I was a mechanist.' Already the ground was prepared for Reich's mechanist-vitalistic synthesis: it would be a synthesis of two halves of himself.

After this Reich hardly mentions Bergson, and indeed rushes on to the pious assertion that 'These early stages of my scientific development are important because they prepared me for the accurate comprehension of Freud's teachings.' But Reich's possible debt to Bergson should be assessed. Some basic similarities are:

- The postulate of a basic life force: Bergson's 'elan vital', Reich's 'orgone' or 'life energy'.
- A distinction between this life force and the matter which it is assumed to create. Bergson's élan creates matter in the course of its movement as 'congealed parts of its own substance which it carries along its course.' In Reich's later work, orgone is seen as creating particles of matter through the superimposition of energy streams in the atmosphere.
- An emphasis on mind-body unity.
- A rejection of 'psychologising' (making conceptual statements about human functioning) which is seen as an artificial reconstitution of experience. In Bergson this rejection deteriorates into a ferocious anti-intellectualism. Reich wrote respectfully of 'intellectual primacy', but he neglected the subject of consciousness and (as Leo

Raditsa demonstrates) his work can in some hands also degenerate into anti-intellectualism.

- Constant emphasis on experience, and sensory immediacy, as the basis of knowledge. (This has tended to attract literary writers – e.g. Norman Mailer to Reich, Marcel Proust to Bergson). For Bergson consciousness, through feelings and affections, gave man freedom through being a check on movement which would otherwise be automatic, machine-like. Similarly with Reich, freedom comes with feeling and sensation, which can be blocked by a habitual, mechanical 'armour' in the musculature. But Reich would not have agreed with Bergson's point that such resistance is what makes humans more than mere automatons.

- A 'psychoenergetic' terminology. This was much more developed by Reich. But Bergson too wrote of 'psychic tension'. He emphasized concrete experience of the human body, 'the empty vessel, which determines by its form, the form which the fluid mass, rushing into it, already tends to take.' (This logical fuzziness in discussing cause and effect is typical of Bergson). Similarly for the later Reich, atmospheric orgone is seen to create characteristic forms in organisms by filling them – the 'open orgone' becoming' closed'. (The cause and effect problem was resolved in Reich's assumption, without discussion, that the main directional flow was from atmosphere to organism). Bergson, like the later Reich, used a terminology of expansion and contraction, although on a more metaphysical level, with time seen as a contraction of human consciousness, matter as an expansion. Some of Bergson's hyperfluidic concepts emerge in Reich's later work in a physicalized form: Reich, in a sense, took up the challenge of trying to construct a physics which could include a vitalism such as Bergson's. Bergson was an ex-mechanist converted to mysticism, so anti-mechanistic that he saw no virtue in physics.

This was not the case with the other main influence on Reich, the biologist Paul Kammerer. Kammerer would have denied being a vitalist (or any '-ist' other than a communist) but his work has an undeniably vitalistic tendency. Reich gives little space to Kammerer in *The Function of the*

Orgasm (1927) but notes: 'he was a convinced advocate of the theory of natural organisation of living matter from inorganic matter, and the existence of a specific biological energy.' In *The Cancer Biopathy* (1947), having paid his dues to psychoanalysis for over twenty years (in spite of the fact that the psychoanalysts brutally rejected him), but now fully involved in biophysics, Reich gives only a few passing remarks to Freud but honours Kammerer with an unusually long quotation from his basic text *Allgemeine Biologie* (1921) which includes the following:

> The existence of a *specific life force* seems to me highly plausible. An energy which is not heat, nor electricity, magnetism, kinetic energy (including oscillation and radiation) , nor chemical energy, and is not an amalgam of any or all of them but an energy belonging specifically to only those natural processes we call 'life'. That does not imply that its presence is limited to those natural bodies that we call 'living beings' but that it is present also at least in the formative process of crystals. A better name for it, to prevent misunderstanding, might be 'formative energy' instead of 'life energy'. It possesses no supra-physical properties, even though it has nothing in common with physical energies already known. It is not a mysterious 'entelechy' (Aristotle, Driesch), but a genuine, natural 'energy.'

Reich followed this quotation from Kammerer with the conclusion that 'in the work of the vitalists, the life force became an elusive specter, while the mechanists converted it into a lifeless machine.' But the energy in Kammerer's description is no elusive spectre. Since Reich had evidently studied this passage while still a medical student, it must have been a key element in the formation of his life-long research programme to discover the functioning of just such a new 'physical energy.'

Reich visited several scientists and analysts in Vienna (Kammerer, Steinach, Stekel, Bucura, Adler and Freud) in order to 'procure literature' for his sexological seminars. He seems to have disliked most of them for their grandiosity. But 'Freud was different' – natural, seemingly honest, and interested in Reich: 'I had come there in a feeling of trepidation and left with a feeling of pleasure and friendliness.' Although eventually Reich was to feel 'bitter disappointment' with Freud, he could still reverentially say in 1952: '*Libido as a physical cosmic reality – that is my work.* Freud provided the concept. This is where he came in. This, to my mind, was his greatest deed. He was a very great man, a very great man.' Thus Reich, in writing his own history, wanted to base his own work in Freud's great success. But what if Kammerer, whose star crashed to earth in 1925 in an explosion of persecution somewhat like the one which Reich was to suffer thirty years later, had been as interested in Reich as Freud was? Reich writes off the meeting: 'Kammerer was intelligent and amiable, but not particularly interested.' Reich had to pursue his research programme through the medium of psychoanalysis, not biology. But the research programme was already formed: the central interest in sexuality, plus the drive to synthesize vitalism and mechanism, almost guaranteed that the 'specific life energy would first be delineated in its sexual aspect.'

It is ironic, and no tribute to Reich the 'character analyst', that he should have found Freud less grandiose than other researchers. (To use a common German expression, he was not a good 'Menschenkenner' – 'people-knower'). Freud the self-proclaimed 'conquistador' imbued the psychoanalytic movement with a grandiosity which left no psychoanalyst, and certainly not Reich, uninfected. Reich was never intellectually fraudulent, in distorting case histories and committing plagiarism, as Freud and other analysts (notably Jung) demonstrably were. And he had a natural scientific distrust of 'psychologising' and 'literary' (meaning bad literary) interpretations of human behaviour. Not that he would have been any better off with the rather suspect Kammerer as a father-figure.

Reich's experiments with pulsation and streamings (following Friedrich Kraus) were all carried out with a view to establishing that these were life energy (libido) processes. His first experimental hypothesis was that libido was bioelectrical. He devised an apparatus for measuring the wandering of galvanic skin potential. The skin of experimental subjects would be stroked by an electrode, or have the electrode taped to it, while the person was subjected to pleasurable and unpleasurable stimulation, often in erogenous zones. (Thirty years later, Masters and Johnson attempted something similar on a cruder scale). Results showed a distinction between merely mechanical events and events accompanied by sensation. For example, a penis which had been caused by mechanical stimulation to become erect would register a neutral tracing on the electrical measuring apparatus, but if the erection was associated with pleasure, the tracing would show a characteristic wandering of potential. Reich's 'orgasm formula' or 'life formula' could now be phrased in a form which expressed the distinction between mechanical tension and charge, and energetic (electrical) excitation and relaxation: Electrical charge > Mechanical tension > Electrical discharge > Mechanical relaxation.

The electrophysiological experiments produced data which prompted Reich to write that he had resolved the basic conflict between mechanism and vitalism. He had already concluded from clinical observations that psyche and soma functioned as a unity, since (as he expressed it later): 'sensation is a function of excitation… in other words, there is a functional identity between the quantity of excitation and the intensity of sensation.' Now he concluded:

> As a matter of fact, living matter does function on the basis of the same physical laws as non-living matter, as is contended by the mechanists. It is, at the same time, fundamentally different from non-living matter, as is contended by the vitalists. For, in living matter, *the functions of mechanics* (tension-relaxation) *and those of electricity* (charge-discharge) *are combined in a specific manner which does not occur in non-living matter… The living is in its function at one and the same time identical with the non-living and different from it.*

Like most proposed solutions in science, this offers some understanding but leads to new problems. How can the living be both identical with the non-living and different from it? A combination of the electrical and the material is certainly a different sort of mix from the solely material but mysteriously metabolizing mix of mechanistic science, but there is still a 'ghost in the machine' in the form of the electricity. Reich's statement is a research programme in itself.

Reich went on to face the major problem: the electrical potential shifts involved were not great enough to be able to explain either the intensity of subjective sensation or the extent of physical excitation and movement. There had to be something else. 'The bioelectrical energy which manifested itself in these experiments could not be any of the known forms of energy.'

Reich had long suspected that life energy was more than the psychodynamic libido of Freud or the bioelectricity suggested by the experiments of Galvani. Reich's bioelectrical experiments suggest that he had genuinely hoped electricity would provide the answer. When it did not, at least he had eliminated the possibility through experiment.

Now, according to Reich's account, the specific biological energy forced itself on him in a new way, in the course of still further experiments to demonstrate that a mysterious radiation which had caused his eyes to redden while observing 'bion' cultures (of decaying vegetable matter) through the microscope, and which had burned the palm of his hand holding a test-tube full of the cultures, was some kind of electromagnetic radiation. The Faraday cage which Reich built out of sheets of metal in order to 'isolate' the radiation instead intensified it. His attempt to show the radiation was electromagnetic was thus refuted. The radiation came from a specific culture made from ocean sand which, Reich later concluded, must have been 'energised' by the sun. Already there was a hint that this radiation did not only emanate from the biological cultures, but was atmospheric. At first, though, Reich thought it was confined to the metal shieldings or the room in which the cultures had been placed. He observed that the radiation emitted heat, and that it could be observed as a bluish light. He named it 'orgone'.

From this point Reich was squarely in the terrain of biophysics, and in a sense was taking up the challenge put by Kammerer: he set out to demonstrate that the life energy or orgone was measurable, and quantifiable. His main tool was the 'orgone accumulator', a box made from alternating layers of metal and non-metallic material. This, the first of several devices to channel or intensify the 'atmospheric energy', was a modification of his original steel-lined Faraday cage. Reich discovered that a thermometer suspended just above an accumulator would consistently register a temperature of about 1 degree C higher than an identical thermometer suspended over a control box which was not an accumulator. (The ridiculously accurate figure of 0.9 C was cited: Reich seems to have had little knowledge of statistics, including standard deviations). This 'temperature difference', known as T-To, became a key demonstration of the existence of the atmospheric orgone.

Eventually, when he had come to America as a refugee from that superior mass psychologist, Hitler, Reich secured an interview with Einstein in Princeton and left a small accumulator with him so that he could replicate 'T-To'. Einstein remarked that if this temperature difference was true, it would be 'a bombshell in physics'. He then handed the accumulator to an assistant who could not succeed in replicating the effect, whereupon Einstein returned the accumulator to Reich with an explanation that the effect must be due to 'convection currents'. This occasioned a torrent of abusive articles from members of the Reich group, now becoming a sort of personality cult – not against the rather broad back of Einstein but against the assistant who was claimed to be a communist spy. (This may seem part of the witch-hunting anti-communist paranoia of the USA in the 1950s, but in fact there is much evidence that Reich was systematically maligned by communists, and no less than three of his journalistic attackers, including the main one, Mildred Brady, were Soviet agents.)

But although some replication experiments by DeMeo and others have been impeccably carried out, the temperature difference has proved impossible to replicate *consistently* in laboratory conditions: as so often in scientific studies there are too many independent variables. To explain the inconsistency as due to the orgone being 'life energy' is an 'escape hypothesis', and circular. More often variables such as a humid atmosphere or local radioactivity are evoked. (DeMeo's experiments which confirm T-To are deliberately conducted in a high-altitude dry climate laboratory, far from radioactive sources.)

Other indicators of the orgone were, Reich claimed, a lower electroscopic discharge in an accumulator, and much later a capacity for charging a Geiger counter. Reich began to observe a similar bluish flickering in the atmosphere of the night sky as had been observed within his experimental devices (large accumulators) or a metal-walled room. Although the intensity of this flickering was enhanced by being viewed through a tube with a cellulose disc on the end (which Reich named the 'orgonoscope'), it could sometimes be viewed with the naked eye. Reich only occasionally mentioned a visible field or aura around human beings: his main concentration was on 'lumination' in the atmosphere.

Eventually a whole technology was developed: the accumulator produced vagotonic effects on a person sitting in it (slight rise in body temperature, flushing, relaxation), apparently raised the person's energy level over a period of time; and eventually was claimed to dissolve some cancer tumors (though *not* to cure the underlying disease which Reich saw as an incurable result of chronic emotional stasis). Subsidiary devices, such as the orgone 'shooter', a steel funnel and tube, and the orgone blanket were used for local irradiation. He invented 'cloud-busters', draw-tubes for weather engineering.

Reich's technology was ridiculed: as with Mesmer's magnetic rods and 'baquets', the orgone accumulator's effects could be dismissed as 'suggestion' by those who did not bother to test them. And indeed some who tested them felt no subjective effects. Finally, since Reich and his associates were renting out accumulators, with at least the implication that they might help with disease and cancer, and one of his psychiatrist associates transported accumulators across state lines in defiance of an injunction, Reich ended up being jailed after prosecution by the U.S. Food and Drug Administration which declared his whole science to be fraudulent. All of his published and unpublished works containing references to 'orgone 'were called in and burned in the public incinerator. This *auto da fe* of 1950s American science and medicine burned even original psychoanalytic and sociological texts by Reich (such as *Character Analysis,* on the grounds that revised editions included reference to the dreaded orgone). In jail, he died. His work rests mainly with his successors, the 'orgonomists' a small group of psychiatrists (descended from or trained by the original American disciples who gravitated to Reich from State Mental Hospitals or psychoanalysis when he arrived in the USA in 1940) and their analysands who have claimed on often flimsy grounds to replicate his basic experiments. They cannot entirely be blamed for their difficulties: Adolph Smith has commented that by the turn of the millennium, less than 50 years after Reich's death in 1957, scientific method was 'centuries ahead' of what he knew. (This is why I refer in this book mainly to DeMeo's experiments: they are mostly recent, and conform to early 21st century methodological requirements.)

The persecution and humiliation of Reich were so revolting, the official hostility to the orgone theory so irrational and relentless, that it seems to be difficult for many sympathetic students of Reich's work to do less than revere it uncritically but defensively. This tendency is added to by the fact that many of Reich's followers seem to owe their emotional lives to the experience of Reichian therapy: to deny the truth of his scheme risks denying the emotional gains they feel they have made. But there are undoubted problems, even within the framework of Reich's own analysis of his discoveries. Even though Reich himself claimed to measure the orgone, through the T-To difference, or through the rate of electroscopic discharge, *these are not direct measurements*. It is admitted in physics that 'Energy can only be measured by its effects on matter.' In other words heat or electricity can be measured only through the movement of molecules or other particles. All measurement of energy is thus second hand. This is also true for the orgone. Since the orgone is postulated as a new energy, it should be possible to measure its effects in isolation. But this is apparently not the case. The orgone is supposed to be everywhere in the atmosphere, and so only relative concentrations of it can be measured. Even these concentrations should be measured *in the absence of known energies*, otherwise results can be explained away as 'just convection currents', or 'electromagnetism'.

As the physicist Leonard Burr pointed out, thermometers measure heat, electroscopes measure electricity, Geiger counters measure nuclear radiation – and they are *designed* to measure these things only. Geiger counters did go wild in Reich's orgone accumulators on at least one occasion, suggesting another source of energy, but this is another effect which has proved hard to replicate in controlled conditions. If consistent new effects and measurements in these areas can be produced by Reich's devices, this will require new explanatory hypotheses. But still a leap is necessary before postulating an entirely new energy, demonstrable by secondary effects alone. Given the semantic and logical difficulties, discussed earlier, with the whole concept of a 'life energy' which is 'mass free' and so on, it might be more productive to explore the characteristics and origins of what appear to be so far undefined 'fields', or the 'aether' which may have been wrongly dismissed from modern physics.

Physics does claim to have defined the laws of electricity, magnetism and heat. But there is always room for expansion. For example, 'electricity' was known in the form of the static electricity which crackled when a dialectric such as amber ('elektrikon' meant amber in Greek) was subjected to friction. The concept later became expanded to include the energy in batteries, and electrical currents produced by dynamos or thunderstorms. Reich eventually claimed that static electricity (whose laws are different from those of electrical currents) was identical to, or a form of, orgone. He saw electrical currents as 'secondary energy', a result of the primary orgone. Adolph Smith, a professional physicist, used to wonder if electricity was 'orgone in wires'. But which came first? If electricity (or an expanded form of it) really is orgone after all, then orgone is electricity, and the new word is unnecessary. There is no way in which measurement by electrical instruments can be used to justify the postulate of a new energy which is something greater than electricity. Rather, the description of electricity must be expanded. On the other hand, if life produces electrical *secondary* effects (as a person can do on a TV receiver) this may provide some means of cross-checking, especially if the *primary* instrument is the one which by definition must be most appropriate in the measurement of life: the living organism. There do seem to be (see Chapter 4) 'fields' around organisms.

One theoretical way out of the problem of orgone/life energy being in a basic way different from secondary energy would be to express it as splitting into energy/matter. In this case, orgone could be seen as 'premeasurable', i.e. a life force pre-existing any physical state. Thus a neo-Reichian, Charles Kelley, has replaced orgone with a 'root' source which he calls 'Radix'. But this is mystical animism, and a metaphysical concept of a life force which is 'everywhere'. Reich's assertions that the orgone was 'universal' are of no help here: any theory of universality rules out scientific experiment. (If orgone is everywhere, there is nothing from which it can be distinguished). But Reich *wanted* to be scientific. In practice he attempted to make distinctions between concentrations or states of orgone. But, again, he sought to measure these with instruments.

Reich often expressed his orgone theory in terms (e.g. the orgone being universal) that are what Popper called, in referring to Freudian theory (in which Reich's work is, by his own claim, grounded) 'refutation proof'. Reich eventually made his work into the self-referring fortress of 'orgonomy'. Soon after reaching the U.S.A., in 1941, he wrote to his friend A.S.Neill in Faustian terms: 'I have in my hands and I dispose of the orgone radiation which exists in the earth and in the atmosphere, and nobody but

I knows how to handle it.' The popular fear of the mad scientist who wants to control the world (life) has a rational basis: by mechanistic standards, all experiment must be replicated and controlled. In fact the only things which replicate motion and are completely controllable are machines – hence, perhaps, their appeal to people who fear losing self-control. Reich must have been frustrated by the failure of his experiments to achieve the required control of results. At times he claimed he could control the life energy itself through his new technology, in a way which seems paranoid (obsessed with control). But he came to think at the end of his life that the cosmic life energy was an 'ocean' which could only be channelled locally.

Reich's key statements about orgone are that it is 'mass-free' and 'primordial'. As a physicist Joe Rosen points out, any universal statement about cosmology is 'metaphysical', in that there is nothing to test it against. And if it is primordial ('preceding the order of things') it cannot by definition be tested *now*. It is not a testable theory. But (*pace* Popper) even if it is not testable it is still a theory in the original sense of the word: 'a way of seeing', or 'a line of sight.' Much science, and certainly most of what I say in this book, consists of invitations to *observe*, to *look*. This is the basis of the science of vision as set forth by Goethe. But it is not as respectable a scientific approach as putting something (inevitably simple) to the test – burning one's tongue on melting toffee, for instance.

So Reich's successors the orgonomists, although they may question random controlled trials on the (reasonable) grounds that they do not take into account the emotional and biological state of the observer, tend to grasp at straws each time a new cosmic theory of 'energy' comes up and hope that this is, finally, orgone, or the return of the all-encompassing 'aether' (or 'ether') which Einstein is supposed to have got rid of. The most recent candidate is Zero Point Energy (ZPE), otherwise known as 'vacuum energy', or 'dark energy', which is proposed to comprise 73% of the total energy of the cosmos. It is impossible to measure, but this does not prevent some physicists from hanging their theoretical hats on it. This is rather unfair considering how many supposed scientists have scoffed at the orgone because it is unmeasurable. ZPE seems to fulfil a mathematical necessity and may be otherwise accounted for by the 'cosmological constant' included in the major theories of modern physics. Nevertheless the 'shape dynamics' of Julian Barbour and his co-workers in theoretical physics threatens to dethrone ZPE. And at any rate, since it is not only un-measurable but invisible and imperceptible it can hardly explain the various conspicuous (for those who observe them) phenomena ascribed by Reich to orgone.

In spite of its failures (and we all fail…) Reich's work provides many pioneering observations and statements which help make the distinction between life and death more clear. Only when we can define life clearly – through the observable presence of pulsation, I propose – can we move to the question Kammerer raised, of a specific life force. He implies this is secondary, not primary. Such a force is likely to be *produced* by organisms, and intrinsic to their pulsation – as, for example, breathing. Here we are back to 'spirit.' It is not necessary to evoke a 'Primum Mobile' either in the form of a creator or a mystified 'cosmic energy' such as orgone. But at the very least we are looking at field effects which demand a testable theory to explain them.

Organisms pulsate. This pulsation produces various effects which we can measure as forms of 'energy'. But 'energy' can also be produced by inorganic events, such as the rush of water through a hydroelectric dam or the radioactive decay of uranium. It is not the origin of life, though it is necessary to life: sunlight warmed the primeval 'soup' in which, Oparin and J B S Haldane proposed, life began. If, in turn, life produces a specific force or energy, distinguishable in its effects from other forms of energy such as heat or radioactivity, and perhaps evident in 'field' effects such as auras, 'animal magnetism', the sensations experienced sporadically in Reich's accumulators – or, for that matter in the glow of falling in love – then this is a legitimate subject for a research programme. But Reich's theory of 'energy' which is everywhere and especially out there – the 'cosmic orgone energy' flowing through us so intensely that we resist it with an 'armour' – can lead to paranoia in those who are afraid of somehow being taken over by it and losing control. Even in many Reichian publications and Internet sites the main emotion is terror: of 'DOR' (Deadly Orgone – e.g. orgone gone stagnant because it is blocked in people by the armour, or blocked in the atmosphere by UFOs and causing desertification); of 'ORANUR' (the crazed orgone over-excited by contact with UFOs or nuclear energy); the FBI; the 'Emotional Plague' of people who can't see the point. The *Journal of Orgonomy* once published an article which claimed that anyone who failed to like the music of Mahler was armoured against the flow of the life energy. 'Orgonomy' has fragmented into factions, as in the Irish joke about the two IRA men who greet each other with the question: 'Did you hear about the split?' Reich's personal agony is visited on his followers – none of whom is noted for taking the kind of risks he did. He was an extraordinary man: 'a fanatic', as Gerd Bergerson wrote to me; the tender lover of a ballet dancer from Berlin who taught him the latest in dance movement therapy; the courageous battler for sexual rights and children's rights; the patient observer of nature working itself through in cells, bodies, emotions, and the atmosphere; a questioning philosopher. He made a great contribution to the science of life. He was, as he knew (and stated immodestly) unusually open. But he became so embattled – and ultimately ill (his heart burst in prison but he had probably been hypertensive for years before that) – so driven, so much the pioneer under attack, that he could not distinguish between what he saw as the life energy out there saturating and forming the universe, and his own lively, and lonely, self.

Perhaps Reich's orgone accumulators swirl with spiralling blue dots when a lively person steps into them on a sunny day and his or her own force field bounces off the metal walls in some process not yet understood. Perhaps the aura that can sometimes be suddenly seen around the head of a person in therapy just before he or she bursts into tears of longing is a sort of biological glow of emotion akin to that of a mating fire-fly. Perhaps when, after an absence from my wife in the first few months of our relationship, I went to meet her at a grimy bus station and a white flash of light burst across the car park and united us as we caught sight of each other, this was a reflection (literally) of *us*.

Is there a cosmic ocean? If so it may be the medium of life, but in itself be no more alive than the sea, teeming with living creatures who even in deepest darkness or even if blind flash with radiant light.

3

PULSATION AND PULSE-WAVES

Streamings

It has been noted by experimenters (starting with Spelt in 1948 – but it still goes on, e.g. in Peter Hefner's prenatal research laboratory in Belfast) that if a clapper (Spelt) or buzzer (Hefner) is sounded outside the abdomen of a pregnant woman, a foetus as young as 4 months will 'startle' in the reflex familiar in the new-born: legs and arms shoot out abruptly. Other researchers (e.g. A.A.Tomatis in France) have demonstrated that babies who have been exposed to certain music as much as 3 months before birth will show signs of recognition when they hear it after birth. (They especially like tinkly piano and thin violin music which may sound as if filtered across the mother's abdomen.) Otherwise the sensory experience of the foetus is a matter for speculations, the most durable of which have been those of the psychoanalyst Sandor Ferenczi about the foetus's 'oceanic' existence, bathed in the amniotic fluid, scarcely differentiated from its mother. Recent research in physiology (best known in Candace Pert's *Molecules of Emotion)* provides some support for this vision: it is becoming accepted that through 'volume transmission', various biochemicals, mainly hormones and peptides, participate in a constant flow of information throughout the body and particularly the brain – and furthermore that this transmission mediates emotions. It is also demonstrable from the study of algae and protozoa that the fluid in cells circulates inside the membrane in a process known as cyclosis.

Reich adopted the physiologist Friedrich Kraus's concept of 'streamings' to describe the person's subjective sensations of pleasure flowing up and down the body, and to and from the genitals, in sexual excitement. These streamings are also felt when the breathing is extended and intensified in body-oriented therapy, and in the common experiences of pleasure in nature, at seeing a loved one, playing happily with children, and so on. Readers of this book will have experienced streamings. It is reasonable to suppose they are associated with volume transmission and perhaps with cyclosis, and that they intensify as the breathing pulsation is intensified by emotion.

The Pulse of Life

The word *pulse* is from Latin *pellere* – to beat. A pulse is a blow. We have come to use *pulse* for any regularly repeated phenomenon – such as the pulse of waves on a shore. Astronomers have discovered that quasars pulse – i.e. they flash regularly – like a light-house. A distant observer cannot tell whether the pulse of light from a light-house is from the sort of light-house which switches a beam on and off at fixed intervals, or the sort in which a rotating beam covers a fixed point at intervals. The pulse of our heartbeat is also just an indication of other events: if we listen to our heartbeat on the pillow on a sleepless night we hear a double thump.

One of the fathers of scientific physiology is William Harvey, a contemporary of Galileo and 'the discoverer of the circulation of the blood'. 'Every schoolboy knows' that before Harvey the blood was simply assumed to fill the body, and the heartbeat was viewed as being a particular function of the heart itself, not the 'pump' which Harvey discovered it to be. The heart is a specialised machine 'for circulating the blood' (mechanistic science often favours this kind of creeping teleology) among organs which are also specialised machines. But this was *not* Harvey's view. Nor did he ever use the word pump or its Latin equivalent (he wrote in Latin). He did discover that as the heart contracted it sent blood spurting down the arteries, and that this caused the blood to circulate. This was, evidently, one of the principal bodily mechanisms. But in its turn it was a result, not the cause

Harvey wrote of watching the cloudy spot in a hen's egg four or five days after incubation:

> In the centre of the cloud there was a throbbing point of blood, so trifling that it disappeared on contraction and was lost to sight, while on relaxation it appeared again like a red pin-point. Throbbing between existence and non-existence, now visible, now invisible, it was the beginning of life.

The throbbing Harvey describes is the sign of alternating contraction and relaxation – as in the heart – and he is using it as a definition of life. Words like 'heart-throb' suggest that 'throb' is connected with the living body. We would not say a light-house beam throbs – or a quasar. So the throbbing of life is more than simply the regular appearance of a pulse or beat.

It is useful to get teleology – explanations in terms of purpose, which suggest design – out of physiological descriptions. (Reich was rigorous about this in what he called 'functional thought.') Harvey did not write teleologically. He did not say or imply that the heart pulsed *in order to* circulate the blood. Rather, the whole body throbbed with the circulation in which the heart was the *main* mover.

Man the machine

Another early medical researcher whose work has become distorted in subsequent interpretations is the 18th century physician Offroy de la Mettrie. His *L'Homme Machine (Man the Machine)* is assumed, understandably if the reader goes no further than the title, to be the quintessential document, a manifesto, of mechanistic science. La Mettrie did pioneer an entirely materialistic way of looking at the body. The point of *Man the Machine* is to read God out of the picture and thus to interpret disease via precise observation. La Mettrie examined bodily functions without recourse to abstractions such as 'humours' or 'essences', which had originated in observation but which had degenerated into Paracelsian balderdash. His observations were entirely *physical*, but this does not mean of mechanisms in the sense that for modern medicine disease is a failure of bodily mechanisms. La Mettrie saw the body in terms of expansion and contraction – oscillation.

Almost all machines, from watches (whether with mechanisms or quartz crystals) to internal combustion engines, contain parts which oscillate. Modern physics is comfortable with the oscillation of magnetic fields or of celestial bodies such as the sun. But there seems to have been something unacceptable in the perceptions of Harvey and la Mettrie of alternating relaxation (or expansion) and contraction as the basic function of life in organisms. The concept of oscillation has not exactly been ignored in biology and medicine. It even turns up, although phrased in different words, in a nineteenth century medical textbook's mention of 'the common tendency towards "pulsatile or rhythmic activity" manifested by all living matter.' And modern biologists pursue oscillatory rhythms in the circadian cycles of organisms.

One unequivocal claim that alternating expansion and contraction are the main movements in the living organism comes from a less reputable figure than Harvey or La Mettrie, although also a physician: Franz Mesmer. Ladies and gentlemen of the French court immersed themselves linking hands in a 'baquet', a huge tub of water and glass tubes filled with iron filings, and succumbed to waves of emotional catharsis as the 'universal fluid' was channelled through them. This was reported to cure various diseases. Mesmer and his successors (including distinguished physicians such as John Elliotson, inventor of the stethoscope, and amateur students of 'magnetic healing' such as Charles Dickens) laid on hands and made 'magnetic passes' along a patient's body, which usually first produced emotional catharsis or convulsive autonomic movements, then led to a period of deep sleep from which the patient often awoke cured.

Mesmer had a tendency to grandiosity. Mozart caricatured him as the village magician Colas in an early opera *Bastien and Bastienne* whose first performance was at Mesmer's house. Mesmer was hounded from France after a royal commission headed by the visiting Benjamin Franklin and including such big guns in science as Lavater, Lavoisier, and the Guillotin who invented the guillotine (and ended up as one of its victims), ruled that the phenomena were due to 'imagination and contact.' (Nowadays the put-down term would be the all-powerful 'suggestion'.) But the commission did acknowledge that the phenomena occurred and even that cures were affected. This is not surprising since cathartic emotional discharges (or 'abreactions' as they are called in psychoanalysis) and autonomic convulsions have been known to be curative since before the days of exorcism, and their modern legacies are well known as intensive psychotherapy and electro-convulsive ('shock') treatment. But there were less dramatic cases of cure after a calm treatment and subsequent sleep. Mesmer's explanation for his cures seems to have been even more unacceptable to the scientists than his techniques. He believed health depended on the free circulation of 'universal fluid'.

The streams of universal fluid can be applied to the intimate structures of muscular fibre exactly as wind or water acts upon a mill. The function of the muscular fibre – as moved by the universal fluid – consists in alternations of contraction and expansion.

Mesmer cannot be claimed to have pursued the concept of alternate expansion and contraction any further than in the quotation given above. He did propose a theory of disease as blocked circulation of universal fluid – a theory very like Wilhem Reich's in the 20th century. But he had an 18th century deistic view of cause:

Within the universe there exists a fixed, uniform and constant amount of movement, which was impressed upon matter in the beginning. This impression of movement was made upon one mass of fluid at first.

Mesmer ends up being as mechanistic as La Mettrie: 'exactly as wind or water acts upon a mill'. And 'movement, which was impressed on matter in the beginning' is as mechanistic as Paley's 18th centry view of God as the watchmaker designing a universe and setting it going. In the 20th century La Mettrie's and Mesmer's views come through in the 'hydraulic' theories of Freud and Reich, of 'libido' or 'orgone energy' pressing against the dams of repression or 'character armour'.

In late 20th century physics the Big Bang theory continues the tradition. Such views cannot admit of movement being *constantly* generated, of *continuous* creation. These possibilities only emerge once the mechanistic view is abandoned along with the theological view which often accompanies it. Paley argued that if the universe is seen as running like a machine, for example a watch, then someone or something must have started it. Or, put only slightly differently, something started the various oscillations of the universe going. Hence a computer scientist can comfortably attend church on Sunday. Science and mysticism become complimentary, each with its exclusive terrain, and this precludes research on the possible borders of life and non-life.

Oscillation and pulsation

In the late 20th century various 'New Age' thinkers (e.g. Fritjof Capra in his *The Tao of Physics*) described the universe as full of oscillations and vibrations – but their function is not discussed. Even Rupert Sheldrake, in an innovative theory of formative causation based on 'morphogenetic fields', although he refers frequently to oscillation does not distinguish it from vibration, nor does he distinguish between its nature in the living and the non-living:

> Atoms, molecules, crystals, organelles, cells, tissues, organs, and organisms are all made up of parts in ceaseless oscillation, and all have their own characteristic patterns of vibration and internal rhythm.

Part of the task of distinguishing life and non-life must be to discover if alternating expansion and contraction, commonly known as oscillation, is a valid criterion for life. If oscillation is as the *Penguin Dictionary of Physics* bluntly defines it, 'a vibration', then it is *not* characteristic of what common sense and ordinary language call life, although it may be considered to be so in the tautological worlds of animism or hylozoism, where everything is alive. In the mechanistic world of modern science, where everything is vibrating at different rates – including the hypothetical 'strings' which many physicists believe are the most basic units of matter/energy – everything is dead.

The way out of the confusion of oscillation and vibration in life and non-life is, I propose, to distinguish a particular kind of *phase unequal* alternating expansion and contraction as *pulsation*, and to claim that it is characteristic of life and life only.

This idea originates in Reich's theory that pulsation is the life function. But Reich nevertheless made no distinction between pulsation and ordinary oscillation. In fact he grafted the word pulsation onto a theory first set out in terms of oscillation.

Reich's research into life functions began when he was a psychoanalyst. Psychoanalysis was characterized by an energy-based vocabulary: of charge, discharge, tension, excitation, displacement, etc. Post-Freudian critics, and by now most analysts, see this vocabulary as an almost 'hydraulic' way of looking at sexuality, pleasure and anxiety. And indeed, as hydraulic imagery it may seem naive as well as unfounded: it implies something solid and testable, whereas psychoanalysis is more pseudo-scientific than scientific, a closed, self-referring system. (As the Viennese journalist Karl Kraus cracked: 'Psychoanalysis is the disease that it attempts to cure.') When Reich eventually moved to biophysics his work was almost fatally contaminated by its psychoanalytic origins.

Part of this contamination was an unacknowledged, perhaps unconscious, tendency towards Cartesian dualism – of thinking, in the Descartes tradition, of mind and matter as distinct. Reich was not much interested in the mind as such but he proposed that 'life energy', which he re-labelled 'orgone energy' was distinct from matter, to the point of being 'mass free.' He had inherited this from Freud's theory of the libido – a psychic energy somehow working on and through the body. This was the conceptual mess Freud had got into when he abandoned neurology, deciding that it was too soon to be able to formulate psychoanalytic concepts in neurological (brain) terms. *Psycho*analysis and *psycho*dynamic thinking are by definition dualistic in the Cartesian sense, *psyche* meaning mind. Hence such concepts as *psychosomatic* medicine, in which the mind/ psyche is assumed to work on the (separate) body/soma.

In 1925 the Russian neurologist Alexander Luria (the father of neuropsychology) tackled this dilemma clearly in an essay called *Toward a Monistic Psychology* (monism being the view of the identity of body and mind). He proposed that *psycho*therapy would eventually be replaced by a *neuro*dynamic therapy. But Luria had to shut up about any kind of therapy once Stalin's communism took hold, and personal salvation was supposed to depend on political changes, not therapy. Freud's impatience and ambition led to a diversion of psychotherapy into a Cartesian approach for most of the twentieth century, and it was only at the turn of the 21st century that the monistic approach of neuroscience began to set the ground for Luria's prediction to come true: finally psychotherapy is being changed by neurodynamic approaches derived from neuroscience, and 'neuropsychoanalysis' is being proposed.

Of all the original psychoanalysts Reich was probably the most thoroughly trained in neurology and biology. He was not only a psychiatrist but a neuropsychiatrist, trained in Vienna by the neurologist Wagner-Juaregg whose physiological approach left no room for the psychodynamic approach that Reich studied simultaneously. However the psychoanalytic and psychodynamic problem of masochism helped Reich formulate what would eventually be a biophysical theory. His clinical work led him to propose that masochistic patients functioned like inflated balloons which were unable to burst. The masochist's inner tension, anxiety and need could only be released (the balloon pricked, as it were) by the intervention of another person whose aggression to the masochist incidentally caused pain but primarily caused pleasure because the inner tension was at last released. Reich eventually formulated this hydraulic view of masochism in energetic terms: the build- up of excessive tension and 'charge' had to be released in relaxation and 'discharge.' Reich concluded that this applied more widely, and that healthy sexual excitation and satisfaction were also functions of charge and discharge.

In another synthesis, his interest in charge/discharge functions became combined with a theory of expansion and contraction in human functioning. Freud had compared the expansion of the 'libido' toward the world in states of excitation to the expansion outward of an amoeba's pseudopodia (the reaching forward of leading parts of its membrane). Reich compared this in turn with the expansion of the penis in erection. Eventually he proposed a theory of human functioning as a process of continual energetic charge and discharge, expansion and contraction. The epitome of this was to be found in the function of the orgasm where sexual tension built up and was released.

'The orgasm shows a function which is composed of tension and relaxation, charge and discharge: *biological pulsation*.' [My italics]. Reich set out the 'orgasm formula': *mechanical tension > bio-electrical charge > bio-electrical discharge > mechanical relaxation*. He stated that 'The orgasm formula shows itself to be the life formula as such.' This 'life formula' governed such processes as cell division: *tension > charge > discharge > relaxation*. This formula Reich also described as a constant *oscillation* between the organism's expansion toward the world, and contraction away from it.

Reich's equation of pulsation with life was what Harvey had taken for granted some 300 years before although the Latin word he used for it, *pulsus,* means simply a pulse or beat. Pulsation is still not defined any differently in Reich's work from oscillation, which can be a mechanical phenomenon. A simple example is a struck bell: it swings back and forth, that is it oscillates, while in a narrower range it vibrates. But it is not alive. Nor does it even need a movement from a living hand to put it in action: the swinging can be started by a gust of wind or the accidental falling of a piece of masonry. Oscillation is characteristic of any material body in resonance in space (e.g. a bell or a violin string) or subjected to regular bursts of force (e.g. the pistons in a locomotive, or the works of a watch). Oscillation of the material itself, rather than in the space it occupies, is less common. It is found in the living – the cells, the heart – but also in what we consider the non-living. Certain stars (Cepheid variables) apparently oscillate, as does the sun which expands and contracts over a range of about 10 kilometers every two and a half hours or so. Astronomers sometimes call these oscillations 'pulsation', but the most recent book on the sun (Varenholt) refers consistently to a huge range of 'dynamic oscillations'. The lid of a boiling pot may oscillate up and down; there is an expansion and contraction of the amount of daylight in any 24 hours; the ice on a frozen lake heaves up and down with changing temperatures; boiling toffee or volcanic mud produces bubbles which swell then collapse.

Definitions of pulsation

The (online) Harcourt Academic Press Dictionary of Science and Technology offers definitions of pulsation under two headings:

> 'Pulsation. *Physiology.* A regular swelling and shrinking motion, such as that of the heart muscle.'
> 'Pulsation. *Astrophysics.* The swelling and shrinking of a star as it evolves from the main sequence to the red-giant stage.'

Although swelling/shrinking is more concrete in English than expansion/contraction (the words being Anglo-Saxon rather than Latin) the definitions still offer no distinction between life and non-life. Furthermore English dictionary definitions do not distinguish between pulsation and oscillation. According to the Oxford English Dictionary (OED), Pulsation is 'Rhythmical expansion and contraction; beating, throbbing, vibration.'

But looked at closely these are distinct functions. Adding to the confusion is the OED definition of oscillate: 'Swing to and fro. Vibrate.'

However the Oxford English Dictionary (OED) does provide a way through, since as it defines itself, it is 'A New English Dictionary on Historical Principles.'

The first meaning of Pulsation (section 1 in the entry) is based on its first recorded occurrences. The earliest is in a translation from the Latin of Galen, in 1541, as 'vehement pulsacyon'. Then in 1615 in Crooke's *Body of Man*: 'This motion of the arteries is called *pulsus* or pulsation... which is absolved by dilatation and contraction.'

The second meaning is defined as 'rhythmical beating, vibration, or undulation: cf PULSE.' Its first record is in 1658, about how worms 'move from place to place with a certain drawing and pulsation.' The first record of pulsation being applied to *non*-organic processes is only later, in 1870, by Emerson: 'The pulsation of a stretched string or wire gives the ear the pleasure of sweet sound.'

As for Pulsate, the earliest record is from Erasmus Darwin (Charles Darwin's grandfather) in 1794, noting that 'The heart of a viper or frog will continue to pulsate long after it is taken from the body.' And the primary meaning is given as 'To expand and contract rhythmically, as the heart of an artery.'

The secondary meaning is given as 'To strike upon something with a rhythmical succession of strokes; to move with a regular alternating motion; to exhibit such a movement; to beat, vibrate, quiver, thrill.' The first record of this meaning is from a *Times* article in 1861: 'The air pulsates with the flash of arms in the sunlight.

The OED does not make a clear distinction between organic and non-organic 'pulsation' in its definitions, but it is clear from them that 'a regular alternating motion' is characteristic of the non-organic. It is also clear from the historical examples, that for centuries the words Pulsation and Pulsate were used exclusively for organic processes. It is only in the second half of the 19th century (1870 and 1861 respectively) that they begin to be used for non-organic processes – and initially not by scientists but by a (mediocre) poet and by a newspaper. In other words, the use of Pulsation and Pulsate to describe non-organic processes of vibration and alternation begins as a literary metaphor – pseudo-poetry. It seems to have had the consequence of confusing definitions of pulsation.

The first meaning of Oscillate in the OED is 'To swing backwards and forwards, like a pendulum; to vibrate; to move to and fro between two points.' And the first historical record in this sense is from 1726.

There is an even earlier record of Oscillation, in 1658 where it is defined as 'a swinging upon a rope whose ends are tyed to several [meaning in 17th century English 'separate'] beams.

It is worth noting that Oscillate and Oscillation from their earliest recorded use, refer to a pendulum or other object which is swinging to and fro while *attached* to 'points' or 'beams.' In the same period (16th-18th century) Pulsate and Pulsation refer to movement *within an organism*. Their meanings are distinct. But when the pseudo-poetry of the late 19th century kicks in, and the word Pulsation is applied to mechanical and atmospheric effects, the result is confusion.

This confusion can be resolved if more clear definitions restore the meanings of Pulsation and Pulsate to their origin in describing organic processes, and reserve Oscillation and Vibration for non-organic processes.

In contrast to the OED, the German Wahrig Dictionary provides a clear distinction between pulsation and oscillation (being technical terms the words are the same in German as in English).

Pulsation is: 'Activity of the heart; the consequently evident pressure-waves in the arterial vascular system' [Tätigkeit des Herzens; die dadurch erzeugten Druckwellen im arterielle Gefäss-system]. Oscillation is: 'Swinging: regular movements' [Schwingen: gleichmässige Bewegungen].

'Vascular system' is the normal translation of 'Gefäss-system' but literally *Gefäss* means a container or vessel. The definition makes it clear that pulsation occurs in a *contained* system and spells out that this is associated with *pressure*-waves. On the other hand oscillation is simply a swinging back and forth (uncontained – as for example a pendulum). Furthermore Wahrig spells out that oscillation is *regular* and furthermore with the nuance in German that *gleichmässig* means *of equal measure.*

The Wahrig definitions in German resolve the confusion of the OED definitions in English, and since science is not merely an English-speaking enterprise, it would be useful to adopt them.

Observing pulsation

Reich, like Freud, could undermine his own work through impatience and ambition. (He was, as he admitted, in competition with Freud as part of working out his *Vaterbindung* – his father-attachment). Although he made pulsation the criterion for life he did not pause long enough to realise that unless it is defined as unequal-phase it is indistinguishable from the equal-phase oscillations and vibrations that saturate the universe. Consequently in his work the whole observable world, from auroras to red blood cells is said to pulsate – with 'life energy' or 'mass free orgone energy'. His work as a therapist was characterised (according to his patients as well as his writings) by subtle revelations of differences between surrender to life and resistance to it – i.e. by an acute awareness of life versus non-life. But in the universe everything became life – for a while, after which he had to re-invent death in the form of 'deadly orgone energy' or 'DOR', and his whole conceptual system became blurred. The life energy could supposedly become a death energy.

Reich seems to have realised some difficulty in his description of pulsation.

In his diary in 1946 he wrote: 'Despite hundreds of different but concurring results of orgonomy, I still have doubts as to the overall concept. It is too *simple*: sexual, chemical, and sidereal superimpositions are essentially one.'

In his late writings he tries to find a way out of the dilemma of non-living things which appear to pulsate, by proposing a distinction between 'bioenergetic' pulsation and 'mechanical' pulsation. But here he undercuts his whole theory. The distinction relies on circular explanations. (Dead material pulsates 'mechanically' because it is dead; live material pulsates 'bioenergetically' or 'functionally' because it is alive.) Reich's 'life science' offers no *observable* distinction (what would now be called an operational distinction) between life and non-life.

Reich also seems to have had a blind spot for time (probably in reaction against his youthful enthusiasm for the philosophy of Bergson), and never examined events in time terms. But time cannot be avoided in his orgasm formula. The pulsation in the diagram accompanying his first exposition of the orgasm formula (in *The Function of the Orgasm*, 1927) is *phase unequal*:

the expansion phase in the rising curve is longer than the contractive phase in the descending curve.

More importantly – although again Reich missed this implication of his own theory, probably because of the blind spot for time – the orgasm formula is a diagram *in time*. It is therefore a depiction of a *shape*. It is a way of *seeing time*.

The orgasm curve is quite different from the graph of a normal oscillation or vibration, which is expressed as a sine curve or wave and is *phase equal*. A heartbeat can only be diagrammed in a sine curve if time is disregarded. Otherwise the heart's diastole and systole must include *phase-unequal* curves. An ECG (electrocardiogram – a direct recording of electrical impulses between "lead" points as the heart beats) traces 5 forms, known as P, Q, R, S and T (with sometimes a faint concluding wave known as U). P represents a build-up of potential as a slowly rising curve which descends more quickly: it is phase unequal. It is followed by QRS which is a sharp spike (Q is the start, R the peak, and S the end) representing the mechanical release of tension in the "beat": it is phase equal. T is again more gentle: it is phase unequal.

Other directly recorded electrophysiological processes such as activity in the brain on electro-encephalograph (EEG) register as phase unequal, although as rapid spikes and domes, not waves.

Breathing is observably a pulsation. Normal breathing *in* is always shorter than breathing *out,* wherever it is observed, in infants or adults – or in animals, such as cats or dogs. It can be willed (pushed 'mechanically') into a phase-equal or phase-reversed rhythm, but this cannot be sustained for long, and would revert to phase unequal in sleep. It may also, in anxiety states, show a phase-reversal (where the in-breath takes longer than the out-breath) although this leads to hyperventilation, and cannot be sustained: the person must stop or loses consciousness. In normal breathing the long phase, breathing out, goes with contraction of the ribcage, lungs and abdominal wall, but with expansion of the diaphragm which is its centre.

A study of pulsation in the body shows a series of interrelated levels, sometimes expanding and contracting reciprocally, which can be called pulsations within pulsations. The point is not that there is an absolute link between contraction (or expansion) and one side of the phase unequal process, but that phase inequality is characteristic of pulsation and of life. In this book, the words *oscillation* and *vibration* are used to describe *phase equal* (mechanical) processes, but *pulsation* describes *phase unequal expansion and contraction* visible when charted out as asymmetrical.

Another example is the pulsation of a jellyfish. (This was one of Reich's paradigms of pulsation, though he did not discuss it as phase unequal). In my observations, mainly of *Aequorea aequorea*, a small jellyfish which swarms in summer in the NW Pacific, phase inequality is marked and consistent. The main pulsation is in the 'curtain' which forms the jellyfish's circumference and from which the tentacles trail. As the curtain expands, water is pushed behind the jellyfish and it then drifts with the curtain expanded; the curtain then contracts abruptly and is gathered in before expansion is repeated. The expansion phase is approximately twice as long as the contraction.

One recent area of investigation which produces evidence of unequal phase pulsation is brain imaging, and in particular high intensity functional magnetic resonance imaging (fMRI) in reflecting the response of deoxyhaemoglobin in the blood of the brain to the fMRI radio pulses. This investigation, known as BOLD (Blood Oxygenation Level Dependent) fMRI, is used to determine blood perfusion. The haemodynamic response, i.e. of biological activity in the brain, shows unequal phase pulsation. In contrast the fMRI radio pulses show as equal phase.

Pulsation and the definition of life

A preliminary theory might be that *phase unequal expansion and contraction are characteristic of life only, and thus distinguish it from non-life.* But this can be swiftly refuted with inference to a whole class of phenomena in which mechanical pressure is followed by release. Take a bubble in boiling toffee: it swells (expands) slowly, then bursts (contracts) quickly. If the bubble is so elastic that it collapses rather than fragments on bursting, as does a bubble in toffee, the process can be depicted by a phase unequal curve like that of Reich's orgasm formula. This was in turn based on a mechanical-hydraulic analogy, the bursting balloon, although a balloon's bursting is more abrupt than that of a toffee bubble.

Does this mean that the bubble has been alive? Or that a volcano which expands and bursts is also alive? Surely another criterion must be added: that of *repetition*. Repetition is a necessary attribute of life pulsation, as is acknowledged in the recent mechanistic addition of 'rhythm' (or 'rhythmicity') in definitions of metabolism. As noted above, the Oxford English Dictionary's definition of pulsation is 'rhythmic expansion and contraction.' The heart pulsation, or the breathing, observably repeat themselves until death occurs. The bubble or volcano do not repeat. A new bubble is unlikely to form in exactly the same place (because local tension has been released by the previous bubble's bursting), but even if it does it cannot be considered the same bubble. A volcano may indeed erupt more than once, but each time it does its configuration is different. Each eruption changes its form.

In fact, although Reich's 'orgasm curve' depicts a single unequal phase expansion and contraction, it is *not* a representation of pulsation, any more than a diagram of the swelling and bursting of a toffee bubble would be. It is a diagram of a one off event. Reich himself muddled it with his own descriptions of what actually happened in orgasm, the *orgasm reflex,* which *is* a pulsation. The orgasm reflex is simply the involuntary (autonomic) convulsion of the body that occurs at orgasm for those in whom it is not blocked by stiffening or holding in the musculature. This convulsion is an intensification of the breathing pulsation that occurs a number of times in succession – thus satisfying the criterion for pulsation that it is *repeated* unequal phase expansion/contraction. The orgasm reflex (or 'orgasm pulsation' as Reich accurately called it) is a series of intensified pulsations within the longer series of the breathing. Orgasm is a paradigm for pulsation (see Chapter 7) since it involves the whole body and so the pulsation can be described in extended detail – as well as experienced totally by the person.

The orgasm pulsation is demonstrably real: it can be confirmed by observation and is a usual experience for at least some people. But one of Reich's central assumptions seems to be wrong: that the orgasm pulsation is natural to 'the organism' – meaning the person as animal, rather than simply human. If this were so, it might be expected to occur in similar organisms, such as the other primates – who have the bonus of not being subjected to society's compulsory repression and defenses against feeling. However, as Adolph Smith points out (unpublished) following a search on the literature of primate sexuality, 'out of the 200 odd nonhuman primates, there is only one species, the bonobo, which leads what Reich would call a sex positive life.' Coitus in many animal species observably consists of 'Wham, bam, thank you Ma'am', and often without a discernible thank you. Although dogs and cats (and lions and other big cats) for example may show apparently reflexive undulating pelvic movements, the moment of orgasm is often accompanied only by a stiffening tremor. Similar phenomena were observed in human beings in the laboratories of Masters and Johnson who did not describe pulsation in orgasm. But perhaps a full surrender to autonomic movement is unlikely in a laboratory in subjects who can probably be described as at least situationally 'uptight.'

The orgasm convulsion was described by Reich at one point as 'physiologically identical to vomiting' – which if true would mean we would vomit during orgasm. Perhaps it is more like the mechanical contraction of a squid to expel a cloud of ink. But these images arise from Reich's view of the orgasm as 'energetic discharge' – again here is the contamination by Freud's libido theory. Reich even developed a view of 'sex economy', which became part of his political agenda in the 1930s. At the time ideas of 'sexual hygiene' were also common. They had originated in the 19th century when various medical doctors (for example William Acton, the Victorian expert on masturbation) took an economical view of sex in terms of saving and spending. The Victorian equivalent of 'Did you come?' or 'Did the earth move for you?' was 'Did you spend?' (See *My Secret Life* by 'Walter' for many examples of this sort of thinking.) Reich's *The Mass Psychology of Fascism* although its explanation of how sexual repression feeds violence is still valid for the 21st century (the book could do with a revival), also discusses 'sex economy'. Reich could not escape being a man of his time. But 'sex economy' has a mechanistic ring, and it seems to exclude, above all, *emotion,* whereas in his therapy and in his later development of 'orgonomy' Reich was always aware of emotion.

Some women who have read *The Function of the Orgasm* have found the 'orgasm formula' to be a masculine model, its convulsions associated with penetration and ejaculation – yet Reich maintained consistently that, like all emotional expression, it showed itself identically in men and women. A subversive poet Martin Seymour-Smith suggested in his *Sex and Society* that Reich fulfilled the common male fantasy of 'teaching' a woman to enjoy sex. (This is always a doomed enterprise: as the witty Karl Kraus pointed out, a man who hopes to teach a woman to enjoy her own body is like someone who arrives at the railway station of an unknown city carrying a map.) At times Reich appears to propose the 'correct' orgasm, but to both sexes. But this is difficult to avoid in discussing a natural phenomenon that is often blocked by an 'armour' resulting from the suppression of emotions. For example, to state that in deep sobbing the body convulses is not a prescription of correctness, it is a description of an unimpeded natural process.

If the breathing is intensified in Reichian therapy by asking the person to breathe all the way out repeatedly, and if the person is able to let go fully, the result is often that the breathing becomes the autonomic convulsion of the orgasm reflex – without the orgasm of course. Over-breathing may also lead to anxiety or to an emotional outburst ('abreaction'). The softer emotional outbursts such as reaching out in longing, or crying, also lead to convulsions similar to those in orgasm. Deep sobbing elicits convulsions of the body very similar to the orgasm reflex. And the 'orgasm reflex' itself is well documented. (See Chapter 7).

Whether the capacity to surrender to the orgasm reflex fulfills all the claims Reich made for it, in corresponding to emotional and physical health, is a further question. But, like sobbing or, yes, vomiting, it is an intensified version of the breathing in which pulsation occurs over an observably wider range, involving the entire body. A less dramatic involvement of the entire body in the breathing pulsation can be observed in babies. As they breathe in, their head tilts slightly forward (chin going down) and their toes tilt slightly forward and down. As they breathe out, in the longer phase of the pulsation, their head tilts slightly back and their toes tilt slightly upward. Physiologically this is an alternating extension of the body with the inbreath and flexion with the outbreath.

I propose that: *Life is distinguished from non-life by the presence of enclosed pulsation consisting of repeated phase-unequal expansion and contraction.*

Pulse-Waves

Words such as vibration, oscillation, and scintillation (e.g. of light through a whirling propeller blade) have different applications in scientific usage. But all suggest a regular mechanical movement back and forth, in and out, or up and down, in which phases are observed or measured as equal. In biology they may aid description (e.g. of the movement of cell contents) but do not make a statement about life functions as such. Pulsation, in the sense proposed above, is particularly useful in discussing the functions of cells or of the body and many of its organs. But in observation of organic life, pulsation is often apparently bound up in another kind of movement, what I shall call for now (following the Wahrig definition of pulsation) *pressure-waves*.

In the inorganic world waves are common. In the sea they occur as propagating swells across the surface, as well as breakers coming into shore. No one claims they are alive, although they have a breath-like rhythm or beat. Each 'one off' breaker which slowly rises then falls on the shore can be seen in terms of phase unequal expansion/contraction. There is also an element of repetition not only in the sequence of the waves but in variations of the sequence, in particular the often observed phenomenon of the 'ninth wave' which tends inexplicably to be stronger than those preceding. Each wave is unique, not self-repeating, and open, not enclosed. So even though phase unequal, waves cannot be described as pulsating. The waves of the sea are not like the pressure-waves of pulsation along the arteries.

What about a flow of water along a closed pipe from a mechanical pump? The pipe, being narrow, provides resistance. Nevertheless when you open the tap the water does not come out in pulsatory spurts as blood would from a severed artery. Unlike the heart, a mechanical pump does not pulsate, it provides a steady pressure through the rotation of a vane or blade. Water does come out in spurts from a hand pump, according to the action on the handle. A heart pacemaker provides a regular electrical pulse which is sufficient to stimulate the heart to pulsate and pressure waves to travel along the arteries causing measurable pulsation all over the body. Strictly speaking 'taking the pulse' is taking the pulsation: it is unequal phase. During surgical operations the circulation can be maintained by the use of an artificial heart – but not for very long. It does not seem to be possible to sustain life in the body simply by pumping the circulation mechanically. Arterial walls *contain* the circulation, and whether initiated by the regular pulses of an artificial heart or not, the 'pulse' at the wrist is an unequal phase pulsation.

One curious observable pulse in nature is that of maple sap as it spurts out of the tree in the early morning when the sun warms the frosty ground and the sap rises – not in a steady flow but in a series of gushes. The series is highly irregular, however. One gush of sap down the 'spile' (the tube inserted into the bark) and into the hanging bucket, is followed after a while by another gush. It might be interesting to compare a graph of this gushing of the sap to one of the gushing of semen during ejaculation. In ejaculation the first gush is the strongest then there is a rapid series of gushes diminishing in strength. Ejaculation seems more obviously pulsatory then the rising of the sap. But if it is partly suppressed by either a voluntary squeezing of surrounding muscles, or the chronic contraction of these muscles which occurs in some people who, as Reich would put it, are 'armoured' against sensation in the genital area, then the ejaculation is a brief steady flow or a more prolonged trickle.

Even if it is possible to define pulsation in fairly simple terms, the *dynamics* – meaning the *interaction of forces* – during pulsation can obviously be quite complex. One element is clearly *resistance*. Another is the interaction of different pulsations, which can be reciprocal. For example in the breathing pulsation, the abdominal wall and rib-cage expand while the diaphragm contracts – and vice versa. And when two people make love – 'it takes two to tango', after all – there is an interaction between two pulsations. Then there are unexplored possibilities such as the probable *acceleration* and *deceleration* of the unequal phases of pulsation. When acceleration, rather than velocity, began to be measured in physics by Galileo the result was a scientific revolution.

These details with regard to pulsation remain to be explored in neuroscience and biophysics. In this book details are only important if they refute the definition. It would be refuted, for example, if pulsation, as defined, was found to occur in something which we otherwise agree not to be alive – such as a star or a rock. But there is sometimes uncertainty about where to draw the line between life and non-life. An oceanographer, John Baross, who studies organisms that live around deep sea volcanic vents without light or oxygen, at a session on astrobiology at the 2003 annual meeting of the American Astronomical Society, remarked about definitions of life based on complexity, activity, reproductivity, metabolism etc: 'It's pretty contentious. Nobody agrees.' It might be useful to know if these putative organisms *pulsate* – in which case they *are* organisms.

In physics waves are identified in the transmission of sound, electromagnetic energy, and light. They are depicted as phase equal 'sine waves'. But it must be noted that this apparent phase equality may be in some cases an artefact of the measuring technique. It would seem logical that a guitar string vibrating over a given range in an observably phase equal way would produce sound waves which are themselves phase equal. However, if a stick is oscillated back and forth phase equally in a pond, the waves which propagate outwards in circles are phase unequal because of the water's resistance. Resistance of the air to sound waves may produce a similar effect. Perhaps atmospheric resistance to electromagnetic waves also produces phase inequality. This is, so far as I know, not observable. Nor is it important in physics: what counts (literally is counted) is the frequency of the wave's propagated pulse, and its amplitude. Similarly a wind turns a windmill slow or fast according to its speed, and wind speed is calculated by timing the turning of a vane. But these mechanical effects are averages of the wind's activity. If you stand in a breeze you can note that not only is it not steady (although it may turn a vane steadily next to you), but that it is hitting you in the form of rhythmic pulses. The trembling of leaves in a nearby tree may reflect this. What is more, apparently because of resistance (they are attached by their stalks), the leaves' movement away from and back to the direction of the wind is phase unequal.

Just as phase equal oscillation is different from phase unequal pulsation, so phase equal waves seem different from phase unequal waves. Since physics has appropriated the word *wave* to describe any phase equal vibration across space (though extrapolating, in a false analogy, from waves in nature such as the sea's, which are observably phase unequal) it is impossible to deny physics its terminology. But strictly speaking what physics calls a wave is an abstraction. Sound waves may indeed be waves, since they work against resistance. But electromagnetic (EM) waves which can travel across a vacuum, can most accurately be called a *pulse sequence*: no more a real sequence of waves than a sequence of machine-gun bullets. The particle theory of EM transmission expresses physics' own distrust of the wave analogy. But physics assumes all waves are equal phase 'sine waves', unless they are 'distorted.'

If particles are assumed to travel *on* waves, then an 'aether' must be assumed (anathema to physics which has ostensibly abolished it): a kind of cosmic ocean. Or if particles disappear and *become* waves, this is an abstraction from the fact that the particles can be caught en route, the catching suddenly rendering them, or a spiral track, visible. Whether they travel in spirals – or spiralling waves – or merely impact as spirals is another question. The waves observed in quantum physics (at other times observed as particles, according to the conditions of the observation) are represented as sine waves in any diagram I have seen, and I assume can be determined to be such. Apparently rotation of any object or celestial body produces, mechanically, sine waves of electromagnetic energy. At any rate – listen to the static on the radio! – the universe is permeated by them.

Reich seems to have sensed that he had not grasped the distinction between pulsation and pulse-waves. In a notebook in 1948 he wrote: 'I had thought that pulsation *consists* of pulses. Now I knew: Pulsation functions in the variations, pulses and waves. SIMULTANEOUSLY.'

This is a useful restatement of his former confusion. Perhaps he was getting there... only to be swept away in the battle of his late years.

Cycles, Flow, Time

Our local environment is dominated by cycles which have some similarity to pulsation. For example, the further we live North or South of the equator, the more dramatically we are exposed to a cycle of lengthening days and shorter nights, then vice versa. Could the origin of pulsation in organisms be due to their adaptation to this asymmetry? First protists (protozoa, algae), then plants, then animals, all living under the sun, developed under a regime of opening and closing (or expanding and contracting, acting and resting etc.) every day. There is even evidence that some organisms function in a somewhat shorter cycle of 23 hours or so, and it is proposed that this is because they adapted to their environment when the earth was rotating faster. Then there are those famous experiments where oysters were taken to Chicago and within a few days had adjusted their opening and closing cycle to the tides in the Atlantic 1,500 miles away. Darwin, who tried his hand at almost every experimental question of interest, towards the end of his life did meticulous work with 'circumnutation', the way plants turn to follow the sun. To his surprise he found that circumnutation was intrinsic. Wherever he put the plants, in or out of the sun, they needed to turn. If stopped, they died. Some plants expanded their leaves every day and closed them at night. If he bound their leaves so that they could not expand, they died. But the asymmetry of day and night throughout the year is not a pulsation as defined here. Even as days lengthen, they are symmetrical and equal phase from the point of view of an observer. On any day of the year the sun rises and sets at almost equal times from its apogee at noon, i.e. every day is equal phase, like all non-organic regular expansion and contraction. (Exact equality of phase is complicated by the slight lengthening or shortening of each day). Unequal phase pulsation may be dependent on the environment for its timing (as we breather faster and more shallowly when it is 20 degees below zero) but the pulsation itself is independent.

Reich wrote: 'For the moment we assume that emotion is tied to the existence and movement of protoplasmic substance within a circumscribed system and, without this precondition, does not exist.' Neuroscience can now demonstrate more accurately than in Reich's day the mechanics and biochemistry of neurotransmission – and for that matter of the 'volume transmission' of chemicals through the interstitial fluid which surrounds the neural network. What we experience as emotion is *internal* movement, its *containment*, and its *external* expression. Reich's definition above, although he considered it provisional, is a valuable step toward the understanding of life experienced as emotion. Jaak Panksepp's *Affective Neuroscience* documents the modern equivalents of 'the movement of protoplasmic substance'. One of Panksepp's conclusions is that on the observable ('objective') evidence of animal behaviour and the neurochemical events that accompany it, we must conclude that animals too experience emotion. Descartes' idea that 'I think therefore I am' has in effect been rephrased by Panksepp as 'I feel therefore I am'. It cannot be claimed that a rat or a pigeon think – but the evidence is that that they feel.

Is it possible that the resistance of a membrane (the 'circumscribed system') to the flow of pulse waves is what seems to convert them into pulsation? The nature of this resistance must be explored further before the containment of emotion, and perhaps the subjective sense of being alive – the most simple kind of consciousness – can be understood.

Bergson's philosophy took off into the blank of intellectual outer space from the launching pad of a single original intuition of the function of time. Originally an almost fanatical mechanist working to conceptualise a philosophy which would be *entirely* mechanistic, he stumbled upon a block which completely reversed his course. It was in a study of the famous Zeno's paradox (in which Achilles can never catch up with the tortoise, since every time he completes half of the distance half of it remains to be covered) that Bergson came to the conclusion that there was a difference between the mechanistic view of time and the actual experience of time. Time is measurable by increments in the same way as the distribution of matter in space. Thus the running Achilles cannot logically ever catch up. Zeno's paradox, though a *reductio ad absurdum,* is impeccable, and mechanistic analysis simply does not offer a way out. What we know, though, from common sense, is that the action of Achilles' running will eventually carry him past the tortoise. In other words there is a difference between the action of running, and the chopping up of this action into spatial increments. This is similar, Bergson notes, to the difference between life and the examination of a piece of dead tissue by a mechanistic biologist. The procedure is to kill the action and subject it to an analysis in terms of its spatial configuration. But this configuration has already happened: it is not the story of what is, but of what was. Time as experience and action, and time as the measured course of the action afterwards are quite different. The first kind of time Bergson renamed *duration* (la durée). It is real time. The second kind, what we normally know as time, is a *spatialisation*. This is obvious from the figures on a clock or sundial. More recently, the physicist Julian Barbour has stated flatly that intervals of time are in fact lengths in space. An example is the passing of a minute on a clock face. Barbour dismisses all time as an illusion. (He rejects duration). Bergson split time into two: spatialised time and lived time. Lived time, which Bergson considered to be real time, could only be understood in terms of such concepts as action, duration, impulse, and the energy behind the impulse. This insight into time led Bergson to the vitalistic concept of the élan vital – the force behind duration.

The insight itself is not new. Three hundred years before Bergson, the poet John Donne wrote: 'If this *Imaginary halfe-nothing, Tyme*, be of the Essence of our *Happinesses*, how can they be thought *durable? Tyme* is not so; How can they bee thought to be? *Tyme* is not so; not so, considered in any of the *parts* thereof.' Donne may have been thinking of Heraclitus who thought that everything was in flux or change and wrote that 'all things are one...an everlasting fire, flaring up in measures, and dying down in measures.'

The metaphysical possibilities of Bergson's theory are large since measured space is cut off, as it were, from the process of real time. Even classical physics, viewing time as an extra-spatial dimension (a description Bergson rejected), at least sees it as one dimension among others. Bergson's theory is particularly abstract to readers in the English-speaking empiricist tradition (although it forms the basis of continental 'phenomenology'). It does nevertheless solve Zeno's absurd paradox, and its basic appeal to the person's understanding of time through experience is true 'common sense.' It makes a vital distinction between duration, or 'lived time' and the spatial time which mechanism offers as basic to its understanding not only of material geometry but of life itself. Bergson's argument is a powerful starting point for the contention that the study of life must be in terms which are not mechanistic.

Bergson had a role to play in the fashions of 20th century philosophy, especially as the grandfather of phenomenology. But it must be admitted that he was largely re-hashing Heraclitus.

Paul Kammerer's interest in time was not philosophical. But he collected hundreds of examples of coincidences, in his own life and from anecdotes by others, to support a theory that some events tended to occur in series, and wrote a popular book, *Das Gesetz der Serie (The Law of Series)*, 1919 – never translated into English. As Koestler points out, Kammerer's law of series has been absorbed by Jung's much better known theory of 'synchronicity' which was propounded some years after Kammerer's death. Jung's definition of synchronicity is almost word for word identical to Kammerer's definition of 'seriality'. In fact, seriality is a more accurate description of Jung's basic theory than the word 'synchronicity' which, as Jung has to explain, is not strictly accurate since the coincidences under study in fact occur in series (clusters in time) not synchronously (at the same time). Koestler, in a gentlemanly way makes a very strong case that Jung stole the idea from Kammerer's book, relabeled it, diluted its implications, and could get away with this since Kammerer's work was discredited because of the scandal of 'the midwife toad' following which Kammerer shot himself.

Kammerer did not, as Bergson did, spell out a connection between time and life energy. In spite of Kammerer's interest in the concept of life energy, most of his work takes an opposite tack: he maintains that biological evolution occurs through a process of pattern formation through seriality. Reich, whose life's project was research into life energy, completely disregarded the functioning of time. Although ready to acknowledge that he was seen as 'a crazy Bergsonian', he seems to have been uninterested in Bergson's concept. He does mention it respectfully at least twice: 'His explanation of the perception of *time duration* in mental life and of the unity of the self only confirmed my inner perceptions of the non-mechanistic nature of the organism.' And 'Bergson's brilliant formulation of the "experience of continuum" made the mistake of describing these biopsychic processes as "metaphysics"'. In both these examples Reich describes Bergson's idea as applying to mental or psychic events. He does discuss it the second time in the context of describing the flux and flow of natural processes. And *flow* is possibly the best English word for what Bergson meant by duration. (See Paul Cynzmenty's book, *Flow*, which had such a popular success in the 1990s). Probably for Reich, as for many others, the duration concept became swallowed up in Bergson's metaphysics.

Reich strongly rejected all abstract philosophising, and time seems to have been an abstract concept for him. He wrote in an essay:

> The behavior of our society toward its body odor is not different from that of the people of the Rococco period. It glorifies flights into the stratosphere but does not allow the Augean stable to be cleaned, which poisons everyday life. He who, instead of meditating about space and time undertakes to clean this stable or even to suggest ways of doing it, is called crazy.

Reich did not see the possibility that there was some fundamental connection between 'life energy' and 'lived time', and that the exploration of this might resolve some of the problems he encountered in his attempt to develop a science and technology of this energy (and even to help clean up the Augean stable).

It proved impossible, in measurements of the effects of life energy on its surroundings, to match mechanistic precision. But Reich doggedly pursued the goal of measurability, and at times wrote as if the success of orgonomy depended on it – while at other times admitting it was unreliable. Bergson's contention that spatialized time can never be a just measurement of life processes might have been a help to him – but only if he had turned frankly metaphysical, and mysticised the life energy. Bergson, as a true metaphysician, rejected the concept of measurement altogether for anything to do with human life. A theory of life as pulsation provides a way out of this dilemma in proposing that the source of the usual physical energy of metabolism and of whatever radiation is specific to the organism's pulsation. It seems unlikely that the reductionism, abstraction, and averaging of mathematics – so useful in technology – or even a topographical and qualitative mathematics like Thom's catastrophe theory, can express the irregular rhythms of lived time.

Streamings and pulsation can be *depicted* (though not strictly speaking spatially measured) through *graphs in time* – as when an EEG graph is studied for the recurrence of such patterns as 'spike and dome'. The crucial point about Reich's description of the orgasm (in a person who is able to give in to it) is that the rise and fall of excitation follow a specific curve (or flow/duration) in time. This is a demonstration of what distinguishes pulsation from similar processes such as vibration or oscillation. Reich's claim that the 'orgasm formula' is the 'life formula' can be rephrased in a testable way (or in Popper's rather extreme term in a 'falsifiable' way) as the statement that: *pulsation is the main criterion of life, and where there is no pulsation there is no life.*

Reich may not have realised how much his early work, with its diagrams and curves and verbal descriptions of events, does in fact fulfil many genuine scientific criteria for the making of testable statements. His pursuit of mechanistic precision in measurement with various instruments modified from pre-existing devices for the measure of radiation or electricity may not have been necessary: his procedures are legitimate once it is recognized that they are adequate expressions of events in time.

Furthermore, the apparent connection between time functions and life functions may be more than of philosophical interest. The current physical world view rests on assumptions that there is no specific life energy, and that there is no non-spatialised time in Bergson's sense of duration: there is no flow, either of energy or of time.

Boucroux, a predecessor of Bergson, pointed out that our experience of personal freedom is enough to provide a refutation of the deterministic view that we do not have this freedom. Similarly, in Bergson's view, our experience of duration is enough to refute the view that spatial time is the only time.

Until recently physics did not admit singularities. Even now, when singularities are a common place of both quantum physics and the astrophysics, any event which cannot be dependably reproduced in a laboratory is like evidence ruled out of court. But, for example, many people have experienced precognition, and almost by definition it is singular, not repetitive.

Reich frequently wrote that the researcher's own body sensations were the primary tool of research into life. But he did not seem to believe that inter-subjectively cross-checked human experience could be an adequate base for the establishment of scientific laws. A true life science may have to rest on a kind of experiential 'common law', rather than on mechanistically precise 'statute.' And this common law does not permit the isolation of a particular life function for the purposes of laying down statutes. Reich attacked biologists for killing living organisms and chopping them into pieces for examination – what Chargaff would call necrology. But Reich too could chop life into pieces: in particular he isolated the sexual function from the experiential continuum and derived a descriptive 'statute' from his observations. His emphasis on pulsation was of vital importance but it was sometimes left behind in his emphasis on 'the energy' in the 'orgasm formula'.

A succinct dismissal of the relevance of an 'energy' concept to human life has been offered by Gregory Bateson: 'If mass and length are inappropriate for the describing of behavior, then energy is unlikely to be more appropriate. After all, energy *is* Mass + Velocity, and no behavioral scientist really insists that "psychic energy" is of these dimensions.' And: 'The conservation laws for energy and matter concern substance rather than form. But mental process, ideas, communication, organisation, differentiation, pattern, and so on, are matters of form rather than substance.' So for Bateson, as for Capra and for Sheldrake, the way out of biology as a valid life science is to concentrate, through systems theory and morphological analysis, on the *forms* life takes.

Bateson, in fact, came near to formulating a theory which might have matched Reich's in daring, when he proposed that there was a process of increased intensity in human interactions which led to a cumulative tension which resolved itself either in a split ('schismogenesis') or, in the case of sex, into fusion. He compared this to the process in orgasm, and pointed out that the *curve* representing this process in time (or, as he put it in another context, in 'the stream of events') was not the usual exponential curve but one of a new type. In effect, without reference to Reich, he was on the edge of making the same point (that the orgasm curve is the curve of basic life functions) without Reich's energy concept. But Bateson stopped short of making the point clearly or developing it, leaving it 'to be explored.' And possibly this is because without an *equivalent* to 'energy' the purely formal diagrams of this or that curve are empty. Something is missing.

A theory of life as pulsation provides a way out of this dilemma in proposing that the source of the usual physical energy of metabolism and of whatever radiation or 'field' is specific to the organism is the pulsation acting within its necessary membrane. Biology can analyse some of the effects of this pulsation. Systems theories may be of help in analysing its *forms*. The pulsation itself is not yet understood.

Subjectively, if I pay attention to the pulsation of my breathing, I am aware of an easy expansion of my abdomen and chest then a 'turn-around' moment when the in-breath seems to meet resistance: my lungs are full. Then I experience an easy and prolonged letting go on the out-breath as my chest and abdomen go down and contract. Then the expansion almost magically begins again. There is no sense of resistance at this point, only when the expansion phase reaches its limit again. Although breathing in and breathing out are both effortless (and usually out of consciousness), there is that one point when the lungs are full when there is a sense of resistance. It is like a sort of 'Heave-Ho' in which, for example, sailors take a pull on a rope, then reach a limit, then relax, then heave again. This is pulsatory, since the Heave is shorter in time than the Ho. There is an element of tension on the in-breath, relaxation on the out-breath. Yet I have to breathe in. What am I breathing in? Here is where an 'energy' explanation can jump to mind: something insists on filling my lungs, until it meets resistance, whereupon it has to relax. Is this 'something' a life force? An energy?

I don't think so. We need to breathe, biochemically, to fill our lungs with oxygen. Before we began breathing, in the womb, our heart (and probably other organs) pulsated: we were alive since our heart began as that pulsating speck described by Harvey. And in our first spontaneous breath we began to pulsate as a whole, as one organism. Pulsation does not require an energy. Our lungs, although they contain the pulsation as a bicycle tyre contains air, do not need to be pumped up. They simply pulsate, as part of a whole body pulsation which is not usually totally visible, but which can be seen in a new-born baby and in orgasm where we pulsate from head to toes. The pulsation does not require an energy, it is an end in itself. It is a process, an event in time – or if there is no universal time it is a pulsation shape in the universe.

4

MICROSCOPIC LIFE

Form and function

In vitalism an outside life force permeates organisms. In animism everything is alive. There is also a modified vitalist view (called by Koestler, Sheldrake and others 'organicism') that there is an 'immanent' life force acting only within organisms. But the standard scientific view is the mechanistic one that life is determined by *structure*, which is in turn determined by genetic blueprints. (If you find this bleak, then Richard Dawkins will console you with the news that all this enables our puppet-masters, the genes, to replicate themselves)

There are strong arguments for the mechanistic view. For example, brine shrimp eggs may be boiled or frozen but once restored to the appropriate temperature and conditions they will begin to develop. There is no life force within them to be 'killed' by the boiling or freezing. Their structure, so long as it remains intact, will ensure that the process of growth occurs under the right conditions. Similarly, artificial insemination can occur successfully from frozen sperm and ova. Presumably, as suggested by observation of the tiny throbbing in a chicken egg yolk, at a given moment when the fertilised egg is planted in the pulsating body of the mother, its own pulsation kicks in.

Sheldrake suggests that although life needs intact structure in order to function, structure may be analogous to a radio through which music is channeled but which is not itself the music. (Popper and Eccles made the same point in *The Mind and its Brain*). Sheldrake develops the idea, following Waddington, that structure canalizes a formative agency. This is not, however, thought to be an energy either from outside or immanent, but rather a 'morphic field' which Sheldrake compares with a plan for a house. Any possible energetic factor is disposed of by a concept of 'morphic resonance': the plan resonates with all previous similar plans and may be somewhat modified in this process. Sheldrake's theory at the very least plugs the many holes (which he skilfully exposes) in the mechanistic view of life. The theory does not provide a distinction between life and non-life: an atom and an organism each have their own 'morphic resonance'. But it brings forth evidence that movement and behaviour must be considered in terms of form, and by its recurrence. Earlier morphologists, notably Goethe, made similar points. D'Arcy Thompson's contention that every form is 'a diagram of forces' opened the way to the concept that form not only channels energy (in the basic sense that all energy is movement, as Sheldrake remarks, and as such is reciprocal to form which is in itself static) but is in some way laid down by energy.

This was Reich's view, with life energy from outside becoming 'trapped' in an enclosing membrane and tending to form certain basic shapes – bean-like, ovoid, spiral etc. Furthermore Reich proposed that any structure was simply the 'frozen history' of the movement which preceded its formation: 'function precedes form.' This would now be disputed in physics where (see below) form is seen as constraining function. But here he is introducing the 'life energy' in a sort of ghost form – as existing before material life. (This is a Cartesian dualistic position). As always, though, Reich emphasises observation. Movement (particularly if pulsatory, meaning in effect for Reich oscillatory) denotes life, but also certain non-moving forms are a history of the past movement of life. Thus, the distinction between life and non-life can be made in the past tense by studying structure for evidence of where pulsation or other movements specific to life have occurred – which makes sense, being not much different from studying fossils for evidence of past life functions. This kind of observation can even work in psychotherapy, where a person's clenched jaw, for example, contains the 'frozen history' of childhood defiance.

For Sheldrake, a discussion of the origins of morphic fields can only be metaphysical, not scientific, because not testable. Less cautiously, Goethe developed a neo-Platonic theory that all forms descend from an ideal ancestor – that all plant forms, for example, descend from and are still part of an 'original plant' – 'Urpflanz'. (Although Goethe did not use this example, the potato is an Urpflanz in that every existing potato is not only descended from an original potato, all potatoes are related to each other as parts of one huge plant.) The concern with ultimate origins can still be found in both religion and science: 'in the beginning was the Word', God, the Big Bang, or DNA in a primeval soup. Stephen Hawking, author of *A Brief History of Time* and a successor to Newton's chair at Cambridge, is consulted by journalists about the nature of God. But perhaps the creation of forms, and the movement through which it acts, are not the descendants, mechanical effects or resonances of past processes, but continuous processes occurring *now*. In a universe of pure shape as proposed by Julian Barbour, everything is happening at once, in a succession of contiguous *Nows,* and forms or structures are 'time capsules' with awareness and memory built into them. This is not incompatible with Thompson's idea that form is a diagram of forces – so long as the forces are seen as the 'fields' in which all matter is distributed, not as external. As Mae Wan Ho puts it simply, 'the act is the cause.' Form and function are identical. (In time terms these statements appear illogical, but they come into their own if Barbour is right and the universe is timeless and consists of pure shape.)

The identity of form and function has recently returned into discussions of evolution, having been abandoned for most of the 20th century, as it becomes clear that Darwin's theory of natural selection must be modified to include findings in genetics as well as the discovery of universal patterns of forms across nature, in both the living and the non-living. Fodor and Patelli-Palmarini in *What Darwin Got Wrong* include a chapter on 'The Return of the Laws of Form', in which they discuss, among other forms, the prevalence of the Fibonacci series (each number being the sum of the two preceding numbers: 1, 2, 3, 5, 8, 13, 21 etc.) in everything from sunflower heads to galaxies. These forms represent the physical constraints of the universe at levels from the microscopic to the macroscopic. They do *not* support Reich's idea that form is 'frozen history': the reverse in fact, since function does not precede form, but form constrains function. It is not so much a diagram of forces, as Thompson thought, as something that restricts forces. The constraints of physics come first. Organisms – life – must fit in. As must galaxies – non-life. The Fibonacci series, for example, would be seen as a recurring shape in Barbour's shape universe. Perhaps a future research programme focused on pulsation in a timeless frame of reference could explore the *shapes* of pulsation – in effect the shapes of the living as distinct from the non-living, although both are constrained by the structure of the universe.

One arena where continuous processes involving biological forms can be studied is microscopy. But the study of micro-organisms while they are alive, not freeze dried and sliced, is a dying art.

Necrology

The biochemist Erwin Chargaff who contributed to the discovery of DNA lamented that biology, the study of life, had become a necrology, a study of death. By the end of the 20th century this necrology was so well established that such laments were just old hat – ignored. After all, the necrology has been so productive: babies are born from deep frozen sperm and eggs, Dolly the sheep has been cloned, the HIV virus has been identified, genetically modified (GM) foods are cheap to produce, cows and sheep are kept free from disease by the prophylactic use of antibiotics. If the future physical and emotional health of the babies is still an open question, if there is the temporary glitch that Dolly's cells are already half way to death a year after her birth, if the life of AIDS victims is something less than optimal due to the side effects of anti-viral drugs, GM crops spread disease-prone mutations to neighbouring fields, and millions of farm animals must be slaughtered and burned in a foot-and-mouth epidemic – the health bureaucrats are ready with messages of reassurance. But something more is wrong: tuberculosis is back to stay, Western populations are becoming more and more obese, lesser STDs than AIDS are becoming endemic (30 – 40% of sexually active British teenagers carry chlamydia), the sperm counts of men born after 1950 or so are at half the levels of their fathers, a stay in even the best hospital is fraught with the danger of catching the penicillin resistant infections MRSA or C Difficile. In the UK and US about 20% of people seek help from their doctors every year for symptoms of depression, which normally include sexual dysfunction. Most are treated with anti-depressant medications whose major side-effect is sexual dysfunction… Even the contraceptive pill reduces 'libido' in about a third of women who take it.

Goethe prophesied in 1800 or so that within a century the world would become one huge hospital. Now that the 18th century death of God has been followed by the supposed late 20th century 'end of history', and people without a sustaining religion are left with one burning concern – their personal immortality – Goethe's prophecy has come true. Since I have worked in hospitals I can hardly complain. I have seen people who have lived longer in years than they could have ever have hoped when they were young. But from late middle age (about average life expectancy when they were born) for most people things start going wrong. Of people aged 65 about 10% have a degree of cognitive impairment, 20% are taking anti-depressant medication, 40% or so take medication to reduce blood pressure, or blood sugar or cholesterol levels, 30% or so have ceased to have a sex life.

Well, that's life: it includes eventual illness and death. And there is a place for care, the reduction of suffering, the management of illness. But why accept the illusion of Goethe's hospital: that everything is in hand, is improving, is understood by the experts? In fact most of the improvement in mortality statistics during the 20th century was caused by improvement of sewage systems: engineers, not doctors, should be thanked for increased life spans. Could public health be one of those vast self-deceiving conspiracies – like the culture industry where people pretend to be artists and other people pretend to appreciate them, or like the late Soviet Union where the witticism was that 'we pretend to work and they pretend to pay us?'

Against this background, books about what necrology has identified under its electron microscopes in microtomed freeze dried slices or smears of centrifuged molecules become best sellers. The most famous is probably Richard Dawkins' *The Selfish Gene* which Dawkins has followed with various clones. In 1999 the favourite was Ian Stewart's *Life's Other Secret*, on 'the mathematics of the living world' – a study of morphology taking off from the work of Darcy Thompson. These two books, and many others, have something in common: a cosy anthropomorphism, evident even in the titles. Here is Stewart discussing (with illustrations from electron microscopy) how the tobacco mosaic virus follows 'a natural growth process' in which, something like crystal, its various parts accrete in different ways according to the composition of the intracellular liquid in which it finds itself:

> That protein assembly takes place at low pH, even without the RNA coil, is a natural inorganic pattern on which evolution can build. It does so in an amazing manner... The problem,

for the virus, is to cause helical growth to occur at neutral pH, where it is *not* going to happen spontaneously without an RNA coil. How does nature use RNA to achieve this construction?

This is intrinsically dull stuff: chemistry, in fact, and how many of us found chemistry our favourite subject at school? (I must admit I failed it.) It is also difficult to explain in an unadorned way without syntactical confusion amounting even to nonsense ('That protein assembly takes place ... is a natural inorganic pattern'). So the explanation, after the disastrous first sentence, is tarted up with anthropomorphism. 'Evolution can build...in an amazing manner'. And the cute little virus has a 'problem'. Then 'nature' – straight from classical allegory – steps on stage and is about to 'use RNA to achieve this construction.' In five lines no less than three personifications are invoked. But evolution and nature are abstract constructs, and the dear little virus is generally agreed to be incapable of thought. What is *happening*? As the philosopher Richard Spilsbury put it in a discussion of how the language of purpose creeps into Darwinism, this is 'an attempt to to supernaturalize nature, to endow unthinking processes with more-than-human powers.'

David Stove (in *Darwinian Fairytales*) has attacked *The Selfish Gene* along similar lines, and quotes Dawkins' excuse that these are only 'figures of speech' to enliven the text. Stove replies with the challenge: write a text without these anthropomorphic 'figures of speech'. In effect, 'Put up or shut up.' Until a Dawkins or a Stewart is capable of writing a clear explanatory text about genetics and biology without resource to anthropomorphism their texts are too rife with the 'teleological fallacy' (that event X occurs *in order to* produce the following event Y – as when the dear little virus ingeniously solves its problem) to be logically acceptable. This kind of 'biological teleology' has contributed to the logical quagmire that is the modern version of natural selection, as exposed in Fodor's and Piattelli-Palmarini's *What Darwin Got Wrong*.

What would remain in the above quoted text if it were stripped down to observables? What remains in any journal paper in modern biology: a dry recitation of unconnected necrological observations. And no clarity whatsoever about what is alive or dead.

Protoplasm

It is worth taking a look at what preceded the structural approach in biology whose triumph over 'protoplasm' Peter Medawar so cheerfully celebrated. It was the study of colloids, literally 'sticky solutions' – or 'slime, snot and protoplasm' according to a Victorian writer quoted by Darwin – under the light microscope with living preparations. Darwin himself, on and off throughout his life, studied microscopic cells in plants, which he called 'gemmules' or 'living atoms' and viewed at one point as signs of 'pangenesis' – generation from all. However Darwin's disciple Huxley and others argued logically that there could only be *one* origin of life, at the very beginning of evolution. They kept Darwin honest to his own statement in *The Origin of Species* about 'one primordial form into which life was first breathed.' He later wrote, apologetically (which was uncharacteristic): 'I ought perhaps not to have used such terms; but they will serve to confess that our ignorance is as profound on the origin of life as is the origin of force or matter.'

James Strick in *Sparks of Life* has summarized the late 19th century battles between Darwinians and others, and among Darwinians, about 'spontaneous generation' – the idea that microscopic life emerged from inorganic tissue or organic tissue which has supposedly been sterilized. Insults were exchanged about contaminated solutions and incompetent microscopy. (Darwin held back while his intellectual hit man Huxley got to work). As Strick remarks, this Darwinian struggle for survival among Victorian men of science certainly exemplified Darwin's point about the struggle for existence. No wonder the physicist Kelvin, perhaps reinforced by his Ulster 'dissenter' background, made his own entry into the fray by in effect banging the heads of both sides together with the stunning suggestion – taken up by NASA and others in the late 20th century – that the first micro-organisms may have reached earth on meteorites or comets.

The animus on both sides of the battle arose because the question of the origin of life was theological: evolution, starting at one original point in time, became a substitute for God's creation. Hence the anxiety Darwinism caused among Christians. On the other hand, on the opposite side of the battle, spontaneous generation, amounting to *continuous* creation, also threatened the Christian view.

Spontaneous generation was not disproved. It was simply replaced by the Virchow statement, now classical, of 'omnis cellula ex cellula' – 'every cell comes from a cell'. In turn this echoed William Harvey's statement 'omne animal ex ovo' – 'every animal comes from an egg.'

Research on protoplasm became obsolete with the invention of the electro-microscope. Suddenly the 'eyes' of biologists became electronic. But in electro-microscopy it is necessary to kill the specimen and freeze-dry it. Microtomed slices of freeze-dried cells can no more indicate life processes than a formalin-soaked, brown, soggy cardboard-textured human cadaver in an anatomy laboratory. They show anatomy (of a sort), but not functioning. Of course it is exciting that electron microscopy reveals hitherto unthought-of levels of structure crystallizing out of dead tissue. But what do these microstructures do? Biologists analyse them chemically and deduce functions of energy transport and metabolism. But most cell structures are, with present technology, too small to observe *alive* under a light microscope whose powers of resolution are limited (to about 1000×) by the physics of light.

Fortunately the larger cells in protozoa can be observed in the light microscope, and protozoology, especially in the work of the great R D Manwell (*Introduction to Protozoology*) still retains some life. But even Manwell was mainly observing killed and stained structures in the light microscope. He reconstructed the life cycle of a protozoon through a series of dead and stained 'stills.' Structure is most easily revealed in immobility. In physiology the work of Marcel Bessis, for example, has been left as a dead end, although its implications are fascinating: he established a correlation between the health of red blood cells and the intensity of their scintillation and of the colouring of their diffraction fringe under the light microscope.

Reich studied movement in microscopic preparations over periods of days and weeks recording it through time lapse film – in which he was something of a pioneer. He did not ignore structure, and studied the nerve fibres of small worms. But he was looking primarily for their movement, and found it in a constant expansion and contraction. This led him to propose that the fibres of the autonomic nervous system in humans also expand and contract – a hypothesis that has not yet (2013) been confirmed by observation, and by definition cannot be under the electron microscope, but which is recently being supported in discoveries that chemical neuro-transmitters travel alternately in both directions along the tubules of the dendrites. Since the analogy has already been made in the very word 'dendrite' (from 'dendros' = 'tree' in Greek) between these long nerve fibres and the structure of a tree, it may be relevant to note that in trees also a process occurs of nutrients passing one way through the tubules of roots and branches, with waste material passing the other way. (Back to the maple tree again.)

The body and its cells are only 10% structure, 90% fluid. One of the few modern studies of protoplasm, Buvat's *Plant Cells*, which is partly valid for animal cells, constantly draws attention to the basic functions of 'cyclosis', the circulation of fluid in the cell – and of alternating expansion/ contraction of the plasmatic 'gel'. (Whether or not this is phase unequal is not clear from his descriptions.) But most modern biology ignores the fluid (except for its structural inclusions) and therefore the possible pulsation. It must be remembered that, as Medawar's statements unwittingly reveal, the 'upheaval' in modern biology is both technological (the invention of the electron microscope which is expensive and therefore must be used full time) and political (the exclusion of protoplasm research done outside the dominant circle.) The upheaval is not an example of progress in a science which, as in Popper's model, refutes faulty theories and replaces them by better ones. Protoplasm study is not dead – just sleeping. Recently there are signs of movement from this sleep. The biochemist Candace Pert's *The Molecules of Emotion* describes the role of peptides communicating almost instantly through the fluids of the body. The neurologist Richard Cytowic describes the 'volume transmission' of information, outside the neural network. The medium of these startling transmissions of information via biochemicals is the interstitial fluid – a colloidal solution, in effect protoplasm.

The importance of studying protoplasm is that, like the aether concept abandoned in physics, it provides a continuum. Protoplasm is the fluid in which cells (cytoplasm) exist. The observation of life and death, movement and stillness, growth and decay of structures within their context, the fluid of protoplasm, opens the study of life to such possibilities as continuous creation and generation – or at least *re*creation and *re*generation.

Following the invention and development of the microscope, biologists such as Buffon and Needham in the 18th century studied microscopic life forms such as protozoa and other 'animalcules' in hay infusions or other infusions of organic matter. (Again Strick provides the definitive history). And in the early 19th century Robert Brown – after whom the 'Brownian motion' of microscopic particles under 'atomic bombardment' is named – also observed what he called 'active molecules' which he at first concluded were alive. Reich made further observations of what he called 'bions'.

A philosopher of science, Mathias Grote, has written about the Indian biologist Krishnan Bahadur who, unaware of Reich's work, continued working in the field of protoplasm studies long after they were replaced by electron microscopy in the take-over Medawar was so pleased about. Bahadur observed under the light microscope what he called 'Jeewanu' – the Sanskrit for 'life particles'. These are similar to the bions, as was noted by Adolph Smith who had studied the bions and who visited Bahadur in India in the early 1970s. In turn Smith when he moved to the NASA project on 'exobiology', meaning extra-terrestrial biology, worked at ways of detecting life in supposedly non-life-friendly environments. It would seem that research into protoplasm is not dead after all. It has a continuing, although marginalized, history.

Microscopic life forms
The work on microscopic life which I will summarise briefly here originates in Reich's 'bion experiments.' (These are described, with photographs, in his *The Bions*, and in various books about his work). The bion experiments have been replicated by several biologists but have only been discussed outside the usual academic circles, although they have provoked some theoretical papers (by Grad, Smith and others) within the accepted framework of biology and biophysics.

Reich himself made a point of stating that his *observations* were deliberately 'naive' in order to avoid prejudice. I suspect his work on the bions would have been more convincing if he had grounded it in protozoology, and that his insistence on 'naïve' observation was part of his being, as so often, in an urgent hurry. Similarly, later he made observations of the aurora borealis without apparently reading the usual textbooks, and came up with elementary errors in his theoretical discussion – but, as usual, with fascinating, and replicable observations. And although in his later embattled years he may have felt like like the persecuted 'discoverer' of the orgone, just as in his early work on orgasm he was quick to acknowledge

Freud as a pioneer, he was quick to acknowledge his few predecessors in the bion work. He seems to have read Robert Brown's 'Active Molecules' (1828 and 1829), since he notes in *The Bions* that Brown described not only the 'Brownian motion' of particles but other forms of movement in some particles, characteristic of life. (For a detailed account of Brown's work in comparison with Reich's, see Peter Jones's *Artificers of Fraud*. The title reflects Jones's focus on 'scientific deception' in those who undermined Brown's work, and a century later, Reich's. But the core of the book is a careful re-presentation of Brown's work.)

Brown, in his 1828 paper, stated unequivocally that he observed 'both simple molecules and larger particles of different form.' He described what is now called Brownian motion in the simple molecules in a great variety of solutions of organic and inorganic origins, including pollen, plant matter, burnt wood and charcoal. He described 'spherical particles' in constant motion in the fluid, but also particles which were oblong or cylindrical in shape which not only moved in the fluid but showed changes in their shapes. Furthermore:

> In a few instances the particle was seen to turn on its longer axis. These motions were such as to satisfy me, after frequently repeated observation, that they arose neither from currents in the fluid, nor from its gradual evaporation, but belonged to the particle itself.

But in his 1829 paper Brown reacted, it seems, to interpretations of his observations as suggesting microscopic life forms (with the implication of spontaneous generation), in a long explanation that his 'active molecules' were *not* to be interpreted as 'animalcules.' He notes 'an erroneous assertion of more than one writer, namely that I have stated the active molecules to be animated', and states, 'that molecular was sometimes confounded with animalcular motion by several of the earlier microscopical observers appears probable from various pages in the writings of Leeuwenhoek' (the inventor of the microscope).

Whether this back-tracking was due to colleagues having put the frighteners on him in view of the murderous controversy over spontaneous generation, or whether innate caution took over, I think Brown left the door open to the 'animalcules' in two ways. First, as Jones notes by bolding a passage in Brown's recantation, Brown describes a new experiment in which he compares the particles to 'microscopic drops of oil' which he inserts in the fluid and which remain on the surface 'at rest', while the usual particles are throughout the fluid and 'continue to move with their usual degree of activity'. In other words, while politely bowing out from the idea of animalcules, he provides new evidence of there being two kinds of movement of particles in fluid. And secondly, he is known to have discussed his experiments with Darwin, and it can hardly be a coincidence that Darwin experimented on and off in the decades to come with 'gemmules' in protoplasmic solutions.

It is clear from Brown's two papers, and from Jones's discussion of them, as well as Reich's comments in *The Bions*, that there are two kinds of motion in microscopic particles in colloidal solutions: the random movement now known as Brownian motion, and the movement of life. In the terms of this book, Brownian motion is due to pulse-waves, and the movement of life is due to pulsation.

Amateurs in particular often have bad luck with the bion experiments, ending with stinking effusions of rotting matter – and I was no exception. Reich's theories about the bions – which go so far as a theory of cancer representing a break-down of cells similar to the rotting of protozoa in a stagnant pond (a version, in fact of Warburg's long lost theory of cancer as due to anoxia of the cells) – are only relevant to the present book insofar as they concern pulsation and pulse-waves. And these are, in fact, observables.

The orgonomists provide regular biophysics seminars in which the bion experiments are replicated, and film of these is accessible online. Reich himself invited many of the most eminent biologists of his day – and then just about anybody! – to replicate and test out his experiments. Only a few did, and that cursorily and inaccurately, concluding (without apparently reading Reich's own discussions of this possibility) that the bions were 'spores' or 'contamination'. Reich concluded these biologists were afraid of life. Perhaps he was right. As already noted, biology has become the study of death, not life.

Reich got caught again and again in furious claims that scientists refused to replicate his experiments. Most notably he claimed that his T-To experiments were faultily replicated by Einstein and his research assistant. But the issue of *replication* of the bion experiments may be a red herring – an unnecessary distraction. It turns out that some biologists have indeed, before and since Reich, made similar observations. They have however interpreted them differently. These observations are summarised in a recent paper by Paolo and Alexandra Correia about 'The Heterogenesis of Eukaryotic Amoebae' – 'eukaryotic' meaning cells with a nucleus. The biologists Altmann (1890), Portier (1918) and Wallin (1927) all proposed alternatives to the accepted view since Virchow and Pasteur of 'omne cellula ex cellula' – every cell comes out of another cell. These rebel biologists proposed a 'symbiotic' model in which various cell structures or 'vesicles' interacted in a process of continuous creation of life. The Correias could also have mentioned Darwin who in his Kent greenhouse spent much of his later life observing and describing 'granules' (i.e. vesicles) in plants. Or Darwin's predecessors going backward in time – Brown, Bastian, Needham, Buffon, Spallanzani…

The Correias dispute many of Reich's deductions from his observations, but they accept the observations, and draw attention to his valid discovery that 'microbes that *normally live symbiotically within* the eukaryotic host cell… given the right conditions, survive the demise of the host to autonomously grow and replicate.'

My own amateur observations of the 'bions' support this finding. But I am not going to engage in the debate about Reich's bion *theory*. This includes the inevitable 'life energy' which I think is a mistaken construct. What interest me are Reich's *observations* – of pulsation. I am not a biologist or biophysicist, and I am not a trained technician in microscopy. In fact I am rather clumsy. However I am not ashamed of offering the following 'naïve' account. My main point is that things *can* be observed which raise questions, and provoke thought about microscopic pulsation – a subject which is not rejected in current biology, it is merely ignored. My invitation – like Reich's, although my work was very simple compared to his – is to *look*.

I used a Wild Leitz research microscope, with eyepieces of 10× or 25× and objective lenses of 10×, 40× or 100×. The 25× eyepiece with a 100× objective gives a magnification of 2,500×, which can in turn be magnified up to three times (to 7,500×) with a zoom attachment. It is not possible to resolve any new structural detail above a magnification of about 1,000×, since only details larger than about 0.2 microns are recorded in the light microscope. This has led to some scorn being poured on Reich for using magnifications above 1000×. But Reich's goal at these higher magnifications was not to observe finer structures. He stated that he knew this was impossible. But in the living preparation, higher magnification is useful for studying *movement*.

I used a quartz halogen light source – not available to Reich who apparently at times used the light of the sun via the microscope reflecting mirror to achieve adequate illumination at very high magnifications. My microscope provided normal illumination, plus dark field, plus phase contrast. Phase contrast helps enormously in the resolution of structural detail (up to the 1,000× limit of course), especially of dark bodies, but provides false colours. Reich was expert in the difficult technique of using a hanging drop slide, and improvised several innovations to keep the specimen replenished with liquid over periods of many days. I could not master these, nor the technique of working, as Reich did, with the objective lens immersed in the preparation. I mainly used an artificial enclosure of Vaseline walls, topped by a cover slip, its contents replenished from time to time with sterile water from a sterile dropper.

The first procedure in the bion experiments is familiar in protozoology: making a hay infusion in which protozoa can breed. From now on, though, I will follow recent usage of the word 'protist' instead of protozoon because it includes both protozoa and algae, i.e. both animal and plant unicells, and these are not always possible to tell apart. A few blades of hay are allowed to rot in water and as they decompose, protists appear in the solution.

Reich varied the classical procedure by trying green grass, which as expected was not as productive (it rots more slowly) and, most important, by autoclaving the usual solution of dry hay before observation: boiling it for 25 minutes in a pressure cooker which gave a temperature of over 200C. In Reich's time this was considered enough to sterilize the solution by killing all protozoal eggs (assuming they have eggs, which is questionable), or cysts, bacteria, etc. It is now realised that cysts, in particular, and viruses can survive such extreme conditions. But again it must be emphasised that this does not invalidate Reich's findings – which were that autoclaving had the paradoxical effect of making the infusion *more* rich in microorganisms than before: they seemed to be generating themselves or be to be regenerated from the vegetable tissue which had been thoroughly broken down by the autoclaving. (Similarly Brown noted that he saw more particles in motion in solutions where plant material had been 'bruised' in preparation – i.e. more broken down.)

A drop of the infusion, containing a small fragment of the hay, is examined regularly under the microscope over a period of several days, after which it is usually saturated with rot bacteria and beginning to dry up. Reich succeeded in observing some preparations for weeks using a hanging drop slide, which was technically beyond me – and others have found it hard to replicate. In the following section I will summarise observations under headings which describe each life form *in the order of its appearance* in the solution as the hay breaks down over a few days. At first the solution is apparently lifeless: hay fibres like ropes and saw-toothed edges of grass blades.

Kinetosomes, Vesicles, Granules

These are different terms for the same thing. Since the invention of the microscope by Van Leeuwenhoek who studied spermatozoa – it was said 'at the expense of his own progeny' – it has been possible for any amateur with a microscope to study life forms. The professionalisation of science which led to the kind of orthodoxy in which, as Chargaff lamented, life is now only studied in microtomed layers of freeze-dried tissue, was only achieved in the latter half of the nineteenth century. Before this – just as the most striking observations in natural science were made by enthusiasts such as Goethe, Lyell and Darwin (whose university degree was a BA in Divinity) whose main instruments were their own eyes – amateurs looking down microscopes had identified what seemed like basic units of life, usually known as 'granules' (Latin 'granula'). Darwin miched his Divinity courses at Cambridge to study granules in decaying vegetable matter through his hand held 200× microscope, and from time to time throughout his life (and especially, it seems, after encountering Brown's work) returned to these observations. He noted how granules formed and re-formed but saw no sign of what others wanted to see: spontaneous generation of life from non-life. Reich does not seem to have known about Darwin's observations of granules. He made no grand claims for his observations and did not deny 'Koch's laws' which describe infection by outside agents – exogenous infection. But he proposed *endogenous* infection was also possible.

Granules are the first life forms to appear in the hay solution. They are bubble-like units about a micron in diameter attached to the edge of the blade of hay, within cells of the blade, within agglomerations (clusters, 'packets', heaps), and in mobile protozoa. They can be observed clustering, like fruit along a branch, along the edge of the hay blade, oscillating, twisting, sometimes breaking free, sometimes agglomerating. They luminate, i.e. they reflect the microscope's light, very strongly bluish-green, and have a strong diffraction fringe. If free in the solution, or loosely attached by apparent stalks to the hay blade, they may quiver with 'Brownian movement'. This is supposed to be due to random atomic bombardment, but as Brown himself noted,many of their movements are less random: they spin, twist, accelerate and decelerate. They often scintillate: their luminosity becomes more and less intense in a regular beat, although it was not possible in my observations to identify this as pulsation because of the rapidity of the scintillations. (Slow motion film might test this).

Vesicles are observable everywhere in organic tissue, and as Reich (and before him Brown) demonstrated, also in substances such as earth or coal crystals which are subjected through intense heat to forced swelling and then disintegration. Reich suggested that the traditional concept of *omnis vita ex cellula* (all life is from a cell) should be revised to *omnis vita ex granula* (all life is from a vesicle). This concept might be accepted by protozoologists who now name these vesicles *kinetosomes* – meaning 'moving bodies'. It is recognized that they can 'give rise to different organelles at different times.' This means they contribute to polymorphy (changing shapes) in protozoa by forming together as various organs within the cell. Manwell quotes Lwoff: 'It is possible to describe the morphology of ciliates [one-celled 'hairy' organisms] in terms of kinetosomes and their derivatives. The morphogenesis of a ciliate is essentially the multiplication, distribution and organization of populations of kinetosomes and of the organelles which are the result of their activity.'

But why kinetosomes (vesicles) are so active remains a mystery. According again to Manwell, 'a suggestion made by Weisz and others is that kinetosomal behavior is somehow mediated by the immediate molecular environment.' In other words their behaviour can only be explained by casting the explanatory net a little wider, into the environment. The sequence of events is then: a) changes in environment, b) activity of kinetosomes, c) changing of structure in single celled organisms (unicells) and indeed in any organised tissue.

Reich's observations of vesicles are supported by descriptions in protozoology of kinetosomes. But his naivete, whether deliberate or not, enabled him to notice vesicles where protozoologists would not normally notice kinetosomes, outside cellular tissue and even in certain forms of what is called 'crenation' of red blood cells.

Amoeboid clusters

Some of Reich's most striking observations were of bion vesicles spontaneously organizing into clusters which then displayed mobility and determined action, and in effect turned into protists (consistently with Manwell's conclusions about kinetosomes forming organelles, but one step further in organisation). This happens in the second stage of decay of the solution. Typically, a cluster of vesicles along a decaying grass blade would roll away and behave like an amoeba, complete with pseudopodia and crawling motion when against a surface – even to the point of ingesting and apparently absorbing smaller free vesicles. Some clusters (of which there exist photographs taken from Reich's films) developed a sort of head and tail: Reich called them 'org-animalcules'. Fantastic as all this may seem, I found this readily observable in most bion preparations. There seems to be a constant tendency for fresh vesicles detaching from the hay blade to cluster into 'lawful' forms. At their most simple, these consist of a large vesicle with a smaller one attached as a 'head' (rather as if a pea were sitting on the end of a large bean). Sometimes a passing rod bacterium has apparently been enlisted into service as a tail, with an effect like a legless dog wriggling through the solution. Whether these two- or three- unit clusters really operate as a miniature organism is an open question, but the formative tendency is striking.

Amoebas are of course familiar in protozoology. Although they are consistently found in decaying tissue (the human gut in disease, the blood in malaria, vaginal secretion in infections, advanced stages of cancer in tissue), biologists and cytologists can only answer the question of how they have got there by invoking 'dormant cysts' or 'spores' or 'eggs' which have never been observed actually becoming amoebas. (Some protozoa do 'encyst' under certain conditions, but that cysts are the origin of all protozoa is simply a hypothesis). The close, day to day observations of decaying tissue in hay infusions, under high magnifications, suggests that 'amoebas' can and do frequently develop 'in situ', becoming organized from vesicles which in turn have developed from the decaying tissue itself.

Protists

This is an all-purpose word for a single celled organism such as is called a protozoon by zoologists and an alga by botanists. Protists contain a definite membrane, cytoplasm, nucleus including chromosomes – all the equipment of any cell. They appear in the decaying solution after amoeboid clusters and display a huge range of sizes, shapes, and mobility. An advanced decayed hay preparation may contain slow moving large amoebas, tiny zig-zagging protists, and comparatively huge cucumber-shaped paramecia which streak jet-like across the solution. In my observations the most common was a vorticella, a purse-shaped unicell with flagellae (whip-like tendrils) visible under phase contrast. Unicells contain vesicles (kinetosomes).

Protists *pulsate* at various levels. It is often possible to see a conspicuous 'contractile' vacuole which pulsates rather like a heart. And the cyclosis or 'cytoplasmic streaming' of the cell contents around the inside of the membrane takes on a pulsatory rhythm, especially at the leading edge as the cell moves.

I have not seen the vorticella type of protist detach itself from decaying tissue: they move across the solution. The question of how they arrive in a solution which has been autoclaved is a puzzle: they appear after about 48 hours, moving around freely, then fade to semi-transparent 'ghosts', no longer mobile, as the solution dies. I have observed some vorticella-like protists (about 2-3 microns in size) gradually breaking up over a period of hours, into a debris of components including vesicles, 'T bodies' and rod bacteria (see following sections).

The structure of protists has been mapped out in the taxonomy to be found in textbooks. This taxonomy is a series of stills in which different species of protists are described with as much authority as species of animals are in mammalian taxonomy. But within the texts of books such as Manwell's lurks information which makes it clear that the taxonomy cannot truly be fixed in this way. Dogs do not turn overnight into cats or intermediate forms. But protozoologists must admit that many protists are *polymorphous*. Even within a period of minutes, some may develop from being amoebas into being vorticella-like or vice versa. Manwell describes a slime mould within a few minutes 'taking on the guise of a heliozoidan-like form, or a highly motile flagellate with two flagella'. This is rather like saying a dog turns into a cat and flies away.

Considering that protozoologists probably have a bias towards classification and order, shape-shifting may occur much more often than they wish to know. Protists seem to be constantly changing according to the state of the medium in which they are included.

Bacteria

The most common bacteria in hay infusions are rod-shaped and presumably anaerobic (flourishing in the absence of the constituents of air – oxygen etc.) since they appear after several days, as the solution is drying up. Sometimes heaps of round cocci (round bacteria) are found at the solution edges. I have observed (or think I have observed: this seems fantastic) masses of green grass-coloured bacterial rods peeling off from the hay blade edge and becoming part of the rod population of the solution. That they are genuinely rod bacteria, not mere pieces of grass tissue coincidentally shaped and moving exactly like bacteria (which would be a miraculous extension of Brownian motion into something new), is shown by the fact that I observed some reproducing by fission. Even more odd, I observed the membranes of several (decaying?) unicells becoming split into rod-like units, at first curved, which straightened out, broke away, and moved away looking exactly like bacteria. Whether these are in fact bacteria or simply 'bacterioform' for some unexplained reason, I had no means of knowing. (Or perhaps I was seeing things).

Rod bacteria are familiar in microbiology. As Pasteur demonstrated, they infect from outside – they are exogenous. But observations suggest that they develop endogenously in decaying tissue and detach themselves from it, then undergo the usual process of further reproduction through fission. I would add that they split off from *membrane* tissue.

The South African biologist Adrianus Pijper after long observations of bacteria concluded that their flagellae – their waving hairs (literally 'flagella' is a whip) – were *not*, as usually thought, ways of moving them, like flippers, through their fluid environment, but merely reactive to the environment (like hair in a wind). Instead, he concluded that bacteria moved in a gyratory wriggle of their bodies. This may be true also of protists with flagellae, and was certainly consistent with my own observations where the movement of flagellae seemed random and not necessarily locomotive.

T bodies

This is Reich's term for the smallest moving bodies in view, some as small (about .2 microns) as the resolving powers of the microscope can define. They appear spindle-shaped, or like commas, or teardrops. Reich noted them as occurring in the preparation in an advanced state of decay, and as being extra-cellular, i.e. free moving in the fluid. He postulated an antithesis between the 'life' functions of the vesicles (bions) and the 'death' functions of the T bodies (T for *Tod* – death) which he considered to be pathogens.

I observed T bodies in the same circumstances as Reich did, but also *within* cells. This may be because I used phase contrast microscopy, not available to Reich. In particular the T bodies are found concentrated in the cell nucleus. Either they resemble chromosomes and I am confusing them, or they *are* chromosomes or chromosome fragments which take on a life of their own, in some inexplicable way, when released into the fluid by decaying tissue. (Their movement is more than merely 'Brownian').

T bodies are not mycoplasmas: microorganisms of varying size, somewhere between viruses and bacteria, and greatly varying shapes, found outside cells although they have a noted 'affinity for cell membranes'. This misconception, originally brought up by the 'bioenergetic therapist' David Boadella recurs without question in several descriptions of the bion experiments by sympathetic observers (e.g. Edward Mann, Myron Sharaf). Perhaps these are attempts to legitimise Reich's observations. But T bodies, in contrast to mycoplasmas, are consistent in shape and relatively consistent in size, as well as being found (under phase contrast) within cells.

It is just conceivable that T bodies may be viruses if live viruses are larger than they appear under the electron microscope. They might have an outer layer, similar to that surrounding the cap in a sperm cell, which is somehow stripped off in the freeze drying process. But in theory, viruses are not observable in the light microscope because they are smaller than .2 microns.

Adolph Smith and Dean Kenyon published a paper in 1972 which indicated, following previous work by Howard Temin, that not only is there no evidence that viruses come from outside the cell as generally supposed, but some evidence that they originate *within* the cell. This implies, Smith and Kenyon proposed, that life is originating 'de novo'. Bernard Dixon in an editorial in *World Medicine* referred to this hypothesis and the supporting evidence as world shaking, but the world of normal science was apparently not shaken.

The T bodies are like viruses in that their existence outside the cell is questionable, and they do not seem to live on their own. I suggest that a test of whether they are truly living micro-organisms, rather than some sort of particle associated with life or perhaps the death of life, would be if they can be observed to pulsate. If they do, then Smith and Kenyon are right about life 'de novo'. But existing technology for the observation of living micro-organisms is restricted to light microscopy which cannot decide the issue. And unless viruses can be observed to pulsate they cannot be considered to be alive.

Infection and defection

The initial problem raised by evidence of protists shifting their shapes, and the multicelled tissue of hay blades breaking down into unicells and bacteria, is: what in the environment determines this? Differences in acidity and solution density have been held to explain the polymorphism of protists. But although the *association* between say, high acidity and a rounded shape is clear, it is hard to explain how the acidity can *cause* shifts to one shape or another. Or if 'adaptation' is proposed, then the question remains of how this is functional. Each question leads to the dead end of circular description, and the wood is quickly ignored in an examination of individual trees. But even poly-morphism, striking as it is, is less of a problem than the possibility that a decaying piece of tissue can break down into vesicles which then re-form and re-organise themselves into motile amoebae, or break down directly into motile rod bacteria. As the solution ages, becomes more anaerobic, and changes in acidity and in no doubt many other ways, tissue breaks down into bacteria rather than vesicles. 'T bodies' seem to represent a more advanced state of decay, and a less complex level of organization. But they too may be part of a polymorphic continuum which includes viruses and mycoplasmas and may even include chromosomes (although this is highly conjectural).

In view of the extent of polymorphism it is not yet possible, in my view, to establish a clear gradient of organisational levels. A hierarchy might be proposed with multicelled organisms at the top, viruses at the bottom, but there is too much variation to be able to establish levels in between. There are, however, two visible processes in the preparations: a 'death' process of disintegration and break down, and a 'life' process of reorganization of the break down products at a new temporarily viable level.

The 'heterogenesis' mentioned by the Correias may be more extensive than so far described. Sometimes a viable new organism seems to emerge and to take on a direction of its own. *Infection*, by bacteria or protozoal parasites, may at least sometimes be a process of *defection* of decaying tissue to another organizational level: that of pathogens (which in turn infect healthy tissue and reinfect the unhealthy.) A defection theory of disease might be useful. Brian Inglis has summarized an enormous bulk of un-refuted evidence that bacteria and viruses are not the causes of disease but rather ever-present opportunists, like fifth columnists or looters. A refugee Russian virologist, Yuri Yabrov, whom I met with Adolph Smith in Montreal in 1974 or so, said viruses were like thieves moving down a hotel corridor checking the door locks.

My own observations of vesicles/kinetosomes in microscopic preparations suggest that they are first of all defectors from the normal level of the integrated organism. In a sense an organism is a viable 'organisation' of its various sub-elements. The integrating factor seems to be the pulsation of the whole organism. When this disintegrates and becomes local, various sub-elements defect to whatever level allows local pulsation to be viable.

A similar process may operate in healthy tissue. An example is the formation of sperm cells and ova in the epithelial tissue of the gonads, which is something of a mystery in physiology. This may represent a shift of the local tissue to this new level of organization 'with a life of its own' but genetically the same.

Vitality is an important variable. (Whether or not this can be another word for 'energetic charge', it is the simpler word and does not imply a theory of physics). A grass blade which has been dried into hay decays more rapidly, either with without autoclaving, than one which is fresh and green, and produces a more rapid reorganization into protozoal forms.

Some phenomena of ingestion, for example bacteria being 'eaten' by phages and white blood cells (amoeba-like clusters of vesicles) may be explained as a tendency for neighbouring life forms to combine and recombine at a viable level of organization. Pathology and dying can be seen as reversal of a tendency toward growth and organization: the organic tissue, instead of constantly *integrating* from vesicles etc., *disintegrates*.

Pulsation is observable at various levels of organization:

- Multicellular tissue pulsates in too many ways to be listed here. Multizoa (animals) contain pulsating organs, breathe etc. Plants show rhythmic metabolism and pulsatory circulation of fluids.

- Protists (motile unicells, amoebae) have a pulsating contractile vacuole, rather like a heart, and the cyclosis or cytoplasmic streaming at their leading edge appears pulsatory.

- Amoebae expand and contract in a much slower pulsation, their expansion becoming elongation with locomotion.

- Bacteria and T bodies do not seem to pulsate. The much larger heads of spermatozoa, which have been compared with viruses, and which are black, do show a vigorously oscillating diffraction fringe. It is difficult to determine from microscopic observation whether this is in fact oscillation or pulsation, since the diffraction fringe is a light phenomenon with no membrane to observe pulsating. The same difficulty arises (see Chapter 5) with atmospheric phenomena. Whether or not this oscillation is distinct from Brownian movement, both may be signs of the action of environmental *pulse waves*. Viruses are not normally considered to be alive, and presumably they are not advanced enough in organisation to pulsate. As noted above, current technology cannot show definitively if they pulsate or not, but they do not have membranes, which would seem to rule pulsation out.

The Microscopic Continuum

The diffraction fringe of a micro-organism under a microscope seems to indicate a field. When a diffraction oscillates or flashes, does this derive from the pulsation of a field, or is the oscillation of the fluid as a whole becoming visible around the micro-organism? A similar oscillation can be observed in the haze around a full moon in some atmospheric conditions. (Again see Chapter 5). A mechanistic interpretation would be that the fluid is quivering (not pulsating) because of Brownian motion (pulse waves, in effect) or mechanical factors such as vibration of the microscope stage (the platform on which the slide is placed). The rigorous observations of red blood cells by Marcel Bessis support Reich's contention that their vibration (which Bessis calls scintillation and which Reich, I think wrongly, calls pulsation) is local and not in the fluid as a whole. Bessis went so far as to state that the scintillation of red blood cells and the brightness of their diffraction fringe are indications of their vitality. He even made correlations between various colours and conditions of the fringe and various diseases. For example, he found that in anemia the fringe is not only weak but it scintillates less rapidly.

The mechanistic view of the diffraction fringe is that it is the mere reflection of the microscope's light by molecules which surround the micro-organism, and that its variations are due to chemical factors and the moisture content of the micro-organism. It must be acknowledged that dead bodies in a preparation – the dried up ghosts of protozoa, heaps of inert cocci – do often show a fairly bright diffraction fringe, although more often it is a colourless haze. This fringe may also vibrate with Brownian movement – pulse waves. Two factors seem to distinguish the diffraction fringe of an alive micro-organism: it appears to pulsate (although this would be best established through slow motion film), and it shows variation in colour. These would suggest that the fringe is more than mechanical and represents the illumination or intrinsic lumination of a field. Further observation in experiments may determine whether the oscillation or scintillation of the field around red blood cells is related to pulsation or not. I suspect that the diffraction fields around micro-organisms such as protists do pulsate, or at least reflect the pulsation of the organism, but this is a subjective impression.

Continuous creation, at least of new forms agglomerated from old as well as the transformations of polymorphy, is readily visible in the bion preparations. 'God Reich creates life' headlined the newspapers in Norway in 1938. But grandiose though Reich could be, he never claimed this, nor even that life originated in his preparations. His theory (though he did not spell this out clearly enough) was in effect one of spontaneous *re*-generation – not the 'spontaneous generation' chimera of the 19th century which Pasteur and Koch refuted. The bion experiments provide evidence of continuous *re*creation, *re*organization, and *re*animation of 'dead' tissue, into new forms which show metabolism and growth as well as pulsation and locomotion. At the least this is a local reversal of the dying process. But the question of how long this reversal lasts is apparently impossible to answer from the observations of bion preparations since, even in the hands of Reich (who, whether right or wrong in his theories, was clearly a brilliant technician of microscopy within the constraints of the period in which he worked) the preparations quite swiftly died. After all, the bion experiments may be observations of processes of decay, as in any corpse which is breaking down and becomes a host for millions of thriving organisms – with the added theory that some of these organisms may originate within the corpse's decaying tissue rather than arriving from outside to consume it. Again, heterogenesis.

Shape-shifters

The laws of genetics and DNA have to be stretched into realms of pure conjecture to explain the apparently endless (in some cases) variety of forms available to microscopic 'shape-shifters' – although perhaps recent findings about mitochondrial DNA and 'epigenetic' factors can provide explanations. But in the bion experiments structure is actually *seen* forming through the attraction, agglomeration, and combined locomotion of the micro-organisms's sub-units. This is a dynamic process in which force or energy (in their usual sense of results of processes – not as primary causes) are obviously involved. But Reich's emphasis on life energy is blinding: even the supposedly deadly T bodies are active and appear 'alive.' Most organic life in the infusion has been technically *killed* by autoclavation. (And the observations described above, of vesicles forming at the edges of grass blades in great profusion, are not of certain heroic cysts which have survived autoclavation – though these may be responsible for the various protists swimming in the fluid). There is evidence for organic life reconstituting itself within the solution. But as the Correias point out, some forms of life do survive autoclavation. And the old bogeys of contamination and cysts cannot be dismissed as easily as Reich thought. His assumption a) that autoclavation eliminated all life in a solution, and b) that life forms observable after autoclavation were new is not demonstrable. But the observations are remarkable in any case.

Perhaps whatever remains of life after autoclavation tenaciously *resists death* and the forms which occur indicate the success of the resistance. A unit of protoplasm seems to constitute itself opportunistically in whatever form the environment permits. This is what is so striking in the polymorphic unicells, the microscopic shape-shifters which are visible in primitive forms (vesicles forming into bean shaped 'body' and pea shaped 'head') in the bion experiments, and in more sophisticated forms in the protozoal solutions described by Manwell. What is the constant in these polymorphs?

Polymorphism could be seen as a dazzlingly versatile kind of adaptation, triggered by environmental changes acting on the micro-organism's huge genetic repertoire of options. But the bion observations show even more: part of a unicell (i.e. part of a single cell, not a cell which is part of a multicelled organism and thus contains the organism's 'programme') can break away and become a new organism – or perhaps more accurately proto-organism – on its own. A similar process may be occurring in the formation of germ cells (e.g. sperm in epithelial tissue) and the autonomous behaviour of cancer cells. Cancer cells, of course, are notoriously 'anti-social'. The organization of many cells (or on an even smaller scale, of vesicles) into forms and coherent structures need not imply a 'formative energy', but it must imply a special kind of intercommunication. Most theories to explain this must evoke 'fields'.

Persistence and disintegration

Microscopic observations of life forms reinforce the contention, (already an ancient idea, as the etymology of the word 'life' shows) that life is best defined as opposition to death. The biophysics which tries to explain these observations has to reckon with the *perseverance* of life in microscopic infusions, its *persistence* at whatever level and in *whatever form* it can resist disintegration and organize itself, even temporarily, into an integrated, pulsating whole.

Smith and Kenyon concluded that viruses were originating within the cell, not only inserting themselves from outside. But they may have been describing a process of defection, not (as they thought) origination.

From the 18th century on, observers of 'granules', including the meticulous Darwin, have failed to discover spontaneous generation – but they have discovered a continuum where these basic life forms shift between levels of functioning, from instant to instant. They also shift between processes of growth and processes of decay: granules emerge as breakdown products from decaying grass tissue under the microscope, just as macroscopically flowers emerge from a compost heap. Protists burst from 'cysts' as a plant does from a germinating seed. But vesicles seem to have a life of their own, defecting from decaying tissue, clustering into what look like proto-protists (to coin a phrase). Although shape shifting is dramatic and may seem abrupt, since it so often occurs off stage, as it were, as a parade of stately amoebas is replaced by a rush of whirling flagellates, the glimpses we have of protists metamorphosing in front of our eyes show that there is a continuum from instant to instant. The protists are in their own way what Leibniz called 'monads', and in his 'Principle of Continuity' Leibniz proposed that 'nature never takes leaps'. At times, though, the abrupt changes are nightmarish. The hay infusions seem almost to parody the quantum universe of successive 'nows'. One can feel the horror of Bishop Berkeley's intuition of 'every moment annihilated and created anew' – which caused him to invoke the necessity of God, 'that eternal invisible Mind which produces and sustains all things.' On the other hand, perhaps the shape-shifting protists are like Leibniz's monads constituting themselves in the best of all possible worlds – meaning the only possible world for them at any given moment.

If vesicles do become protists they presumably contain genetic material, whether it has been encysted or not. (Though the clumping of several vesicles together to form one protist is not, so far as I know, described in the textbooks). It is irritating that Reich's work, yet again, points to new observations but fails to acknowledge even elementary existing explanations. Darwin observed granules more patiently and, on and off, over a much longer period than Reich, and his observations of these and of macroscopically visible plants and seeds which he systematically cross bred led him to propose a theory of 'pangenesis' in which the characteristics of organisms were transmitted from generation to generation via hypothetical particles which he called 'gemmules'. Half a century later the patient work of Mendel in crossing sweet peas demonstrated gemmules as 'genes'. Half a century later still, Reich, who was a qualified neurologist, was insisting on observing vesicles 'naively', as if genes did not exist. (As a refugee from Nazi Germany with its emphasis on supposed racial heredity and its eugenics policies, he seems to have had an understandable suspicion of genetics.)

On the other hand, in this age of obsession with genetics, it may be useful to redress the balance with some 'naïve observation' of events which are commonplace in protozooal infusions but which have no genetic explanation yet. The paper by Correia and Correia provides some hope that biologists will continue with 21st century technology the observations of vesicles (or bions) which have been made since the 19th century and in which Reich's work may eventually find its place. But such observations may lead to contentious conclusions. For example, Bernard Dixon (who reviewed Smith and Kenyon' article in 1972) has recently reported on research that shows that amoebas (protists) act as 'Trojan Horses' for bacteria contained within them, and thus as agents of infection: a dying amoeba bursts and the bacteria pop out. But how did the bacteria get into the amoebas? Bion observations suggest that they might have originated de novo as part of a 'defection' process within a dying amoeba. Normal biology suggests that they were ingested by the amoebas. Back to square one…

Exobiology

A brief return to the work done by NASA, as detailed by Dick and Strick in another definitive historical study. The exobiology programme included:

1) Microscopic observation of membrane enclosed 'protocells'.
2) Examination of fossil records.
3) Biochemistry, starting with nucleic acids. This includes experiments in which life-like (or protist-like) 'microspheres' form in a chemical

soup, but these are not considered to be alive by the usual criteria.

4) Study of microbial life in extreme environments such as 'vents' in the deep ocean floor.

5) The 'Gaia' hypothesis of James Lovelock (who worked for NASA): that the planet and the life on its surface formed 'a unified synergistic system…analogous to the body of a single organism.'

With regard to (1), the closest approach to that of Reich in his bion studies, Sidney Fox argued that, as Dick and Strick recount, 'membrane-enclosed "protocells" probably came first and that the development of complex heredity molecules such as nucleic acids came only much later.'

The difficulty of establishing a causal direction in many experiments, and disputes between approaches favouring either a 'metabolism first' or a 'replication first' view presented NASA with a classic 'chicken and egg' dilemma. One way out was proposed by Freeman Dyson with a 'dual origin hypothesis' in which the simplest living systems developed through metabolism, then more complex ones through replication. But this presents a new question of a possible 'missing link'. The debate is not yet resolved.

Exobiology is not devoted to protoplasm studies, and in fact searches for the evidence of life, not life itself. But it appears to open at least three possibilities:

1) Life is generated wherever conditions permit organic structures to occur in inorganic environments.

2) This may be due to some sort of emergence of the organic from the inorganic – life originating *de novo.*

3) Life may be 'seeded' or deposited in favourable inorganic environments if it arrives from another part of the universe where life already exists, perhaps as a passenger on a meteorite or other heavenly body. (A return to Kelvin!)

Pulsation de novo

So is life originating *de novo?* If it is, in terms of this book it will be characterised by pulsation. How can pulsation, then, occur *de novo?*

This book is about pulsation and pulse-waves *now.* It is not about the origin of life – about which I have no idea. However, the question arises of whether or not pulsation *could* emerge from pulse-waves. Pulsation depends on the presence of a membrane. Without a membrane there are only pulse-waves. Are we back with Reich's idea of 'closed orgone' and 'open orgone'? No, because he did not distinguish unequal phase pulsation from equal phase pulse-waves.

But what happens when pulse-waves get into a membrane? One could imagine a colloid solution, for example, a primal soup where the jostling of molecules and the mixing of chemicals in the 'Brownian movement' (pulse-waves) of the soup led to the formation of skins or enclosed sacs or bags or cysts – microspheres perhaps. Would the pulse-waves in these membranes begin to pulsate?

This is a question for biophysicists. As close as I can get to it is the simple example of blowing up a balloon. I puff gas into the balloon (in spurts from my lungs, or as a flow of helium from a cylinder) and it inflates until either it bursts or I stop filling it with gas and I tie the neck. Does the balloon then pulsate? No. It may eventually leak or burst, but for now it is static, fixed.

Or imagine a permeable balloon – one with myriads of tiny holes in it. Does it pulsate? No, although it may gradually deflate. An example is a leather wineskin. I could blow it up. It would gradually deflate because of leaking air.

So whether or not the balloon or sac is permeable or not, filling it with air or liquid or a colloid will not lead to pulsation.

Back to square one. The presence of a membrane seems to be necessary in pulsation, but it does not cause it – no matter what force is applied. Pulsation just pulsates! Life is just life! Perhaps it doesn't emerge from non-life any more than consciousness can emerge from non-consciousness. (Theories of 'emerging' consciousness have been elegantly demolished by the philosopher Colin McGinn).

For me square one is Parmenides. I have discussed in another book *Time / No Time – the Paradox of Poetry and Physics* the world of Parmenides where change both exists and does not exist. Similarly life exists and does not exist. There seems to be this duality in the universe. The chicken-egg problem which torments even the brilliant physicists in the exobiology programme goes back to Parmenides and before. Why assume non-life comes before life? Why assume pulse-waves come before pulsation? They co-exist. Could the universe from the very beginning have contained life?

Continuum

If you stand a quince on its bottom end, the stalk end, and bisect it vertically, you are faced with a vagina! Even to the curve back at the stem as if to an anus, and above the perfect double lips, a lump like a clitoris. The quince was sacred to Aphrodite, Goddess of love. One can see why. But why this resemblance? Goethe, Portman, Thomson, Reich, have all noted the recurring patterns of morphology. This can have nothing whatsoever to do with a causal process, or with evolution: quinces and women are from separate phylae. But quinces and women have developed 'along the same lines'. The hollow core of the quince does contain a few seeds: it is the womb, as it were, of the fruit. Yes, form represents the constraints of the universe, as Fodor and Piatelli-Palmarini point out. But perhaps function and form are identical. Just as pulsation is an end in itself.

At a much larger level, the universe contains recurring patterns – configurations – whose relation with each other may have nothing whatsoever to do with cause and effect. Darwin was driven by a scientific search for cause and effect: he was a mechanist. Mechanism is the method of science. The alternative is vitalism: the evocation of an outside force – orgone, entelechy, the divine will, a mystical 'purpose'. But perhaps neither cause-effect nor a vital force, neither the ping pong of mechanistic dynamics nor the dream in the mind of God are necessary. If time is withdrawn from the equation, then all that remains is a continuum of shapes.

When I was making my 'bion' observations I entered every day into a world where after a while gazing through the microscope the sense of up and down and side to side was suspended. I felt, indeed, as suspended in the solution as the micro-organisms darting erratically across it or crawling along the edges of crystals and fibres. At the same time I used to go skin-diving almost every day in a lake with a snorkel and flippers, losing part of my orientation in a world where light shone at various angles and I was surrounded by bass and perch drifting in schools or travelling individually, and occasionally a diving duck would streak by, or a turtle or water-snake wriggle away from me. In both contexts I experienced a loss of my usual bearings. My memories of the organisms moving among each other in the drop on the microscope slide and in the lake gave me a sense of *relative* motion as distinct from *absolute* motion. Later my reading of Julian Barbour on this subject was all the more vivid. At the time I felt I knew what Reich meant by the 'cosmic energy ocean' – or, as I prefer, simply the 'cosmic ocean.'

5

AURAS AND AURORAS

Fields and Auras

In physics a field is 'a region under the influence of some physical agency', for example 'electric, magnetic and gravitational fields that result from the presence of charge, magnetic dipole, and mass respectively.' A field may also be a more abstract concept 'used in connection with scalar quantities to describe distributions of temperature, electric potential, etc.' The energy of fields is secondary to the physical agencies which create them. In no sense does the field have a life of its own and become a creative, organizing force.

A visible field, as in St Elmo's fire when bluish lumination glows and flickers around a ship's mast, in the aurora borealis, the sun's atmosphere as observed during a total eclipse, or the glow that can occasionally be seen around electric power lines, is called 'corona discharge.'

Some investigators have described 'auras' around human beings. If these are field effects they seem to require explanations beyond that of 'electrostatic fields' – as when a person causes disturbance on a TV screen. This is an area of investigation where mysticism and 'fringe science' flourish. Explanations range from claims that human consciousness/mind/spirit are themselves fields ('ectoplasm', 'aetheric body', 'prana') to the fringe- (no pun intended) scientific ('the Kirlian aura', 'L-fields', 'orgone energy lumination'). This profusion of terms suggests that seeing auras is quite common, although normal science has not provided a definition for this phenomenon – beyond the inevitable 'optical illusion'.

Medieval painters depicted a halo or nimbus around the heads of Christ, the saints, and angels, in the form of either a glow of light or a stylised disc. The word 'aura' used to be more often used in science than now, to describe corona discharge. Derived from the Latin for 'breeze' it suggests a more active force than 'nimbus' which means a cloud. The *Oxford English Dictionary* states that the nimbus was 'imagined' to surround the heads of deities. If a person sees a luminous glow around his beloved – for example the poet Robert Graves claiming that the woman he loved had 'a light around her head', or another poet the Russian Alexander Blok writing that his beloved's head was surrounded by a blue circle – then this is typical of the fevered imagination of lovers and poets. Perhaps a person excited by devotion to a saint or passion for a beloved is susceptible to seeing such luminous auras. Actually a bluish haze or aura is visible around the space suits and helmets of astronauts in some photographs of them walking on the moon. This has been explained (or explained away) by NASA as the 'scattering of sunlight'.

Observing auras

The first person to discuss auras scientifically was Baron Karl von Reichenbach (1798-1869), renowned for his discovery of creosote, who presumably turned overnight from brilliant biochemist to crazed crank when he described observations of light fields around human beings and magnets. (Again and again one discovers that in 'normal science' even researchers considered to be brilliant are suddenly excommunicated, as it were, if they question the prevailing paradigm). These fields were not only visible but could be channeled like Mesmer's magnetic fluid from the body, especially from the finger tips. They did not behave exactly like magnetic or electrical fields. Reichenbach concluded that they came from another force which he termed OD. This yielding to the temptation (like Reich with orgone) to baptise a new discovery with an idiosyncratic name is the first catch in Reichenbach's work. The second catch is that the OD fields were only observable by certain people, whom he called 'sensitives'. But his method was sound: he cross-checked the sensitives' observations. Not everyone could observe the auras but that was not evidence that they did not exist, since those who did have the faculty of seeing them made observations which tallied. (As the poet A. E. Housman wrote: 'Can you hear the shriek of the bat? Probably not; but do you think the less of yourself on that account?' Some people, of course, do hear the shriek of the bat.) Reichenbach's method might be compared to what would be necessary to convince a person colour-blind to red and green that these are separate colours: the best way to do it would be to produce several people who do have the faculty of distinguishing red from green, and have them do so independently, with their distinctions tallying, in the presence of the colour-blind person. This inter-subjective testing must be a valid procedure for phenomena which are not measurable by instruments.

Another investigator, W.J.Kilner, in *The Human Atmosphere* dealt with the problem of not everyone being able to observe the same luminous auras as he could himself, by devising ways in which many people could be trained in this observation through the use of favourable light conditions (observing the subject against a dark background) and coloured viewing filters or screens, notably a blue screen containing dicyanin. Kilner was a physician who used his observations of auras for diagnosis. His use of the words 'human atmosphere', rather than the by then more mystical 'aura' suggests he sought an explanation compatible with physics.

Another medical doctor, John Pierrakos, originally a student of Reich's, also suggested the use of blue filters to observe 'energy fields', which he observed in the earth's atmosphere as well as around living organisms. But he proposed a theory (not, unfortunately, backed with experimental evidence) that auras are registered by the retinal rods which are peripheral to the retinal cones. This theory falls down with the fact that the cones perceive colour and the rods (much more numerous) do not. People who report seeing auras almost always mention colours.

Pierrakos claims that de-focusing the eyes slightly assists in seeing auras and that this is because the retinal rods are being used. In fact de-focusing the eyes and using peripheral vision (not the same as using retinal rods rather than cones) is a common method used by sailors when on watch for distant objects on the horizon, or by astronomers observing faintly visible stars.

My own observations of a human aura have been inconsistent and rare. I have a few times, in states of excitement, seen fields of light around the woman I love. More often I saw such phenomena in the practice of Reichian therapy (in the 1970s). The conditions of this work perhaps favour unusual states of excitement in the patient – and the therapist is, after all, paying total attention – but I myself have never seen auras while deliberately looking for them. I know several highly rational medical practitioners of this kind of therapy who have been startled by perceiving auras from time to time. My neuropsychiatrist colleague Jose Xavier (who is no mystic) reports seeing in therapy sessions both 'heat-wave' phenomena and 'dark moving clouds along the body surface'.

The phenomenon I noted most often was a shimmering cloud-like aura around a person's head, usually silvery blue but occasionally green, or muddy yellow-brown (this has corresponded with the person feeling angry but 'stuck') or rose-pink (one person in whom I noticed this remarked afterwards that he felt 'in the pink'). This vision lasted only a few seconds for me.

I have also experimented with blue filters (though not dyacinin-filled, which are very expensive) and noted a whitish fringe around the subject being observed. Another experiment, without a filter, is to hold one's hands about a foot away from one's face and move them slowly together, almost touching, then apart – either palm-to-palm or fingertips-to-fingertips. Quite often bridges and threads of light can be seen joining between the hands.

All this can be dismissed as 'self suggestion'. But children often report seeing auras, and are dismissed as 'seeing things'. (Children are often taught to distrust their experience if it does not fit the supposed norm). Two of my daughters independently at the age of 3 or 4 remarked on seeing light around people. One described it as 'moving waves.' (And no, auras were not a subject of family talk at the time).

Both Reichenbach and Reich had people sit in totally dark rooms where after one or two hours other people, plants, and organic matter are seen to be surrounded by a glowing field. Not only 'sensitives' report these phenomena, which most people patient enough to undertake the experiment will see. (Some people are upset by the ghostly wisps that emerge). Since there is no light, the phenomena are in no way reflective, and 'intra-ocular phenomena', sometimes proposed, is merely a cop-out term. Reichenbach and Reich explained the phenomena as lumination from organic life. But there is also a more faint, moving luminous mist in the air, and this seems to cling to non-organic objects such as furniture.

Auras and emotion

A few quite startling examples from body oriented therapy have suggested to me that some kind of personal atmosphere can luminate abruptly in states of emotion or, more precisely, just *before* emotional expression. (Interestingly, the epileptic's premonitory change in sensation just before a fit has been labeled 'the aura.')

In one case, a man in therapy had been breathing deeply, lying on his back and looking at the ceiling. Suddenly I saw two blue beams of light – as if from pen-light torches, shoot from his eyes to the ceiling. A second or so later he burst into sobs and the blue beams disappeared. He said he had had a sudden vision of his mother's breast. (Very 'Freudian', but it happened.)

Another man breathing in therapy began to be taken over by a trembling which began in his legs and moved up through the pelvis into the trunk. As it reached his chest I began to see sheets and waves of blue light (like dense 'heat-waves' above a road in summer) rising from his chest as it heaved up and down then 'gave', and he broke into sobbing. The blue light then disappeared.

In another case, I suddenly saw a cluster of black dots forming in the air above a man's forehead. He remarked that he felt a headache beginning.

In another, truly frightening session a man was transported by intensification of his breathing into a state where he appeared to be possessed by the devil – at least, his face went into a contortion of mixed rage and horror (like a caricature of the devil in a medieval painting), and he began to whimper that there was something inside him that he couldn't get out. He began writhing in terror on the mat, and became so lost from contact that I could not get his attention either by touching him on the shoulder or asking him to look at me. He began to thrash around wildly and I was afraid he would hurt himself so I made the mistake of holding him by the knees. At this he burst into screams and a dense brown cloud smelling of sulphur formed around his body and spread out into the room. Eventually he calmed down and the cloud dissipated. I aired the room and burned candles in it but it felt suffocating for some days. The man stopped coming to therapy – understandably – saying he did not want to repeat such an experience. I did not want to either. I was not an exorcist. I became much more careful in my use of breathing methods in therapy.

Auras and electricity

Some people observe auras around inanimate objects such as tables and chairs, and Reich and many or his followers claim to have observed them in the earth's atmosphere. In the absence of systematic investigation by teams of scientists, rather than lone amateurs, it is not possible to address adequately the question of whether every such field, or only a specific kind of field, is characteristic of life.

The Russians Semyon and Valentina Kirlian and their associates in their work on the 'Kirlian aura' in the 1970s, which produced coloured photographs of apparently luminating leaves and hands, ran into a major problem precisely in the area of the distinction between life and non-life. Enthusiasts and mystics seized on the Kirlians' work as evidence for the existence of everything from a specific life energy to an immortal soul. But eventually a damp squib was thrown into the excitement by the announcement by American investigators that the presence of the Kirlian aura depended on the moisture content and the electrical conductivity of the object being photographed. They were simply corona discharge. But water content is a sign of life and the Kirlian photographs which show a luminating 'phantom' where part of a leaf has been removed are ungainsayable. Moss in *The Body Electric* notes counter-arguments to the Kirlian evidence which range from 'just a molecular effect', to 'just heat' to (perhaps the most bizarre) 'just pheromones' – the molecules which transmit smells. These are not attempts to refute by citing facts, but what Popper called 'escape hypotheses'.

The real problem with the Kirlian work was that the photographed object was subjected to a brief but extremely high electrical charge (thousands of volts). Whether the aura is, as the Kirlians maintained, produced by a 'transformation of non-electrical properties of the photographed subject into electric ones', or an artefact of the high electrical charge used, is an almost insoluble problem since the experiments cannot be replicated *without* the electrical charge. This is a problem of all experimental as distinct from empirical investigation: it imposes drastically changed conditions on the subject. So the argument about whether the Kirlian aura is corona discharge or evidence of another kind of field (the Russian Inyushin has suggested 'bioplasma') remains impossible to resolve.

But when evidence from visual observation of auras under different conditions tallies with the Kirlian photographs, this is surely a valuable crosscheck. The Kirlian photographs, the descriptions of Reichenbach, Kilner and Pierrakos, and many informal observations including my own, may vary in some details but all describe luminous haze, waves, and flickering 'flares'. This convergence of data from very different sources (human, and mechanical) is convincing evidence.

Life Fields

Apart from auras the most striking field effects are of the kind reported by various 'magnetic healers' and 'faith healers'. One person supposedly transmits some kind of force or current into the body of another, producing observable dyskinetic movements or convulsions, inner sensations of warmth, electricity, or tingling, and often measurable physiological changes. All this can, of course, be explained away as 'suggestion' – which on the evidence must be such a powerful force that it demands explanation beyond a mere word. But suggestion is ruled out convincingly by at least one experimenter, Bernard Grad, a biologist who studied with Reich and in spite of this and his unconventional experiments managed to hold down a job as a Professor at McGill University in Montreal. (He was eventually starved of resources in an attempt to force him out – but he had tenure).

Grad's experiments used containers of water, each of which had been held in a different pair of hands – of a faith-healer, a depressed person, and a 'normal' person. The container was then held by a subject who reported on the sensations it evoked, or the water could be used on plants. In contrast to almost all neo-Reichian experiments, Grad's were controlled 'double blind'. Water which had been held by the healer supposedly made people feel better, and made plants grow faster and/or more luxuriantly. Grad also demonstrated that the healer could heal sick mice – presumably out of the reach of 'suggestion.'

Following Grad, Sister Justa Smith, a biochemist, demonstrated that the same healer could raise the level of activity of 'damaged' enzymes in a solution. In one experiment the effect was similar to that when a magnetic field was applied – although no magnetic field was detectable from the healer's hands.

Such experiments suggest the existence of a field which apparently emits energy. But what kind of energy? H.S.Burr at Yale, with a colleague L.Ravitz, put in decades of experimentation with what he called the 'L-field' – the 'Life-field.' This L-field was stated to be detectable with a vacuum tube voltmeter which measured not 'the alternating electrical currents which doctors find in the heart and brain' but 'pure voltage *potentials* which can yield only an infinitesimal amount of *direct* current.'

Burr hoped that 'since L-field voltages reveal both physical and mental conditions they can offer doctors a new insight into the state of both body and mind.' The connection between L-field variations and emotional states was documented by Ravitz who concluded: 'both emotional activity and stimuli of any sort involve mobilization of electric energy… Emotions can be equated with energy.' A bit of a leap there! Burr himself discussed 'mental states', not emotion. And 'the nervous system of man is an organized, designed [sic] dynamic machine.' The L-field variations are 'variations in the flow of energy in the system, a flow of energy which arises first of all in chemistry and is controlled and directed by the electro-dynamic field of the whole organism.' Chemistry provides the physical-energetic fuel, as it were and the L-field works on it. But Burr points out that if the L-field is genuinely 'electro-dynamic' (not to speak of controlling and directing) it must have its own energy.

Burr saw embryonic formation as controlled by the electrodynamic L-field. On the other hand 'the field properties of the embryo do not short out in the liquid' – as would happen if they were simply electrical. The L-field, Burr admits, is 'quasi-electrostatic.' (Static electricity follows different laws from those of electricity in a current). But, Burr hurries to correct, 'it is not another name for *élan vital* or entelechy. It is a definable concept capable of precise measurement and is to be thought of in the same terms as fields in the non-living universe.' 'In the same terms' – i.e. it is a different kind of field. Burr then makes an important methodological point that must be remembered in any discussion of the 'energy' in fields:

> Someone once asked the question: 'What is this energy which constitutes a field?' A distinguished physicist gave the best answer that the author knows: 'Electricity is the way Nature behaves.'
>
> This electricity, then, which can be measured and shown to have order and pattern, is not some strange and separate phenomenon but an essential characteristic of the Universe. Numerous names have been given to these electrical fields. We refer to electro-magnetic fields, electro-static fields, and

electrodynamic fields and it used to be assumed that these are different and separate. This is not so. The various names derive from the instruments used to measure the fields.

Thus the 'energy' of a field will be electrical if measured by electrical instruments, magnetic if measured by magnetometers, gravitational if measured by a gravitometer, and so on. By extension, if 'measured' by the 'instrument' of a living organism, is it therefore 'life?' This would be the most extreme version of animism: everything I perceive is alive, as I am alive. So the sun is alive. A rock or a typewriter are alive. We reject this view. How? By falling back on mechanical instruments (thermometers, electrocardiographs) to tell us? No. We seem to have a sense (a measuring instrument) which recognizes life, as opposed to non-life. We are in some way moved (our 'instrument' responds) by the life in a person more than we are by a rock or even a swaying tree. We may also have developed our 'instrument' and in a sense calibrated it according to our *experience* of life: its specific movements, its specific warmth, even its specific light or glow. We may, in fact, have a sense for a person's life field because of our experience in early childhood, or as embryos in the uterus – Burr describes the L-field as a 'matrix.'

He also describes

the pulsating character of the growth of the slime mould under a miscroscope as measured by voltage potential: every sixty or ninety seconds the protoplasm in the veins reverses the direction of flow... In the majority of instances polar reversal of the voltage occurs *before* there is a directional change of the plasmic flow, but also there are many instances where the change in both phenomena seem [sic] to occur simultaneously.

But this is Burr's only mention of apparent pulsation in the life-field, and it may be, strictly speaking, an oscillation.

The implication of an electrical shift *before* a physical shift recalls my observation of events in the human aura *before* physical movement. (It also looks forward to the neurological research by Benjamin Libet demonstrating that a person's nervous system begins to respond to a stimulus before the person is aware of it: the 'half second delay'.) The relation between pulsation and attention remains to be explored.

Pulsation of the human atmosphere

Pierrakos's observations stress that the field, whether as the human aura or as that around crystals or in the atmosphere, always 'pulsates'. Although Pierrakos makes no formal distinction between pulsation, oscillation and vibration, he describes pulsations which are phase-unequal. He observes the human aura swelling outwards for 1 or 2 seconds, remaining fully developed for about ¼ second, then abruptly disappearing, reappearing again after 1 to 3 seconds and beginning to swell again. In other words the visible expansion process is longer than the abrupt contraction. But all this timing is suspect: how was the ¼ second measured, for example?

Pierrakos used a kymograph, a rotating drum with graph paper on which he moved a pen up and down according to shifting light intensity in his observation of the auras of plants and crystals. The result was always a rising and falling curve which, although it varied with a characteristic 'signature' for each object under observation, shows a slower rising side than falling. In other words, these are phase unequal pulsation curves, as defined earlier. A physicist, S.A.Silbey, analysing Pierrakos' charts, pointed out that the 'pulsation waveform' recorded is always 'non-sinusoidal', unlike the sinusoidal wave (equal sided) which expresses alternating electrical currents. He adds that the non-sinusoidal form, unlike the sinusoidal which is limited by its symmetry, opens the wave to many levels of harmonics. This work by Pierrakos and Silbey comes near to the key concept that pulsation is by definition unequal phase.

The question remains: if the human atmosphere pulsates, is this in its own right or because it reflects the pulsations of the physical organism it surrounds? In Pierrakos's observations the cycle of the field pulsation is described as having a duration of between 3 and 5 seconds. This is suspiciously like the human breathing pulsation. Normal breathing is usually reported as 12 to 16 cycles a minute, although relaxed breathing in an 'unarmoured' person may be somewhat slower. Pierrakos does not make the connection. It can only be explored by other observers who perceive the field pulsation clearly. It would be of great interest to know if the field pulsation is synchronous with the breathing, or if it is 'coupled' to it, either preceding or following it. In other words, even if, as some evidence suggests, the human life field is primary, and determines the disposition of matter (rather than a secondary coronal or other discharge of energy from material dispositions) its pulsation may not be primary, but rather a consequence of its interaction with matter.

Earth's Atmosphere

'Does planet X have an atmosphere which could sustain life?' This question has become familiar as various rocket probes measure the atmospheres of planets within our solar system, and even as astronomers attempt to deduce whether planets in other possible solar systems have atmospheres. But surely this is putting the cart before the horse, the chicken before the egg. The only atmosphere we know for sure sustains life is our own. We also know that this atmosphere consists partly of chemicals created by life itself. It may be more accurate to say: 'if a planet has an atmosphere that can sustain life it will have an atmosphere in turn sustained at least partly by that life.' If what James Lovelock calls 'Gaia', including its atmosphere, is in some sense self-regulating in the way a living organism is, this may be because it is largely a product of living organisms. The only atmosphere we know personally has been partly constituted by our presence: we are interdependent. Without our atmosphere we would die. Without us (meaning all earth's organisms) our atmosphere would also, in the long run die, in the sense that its organic elements would dissipate.

The earth's atmosphere is usually considered to be a hydrodynamic system, its movements the consequences of various mechanical forces, such as that of the earth's rotation and the convection currents caused by the unequal distribution and reflection of the sun's heat on the globe. The practical problems of pollution, and the effects of nuclear radiation in peace or in war, the greenhouse effect, or climatic change are nowhere near solution, but they can be discussed in a framework of accepted theory. There is no question of the atmosphere being considered in itself alive. Lovelock has pointed out that the whole biosphere seems to have self-healing or problem-solving attributes, and to function at times as a unit; but this only accidentally simulates conscious behaviour. Lovelock's referring to the biosphere as 'Gaia', after the Greek goddess, is considered a fantasy. But are there any signs of life in the earth's atmosphere?

Auras have been observed not only around organisms but around magnets and crystals. They are similar to lumination phenomena which are observed in the earth's atmosphere, in the form of nightglow and auroras. Furthermore, the same sensitives or visionaries or oddballs who claim to see human auras often claim to see various luminating effects in the atmosphere beyond those discussed in normal physics. I have seen many such effects myself, on occasion, and I am not all that sensitive. I have found that I have been able at least to some degree to train myself to see certain atmospheric phenomena of lumination when the conditions are favourable. My only defense against accusations of self-deception can be to invite the reader to test similar observation procedures, and to reconsider observations which he or she may have been made already but not taken seriously. I shall describe some of my own observations and pay attention to any special conditions under which they have been made. But not all observations of unusual or unexplainable atmospheric movement are made under special conditions or only at the edge of vision. The well-documented phenomena of the aurora borealis is readily visible in places where the atmosphere is clear and relatively close to the magnetic pole.

Observations of spontaneous movement in the atmosphere are mainly of streaming waves. Their rhythm sometimes suggests pulsation. Physics accepts scintillation, and rhythmic fluctuations and oscillations in the atmosphere. But if these are pulsation in the strict sense used in this book, of the phase-unequal pulsation which characterizes life, then two questions arise. First, does life exist in the atmosphere at large? Second, is pulsation is invalidated as a criterion of life if it is found to exist where life, by any other criterion, does not exist?

Atmospheric pulse waves

Atmospheric pulse-waves are visible as the 'heat waves' above tarred road surfaces in the sun. They are also frequently observed through telephoto lenses: most readers will have seen films of animals on the African plains viewed through an atmospheric sea of bluish shimmering waves. They are certainly made visible by sunlight and usually by heat. But are they only 'heat waves'? What are heat waves anyway? Why should the atmosphere be made visible as waves? Explanations are lacking. The most common one is 'refraction', as when a stick is bent when perceived through water. But this does not explain shimmering *movement*. And there are puzzles. Heat waves cast shadows: how does this happen? And they can be observed on cold days, or over cold surfaces. I have seen them along snow covered ridges on winter days with a temperature near -20C. One 'Reichian' observer, Jerome Eden, claimed to have observed them in Alaska at -40C. Reich observed that they usually travel in a West to East direction, as does the prevailing wind, but that their direction shifts *before* the wind changes. These West-East 'streamings', Reich pointed out, are most easily observed through a telescope at about 60× magnification. I have observed them in this way on summer days when the air has been at about 20C, flowing thickly over the water of the Straits of Juan de Fuca (Vancouver Island) where the water temperature has been about 10C.

The following series of descriptions are of observations of pulse-waves with the naked eye, and of associated atmospheric perturbations. Each description starts with an account of the observation (**O**) and the conditions under which it was made, and continues with a brief mechanistic explanation (**M**), and a final section (**Q**) which raises some questions.

Pulse waves over the ocean
O) 6-7 p.m., 22 June 1980, La Push, Washington.

The sun was still high, in a blue sky with high stacked cumulus. There was apparently an unusual weather reversal, in that the norm is for the Pacific North West coast to be covered by whatever cloud is present, with the inland more clear. On this day it was dull and cloudy inland, the coast clear. Standing on the beach looking West out to sea I observed simultaneously:

i)   *Up and down pulsing* in a narrow band on the horizon: a dark blue strip with a white aura pulsing over a couple of degrees. The pulse rate was similar to my own pulse rate (c.68 per minute).

ii) Up and down *shimmering and dancing* of the atmosphere at a fast rate, in vertical waves between me and the horizon.

iii) *Sheets* of light, apparently 10–20 feet high, advancing from West to East towards me, like sheets of rain in a storm, curved and curtain-like.

I made similar observations of pulsing of a dark horizon band and its white aura when near or on the sea on a weekly ferry trip from Vancouver island to the mainland. The pulsing suggests *pulsation: short phase upwards, long phase downwards*. The band flashes up almost instantly, then settles down over a longer period. The cycle is approximately one per second.

M) Optical illusion? Heat waves? But the NW Pacific is still cold in June, about 8C. Air temperature was about 15C. Effect of my heartbeat (similar pulse rates) on my vision?

Q) Does the earth's atmosphere pulsate? Reich suggested that the atmosphere formed an 'envelope' which rotated West to East slightly faster than the earth itself and caused the earth's rotation, as a rotating vortex in fluid would cause a ball to rotate in it. But without measurable evidence this is about as naïve an explanation as the earliest Greek philosopher Thales' theory that the earth is like a boat floating on water. The observations of mainly West to East pulse-waves, where the flow was apparently off the ocean from the West towards my position on the beach, suggest that the local atmosphere was moving in this way. But pulse-waves do not suggest life as pulsation does. The question of whether the atmosphere pulsates at the horizon or only appears to do so is crucial.

Reich mentions no pulsation of the atmosphere. But Pierrakos has described it in detail. He distinguishes three layers of aura above the sea horizon (where I only saw two) which together surge upwards ('Phase I'), then recede fading downwards and disappear ('Phase II'), then are invisible in an interval of apparent rest ('Phase III'). Pierrakos does not give a graph of the wave form of the supposed pulsation. He mentions that the upward surge is ¼–½ seconds and the downward movement takes 1 to 4 seconds. Suspiciously, to my mind, this is exactly what he notes for a human aura or for that of a leaf or flower.

I have also noted that the sea horizon bands (or aura) expand rapidly upwards, then fade more slowly downwards – the *opposite* of such mechanical processes as a bubble swelling and bursting. But I have a problem with this: I have often noted the same phenomenon over any object's edge with a brighter lit background: trees against the sky, roof tops, and clouds. Trees are alive. They sometimes seem to 'flare' with bluish or white streamers of light above the tips, a phenomenon recorded by Van Gogh and other painters. But I have not noted this around clouds or rooftops. A Reichian would maintain that clouds are concentrations of 'orgone energy'. But rooftops? *I strongly suspect that this apparent field pulsation is a product of my own pulsation.* It may not only be 'endoptic' (in my eyes): if I have a force field around me I am presumably looking out through the filter of this field. If it pulsates, my perception through it might be affected, also pulsating. That the pulsation rate of a leaf or the horizon is similar to that of the human breathing makes it suspect. But I do not notice observed pulsations being coupled to my breathing.

Pierrakos does give a graph which shows the rate of observed ocean-horizon 'pulsations' increasing during a 24 hour cycle from around 10 pulsations a minute to over 40 at midday. This suggests a process independent of the observer's condition. I must admit to suspicion with regard to Pierrakos' work because his account is always sloppily written and unclear, but presented with great confidence. No attempt is made to discuss any other explanations for his observations than the one he initially believes in: that they are observations of 'the energy field, life energy, common functioning principle, "aether", "Od", "orgone" and "God"'. Pierrakos is a mystic with an interest in spiritualism. He is also a psychiatrist, and careful in his method in spite of his lack of clarity in writing it up. Having met him once (1974), I think he was sincere in his observations. I wish he had questioned them more. As it is they are idiosyncratic.

If Pierrakos is right, the atmosphere pulsates, and by some of my own criteria for life I must consider it to be alive. (It certainly does not fulfil the criterion of being 'contained'). I hesitate over this because although my own observations, though less vivid, are similar to Pierrakos's, I doubt if the pulsation I have observed in the atmosphere is genuinely external to my own organism or 'field'. I have no such doubts about pulse-waves ('streamings') because they are recorded by many other people, can be seen in any TV film about the Serengeti or other wide space in the sun, and are readily viewed by anyone through a telescope. The same is not true of pulsation. Pierrakos is the only one of many students of the human aura (Kilner, Reichenbach et al.) to state confidently that it pulsates.

Pierrakos' observations of 'pulsation' in the human aura or in the earth's atmosphere cannot be accepted without further cross-checking, which he does not offer. There is also the possibility that he is not observing pulsation but a sudden bright flash of lumination which 'fades' on his retina. Any bright flash seems to 'fade'. It may seem unkind for me to point out that

Pierrakos also suffered from impaired vision which may have affected his observations. Finally, even if the earth's atmosphere seems to luminate in *pulses* (similar to those from a mechanically rotating lighthouse beam) this phenomenon is not necessarily a *pulsation* of rising and falling, expansion and contraction. And furthermore, as noted above, it is not contained in a membrane or equivalent.

It is important to distinguish pulsation from *pulses* which can be of mechanical origin, though they are not necessarily so. If the horizon band or other auras pulse, this is a phenomenon worth investigation. Again, more cross-checking is needed. A regular pulse is a wave phenomenon: cf. the pulse of ocean waves on a beach, which is *not* a *pulsation* (though unequal phase, it is not repeated in the same enclosed unit). Pierrakos compares the 'pulsation' of ocean waves to atmospheric 'pulsation'. But if pulsation is defined carefully, these are pulse waves.

Hearing pulse waves
O) La Push, Washington, as above.

Accompanying the above observations there seemed to be a sound: zing-zing-zing-zing, like a rope being whirled around. It was as if dimly behind the other noises of surf, birds etc., I noticed the sound because of its synchronicity with the pulsing of the atmosphere. I could not be sure whether it was external or inside my brain. Stopping my ears with my fingers replaced it with a circulation roar.

Similar observations: traditions of aurora borealis making a 'swishing' sound like the rustling of a silk dress. Scientists have dismissed this as nonsense, but it is persistently reported, especially by observers in isolated regions, such as the Inuit (Eskimos). There have also been assertions that fireballs make a swishing sound (although when I saw one as a child, it did not – see next section). The Australian aboriginal 'bull-roarers' are used to make a similar sound, considered to be of magical power.

M) This is a phenomenon unrecorded by mechanical instruments, and when reported in connection with auroras is dismissed as an illusion.

Q) Do atmospheric streamings/pulse-waves impinge on the ears as well as the eyes?

Consider the well known phenomenon of ringing in the ears, for example when sitting alone at night in 'silence.' I note that

1. It modulates, is not constant, is sometimes absent.
2. It seems independent of my heartbeat or respiration (unlike for example, placing a shell to the ear).
3. It seems to impinge from outside.
4. If I stop my ears it stops.

I suggest this ringing is the sound of the atmospheric pulse-waves, a sort of perpetual auditory background count, normally obliterated by other sounds or taken for granted and not felt, like air pressure on the skin.

When 'excited' in certain atmospheric conditions it becomes a more lively 'swishing.'

Rainbows and clouds

O) Sometimes a rainbow will appear, then fade and disappear, then appear, disappear, and so on for several cycles. I have not discovered any particular rhythm to this.

M) Not noted. It would be logical to suppose that the air is saturated with water droplets in succeeding waves from passing clouds, slanted into by sunlight. Hence this mechanical cause gives the appearance of a pulse or pulsation.

Q) Unless there is evidence for some unexplainable rhythmic pulse or cycle of brightness, this example is a useful check on speculation: mechanical factors, such as the passing of clouds, can cause successive pulses or the *appearance* of pulsation. On the other hand if clouds pass in rhythmic sequence, this opens a new question about whether they express a pulse-wave.

Atmospheric 'rain'

O) 'Atmospheric rain.' This is the appearance of 'rain' in the atmosphere, without actual rain, although it often seems to precede actual rain. It can also be observed inside a room. I have observed it mainly in the evenings, both indoors and outdoors. After a sunny day, just before sunset, it has a marked West to East drift. It often seems like snow in a car headlight; it is characterized by a slight lumination. There is some random drifting from side to side in a general downward, slanting direction, as with actual rain blown by wind.

On November 26th 1980, at Careywood, Idaho, I noticed 'atmospheric snow' when I stepped outdoors at night. The difference from 'rain' was that it was like many bright points. (These were not the ice crystals which sometimes occur as snow begins, and with which I am familiar having lived for nine years in Quebec). This looked like 'future' light snow, although none was actually falling. I mentioned it to the person I was staying with, Jerome Eden. He quoted me a verse (see earlier, Ch.1) including the line 'It snows before it snows'. Later that evening, about three hours later, it began to snow lightly.

M) Never discussed.

Q) The condensation of rain or snow seems to be preceded by an atmospheric condensation which 'luminates' enough to be visible. (Why rain and snow form drops and crystals is a mystery to physicists, with explanations that they form on random particles such as grit or even bacteria mainly unconvincing). On the other hand it does not rain inside rooms, even though 'rain' can be observed. Perhaps rain follows 'field lines' in a similar way to iron filings arranging themselves on magnetic field lines. Why should atmospheric field lines become visible? It would seem impossible to explore the question experimentally. Nevertheless it can be observed, and inter-subjectively cross-checked. Many readers will already have noticed it.

Apparent oscillation of the moon
O) 8.45 p.m. 28 August 1982, Victoria, B.C.

Apparent oscillation of the moon. The preceding two days had been cloudy. Now the atmosphere was clearing. The moon, three quarters full, was seen in a clear patch of sky with some surrounding clouds. It appeared to dance or bounce up and down, as if seen through a quivering, jelly-like medium, in an irregular rate of vibration over perhaps a degree of arc. This was noticed first by my four year old daughter who called us to 'see the moon moving.' Of note: the clouds around the moon were *not* moving. My wife and I confirmed the marked dancing motion of the moon, and also noted a strong blue fringe or aura along the right or outside side of the moon's disc, with some component of pink. Our daughter saw mainly pink. After ten minutes or so the moon appeared to become steady.

Similar observation: around 11.00 p.m., 6 August 1982, San Juan Island,

Washington, a line of treetops about two miles away appeared to dance up and down against a night sky which was glowing in a faint green colour. Later there was an auroral display (rather rare in this region).

M): Supposed turbulence of the atmosphere. Since cloud fragments were strato-cumulus, normally at about 1,000 feet, and did not participate in the movement, the turbulence would be supposed to be above this altitude. According to a textbook on meteorological optics

> Local fluctuations distort the rays of light and lead to the familiar scintillation or twinkling of the stars. The fluctuations in position consist of a vibratory movement amounting to a few seconds of arc at frequencies which are not constant... because of fluctuations in the density of the atmosphere, a plane wave front is distorted, some parts becoming slightly concave and others slightly convex, a corrugated wave front.

Similarly, in shimmer or 'atmopheric boil'

> Fluctuation in intensity increased with distance and, at night, reached a limiting value of about + 65 per cent at a distance of 1,200 meters. The frequency of the fluctuations was about 9 cycles per second. There was marked diurnal variation, in fine weather. There was a minimum just after sunrise, a maximum towards midday, a second minimum just before sunset and another maximum but much lower than the first, at night.

Q) Why corrugations? Why vibratory? Why the frequency of 9 per second? Why the seemingly lawful diurnal variation of intensity of atmospheric boil? (Cf. Pierrakos' observations). The data require an explanatory theory but none is offered. Tricker gives a similarly careful description of refraction in corona phenomena around sun and moon. But there is no mention of the corona moving (see next example, 6). When movement is noted, as with shimmer, boil and star twinkle, its observable lawfulness is not explained.

Clearly the moon itself, or trees, do not dance. But the atmosphere oscillates with pulse-waves.

O) 30 November 1975, Ladysmith, Quebec. I made a Super 8 movie film of the moon, which shows a wide multi-coloured corona which expands and contracts rhythmically at a rate of about 105 times a minute (as counted with the film in slow motion). This is clearly an equal phase oscillation, not a pulsation.

M) Not noted in mechanistic physics. Probably 'atmospheric turbulence.'

Q) This is *not* evidence that the moon or a hypothetical 'energy field' around it pulsates. But it is further evidence that the *atmosphere* as seen between an observer and the moon, expands and contracts, i.e. oscillates.

Visible light fields in Cloud-Busting
At the risk of ridicule (the bullfighting critics) here is a rather dramatic one off observation (or illusion or self-hallucination if you prefer):

O) In 1974 or so there was a 'Life Energy' conference at York University, Toronto, organised by Theodore Mann who had written a book on Reich. An American operator of a Cloud-Buster was invited to give a demonstration which I attended at the end of the conference, in the late afternoon of a sunny and torrid day. The operator (I forget his name) had driven up in his half-ton truck with a massive cloud-buster – a rack of tubes cranked by a cogwheel – and set it up earlier in the day. The pipes were grounded by cables in a small stream. From my rudimentary work with Adolph Smith some years before, and discussions with Jerome Eden, I knew that the technique recommended by Reich on the grounds of safety was usually to 'draw' from (i.e. aim the pipes at) the prevailing flow of wind and atmosphere from the West. The operator had set up his cloud-buster pointing, at a 45 degree angle, due East. Nothing obvious was happening, and most people had a look then drifted away. I stayed for a while, but I felt uneasy, as I was about to drive home to Quebec, going East. As I watched I began to see a sort of boiling turbulence around the ends of the tubes, a shimmering light in what seemed like all the colours of the rainbow. At the same time there was a sort of throbbing sensation in my ears.

I turned away and went to my car, driving home Eastwards along Route 401. After some miles I noticed that the skies ahead were black, and after another 10 miles or so all hell was breaking loose: a violent thunderstorm with flashes and bangs, gusts of wind that tore at the car, and floods of rain. I drove slowly through it and on the other side the weather returned to normal.

M) Atmospheric 'boil'?

Q) Consistent with the reports by Jerome Eden and James DeMeo of careless cloud-busting experiments. The turbulent aura around the pipes was not like a human aura, but was reminiscent of the aurora borealis on a very small scale. Perhaps cloud-busting channels atmospheric pulse-waves.

Atmospheric oscillation, not pulsation

The above observations provide evidence for pulse-waves and oscillation in the atmosphere. The oscillation seems to be a variation of atmospheric density which causes the illusion that a bright object seen through it is itself oscillating: cf. a lamp seen through a fishbowl of water in which a regular oscillation has been induced through shaking the bowl. The regularity of the oscillation suggests a consistent *pulse* – though, again, not pulsation.

My conclusion is that pulsation in the atmosphere is apparent, not real, but that *pulse waves become visible under some conditions.*

Observations of the 'human atmosphere' and the earth's atmosphere suggest that the former may pulsate but the latter does not. This supports the theory that pulsation is a sign of life, and the common sense view that although we may feel a sense of contact with the world around us and even the cosmos, the world and the universe are not in themselves alive. They are the continuum in which we live. We are like fish living in a sea which supports life but is not in itself alive.

The above point may seem rather banal, but it contradicts theories of animism, New Age pantheism, and even the 'implicate universe' deduced by Bohm from quantum physics.

The aurora borealis

An area of physics where the words 'streaming' and 'pulsation' are used frequently and freely is in the study of the aurora borealis. This study is inevitably technical and the reader may wish to skip or skim the following sections until the end of the chapter. However it is impossible to avoid discussion of the aurora borealis here, since it is a dramatic atmospheric event which is often described in terms of pulsation.

While living in Quebec, from 1967 to 1976, I observed many auroras in winter, mainly as diffuse greenish lights and bands or moving shafts against the N or NE horizon. The more dramatic displays took place in Spring and Autumn. The following description is of a single display, from 11:30p.m. to 12:15 a.m., 25–26 March 1976 (at Ladysmith, Quebec, Lat.46, Long.75.)

1. At 11:30 I noticed extensive Northern lights of the usual greenish luminous colour, in an arc of 'curtains' or 'draperies' from the East around from North to West, reaching up 60 to 70 degrees, sometimes in the form of playing 'searchlights'. At the same time there were huge luminous blobs flickering and darting across the zenith ahead of the main lights, forming and re-forming, appearing and vanishing at a main point 15 degrees or so South of the zenith. Darting extensions of the auroral searchlights from the NE and NW were crossing the zenith to this main point and hooking in circles around the luminous patches as they formed. These extensions seemed to 'swoop' on the main point, now simultaneously from NE and NW in pairs hooking around each other and spiraling into the main point, appearing and vanishing almost instantly.

2. These movements took on a definite rhythm: streamers of light from the auroral curtain rushing across the zenith and into the main point, vanishing, rushing in again, vanishing, rushing in, at the rate of about one of these 'pulses' per second.

3. The various streams of light began to merge and even out into broader streams obliterating the main point and eventually becoming a 'mainstream' extending over the zenith from a double-dome of light in the North, each side of the dome seemingly pushed upward by or containing bright internal shafts of light. The mainstream contained rushing light moving from two opposing directions in various wave forms, some equal phase and some unequal – like the waves moving across a pond after a splash, or waves on the sea. This mainstream was about 20 degrees wide, stretching across the former main point. There were now some luminous patches in the sky to the South, but the North was relatively empty apart from a few greenish shafts of light.

4. It was now midnight. The mainstream had settled down into a

narrower 'rope' of light, about 5 degrees wide and stationary, with a few waves: like a braided rope or silver-green river across the sky, and much brighter. It remained stationary for about 10 minutes while the Southern edge gradually took on a pink colour which then permeated and replaced the green.

5. At about 10 minutes after clock midnight, i.e. at 'true' midnight for longitude 75, the main point suddenly asserted itself again in a 'soft explosion', a sort of starburst or 'unfolding flower' effect, splitting the mainstream back into two again.

6. The streams now diffused quite quickly leaving a sky similar to that at the beginning of my observation, the main shafts of light to the North persisting but less bright, the zenith crossed by vague and diffuse streamers and luminous patches.

My impression was of a process of 1) alternating diffusion and fusion, 2) accelerating pulses, 3) merging 4) total fusion 5) 'burst' 6) diffusion. Although unusually bright and active, this auroral display contained the same sequence of events I had observed in other displays, in what is called the 'auroral substorm.'

The auroral substorm

In conventional descriptions of the aurora borealis the substorm is characterized as having two phases, of *expansion*, and *recovery*. *Pulsation* (although it must be remembered that in mechanistic physics the word pulsation is used interchangeably with oscillation) is noted as occurring around the main point or 'auroral corona.' The word *streaming* is used for 'apparent movements of regions of enhanced luminosity across pre-existing auroral forms.'

Current research on auroras uses electromagnetic measurements of the atmosphere and satellite photographs. [The researchers I quote here were active in the 1970s and early 1980s, when I first wrote these notes, but the accepted picture of auroras has not changed since then and satellite photography confirms it]. Auroras are described as occurring in 'the auroral oval', a doughnut-shaped area of electromagnetic activity in the ionosphere, encircling each Pole but most intense at the North. The oval is broader in the midnight portion, that is away from the sun. The plane of the oval is tilted, its sun-facing or noon portion at Geomagnetic Latitude 76, the midnight portion lower at 67. (These geomagnetic latitudes relate to the *magnetic* N pole, not the geographical pole). The oval tends to contract toward the pole in periods of low sunspot activity, and expand equator-wards during high sunspot activity. Auroral substorms occur as disturbances along the midnight portion of the oval. The auroral oval's position is at the interface between the ionosphere and a major radiation belt, and also coincides with a 'wind' of charged particles, the polar electroject 'which flows westward all around the oval'. According to Akasofu, 'two major geophysical phenomena, auroral and magnetic occur along the auroral oval. The oval can thus be considered to be the natural frame of reference to which some major polar geophysical phenomena can be referred'. The oval is 'a natural coordinate', although a flexible one.

There is some controversy about the real shape of the oval. A Soviet researcher, Nicolsky, identified spiral patterns of disturbance. These spirals were dismissed by Akasofu and others as merely referring to the noon portion of the oval, or as 'fragments' of the auroral activity. But still other researchers have identified possible 'spiral zones of proton precipitation'.

Some difficulty in defining the shape of the oval must come from the fact that 'auroral morphology is a four dimensional problem which investigators usually try to describe on a two dimensional piece of paper'. But keeping this caution in mind, a recurring theme is nevertheless 'the concept of two oppositely unwinding spirals'. The earth's atmosphere is full of various other auroras and airglows: faint 'polar auroras' arcing across the poles in a direction from the sun towards midnight; a reddish airglow known as the intertropical arc, near the equator; and a red mid-latitude glow. Furthermore, according to McCormac, the 5577 Angstrom spectrum line known as 'auroral green' has been observed to be 'present at all times over the entire sky'. The explanation of this basic airglow as well as auroral airglows excited up to pink or red is that they are caused by ionization of the oxygen atoms which float dissociated in the ionosphere'.

Auroral displays occur at periods when the earth's magnetic field is disturbed and the auroral oval expands and bulges southward towards the midnight sector. However, substorms are not themselves initiated by solar disturbances: 'Since there is no visible indication that the substorm is preceded by an auroral motion, and since an enhanced solar plasma does not initiate the substorm, the substorm is most likely to be an internal process within the magnetosphere.' In other words, although solar events such as flares or storms may set the preconditions for auroral activity in general, internal processes specific to the earth's magnetic field trigger the substorms.

'The auroral substorm has a sudden onset, an explosive energy release (the explosive phase) and a slow relaxation (the recovery phase).' (The energy referred to here is electromagnetic). 'The auroral substorm can roughly be described as an intermittent expansion and contraction of the width of the oval in the dark sector'. Akasofu also describes the auroral motions during the substorm as away from the midnight meridian to the E, W, and N to the pole during the expansive phase, lasting 10 to 30 minutes; then equatorwards, to the S and to the E and W during the recovery phase.

Some researchers have trouble with the fact of motion in the auroral displays. 'Bright rayed aurorae, such as the fascinating type B red bands, often give an appearance of a horizontal wave motion… These active bands and draperies may give the illusion that the individual rays are moving, whereas only *the excitation pattern* moves.' But whatever moves, the processes of expansion and contraction are apparent, and between these phases the 'bursting' at the corona which is sometimes known as 'break-up'.

Auroral substorms may occur several times during a night, at the midnight sector of the oval, sometimes as often as every hour during a magnetic storm. The more expanded the auroral oval is towards the South, the more the substorms will occur at lower latitudes: during periods of intense magnetic activity they may be seen as far South as 40 degrees, very occasionally even further South. (I was able to observe them so vividly at Lat. 46 – close to the Latitude of Bordeaux or Geneva in Europe – because of the clarity of the atmosphere in Quebec during periods of high pressure, and because of the relative proximity of the magnetic pole.) The major light phenomena are concentrated at an altitude of about 100 km, though some curtain forms may reach as high as 300 km.

The corona, sometimes known as the 'radiant point', has long been noted to occur near the magnetic zenith (the point vertical to the horizontal plane of a compass needle at a given latitude): 'Since rays are aligned more or less along the dipole lines of force, they appear to converge toward the magnetic zenith. This railroad track effect produces the illusion of a dome or, if it is developed on one side only, a fan.' (Chamberlain is here referring to the 'dome' almost above the observer's head, not the domes often visible rising from the Northern horizon). In other words the corona is seen as an optical illusion due to the relation between the observer and the magnetic zenith. But some doubt is thrown on this by the fact that there are many instances where the corona deviates substantially from the magnetic zenith, as Chamberlain has to admit:

> The radiant point was found on either side of the normal (undisturbed) magnetic zenith, but sometimes measurements of the disturbed field showed that the instantaneous magnetic zenith was lower by 7 or 8 degrees than the radiant point. There seemed to be no relationship between wanderings of the magnetic zenith (as determined from magnetometer readings on the ground) and the auroral zenith (as determined from the radiant point).

Chamberlain concludes that 'Extended investigations of this sort have barely scratched the surface of their potentialities and could conceivably yield important clues to the auroral mystery.' This is rather a mystical way out of the problem.

The magnetosphere

Another problem for physicists with regard to the aurora is to explain where the energy comes from for these vivid events in the ionosphere. Although the auroral oval may be the ideal coordinate, and coincides with electrojets, apparently there is not considered to be enough energy 'in situ' to account for such intense atmospheric excitation. The main theory proposes that in fact the events of the aurora – the motion of various magnetic currents – do not take place where they are observed, but some thousands of kilometers away, in the 'tail' of the earth's magnetosphere. Accordingly, 'the auroral and polar magnetic substorms are directly caused by the sudden reconnection of magnetic field lines in the tail of the magnetosphere. The process of reconnection causes the boundary separating open and closed geomagnetic field lines to move to higher latitudes on the night side.' Or: 'a streamline interface is assumed to exist between the outside magnetosheath region and the inside geomagnetic field region.' Again, satellite photography confirms this.

In effect, plasma instability, reconnection etc., are proposed to occur with the closing/opening of force lines in the magnetospheric tail which extends from the earth in a direction away from the sun, like a broad tapering banner in the solar wind. The events of this closing/opening are projected back along the magnetic field lines or flux tubes to the auroral ovals, where the observer will see them. The analogy is with a television screen: the ionosphere is a screen onto which electron beams are projected from the magnetospheric tail which 'in some way acts analogously to a cathode ray tube.' Again there is the problem of where the energy comes from for this, as well as in explaining the most simple mechanics of the model. Even the Encyclopedia Britannica which struggles to present science as infallible had to state (14th edition): 'Several fundamental questions still puzzle scientists concerning the comparison of the aurora to a television tube. It is unclear what processes play the roles of the tube's cathode and anode in the magnetosphere, or what processes play the roles of electroplate and electromagnet during the auroral substorm...' Then after a list of further puzzles, the encyclopedia concluded with the usual hopeful mysticism: 'Current research efforts may unveil the secret of the aurora.'

Cosmic superimposition

The aurora naturally interested Reich. As often, his theories present difficulties, but more often his observations are pioneering and worth further explanation. Although he did not provide an operational definition of pulsation, he was the first scientific researcher to bring it to prominence.

I would not have spent so much time observing auroras systematically when I lived in Quebec if I had not read Reich's discussion of them in his late book *Cosmic Superimposition*. But unfortunately this discussion is even more rushed than some of his previous writings. In particular he got his mathematics wrong. He proposed that one auroral stream merged at an angle of 62 to the plane of-another 'equatorial' stream, these being deduced from the result of their 'superimposition', the auroral corona being at 31 degrees. This he supposed to be the latitude of the auroral oval at an altitude of 76 degrees (which, minus his own latitude of 45 at

Rangeley, Maine is 31) But if he had lived a few hundred miles further North, at Lat.52, he would have discovered the corona at an altitude of 80 – and so on, since the altitude of the magnetic zenith depends on the observer's latitude. Reich does not discuss the magnetic zenith, nor does he realise, apparently, that the aurora's main events occur at a height of some 100 kilometers, so he ends up confusing the celestial and terrestrial spheres as well as the true and apparent horizon. He did however note that the merging of East-West atmospheric streams was the main event in the aurora.

The auroral streams

In my observations the various pulsing and darting movements observable in the streams seem to have a phase unequal rhythm because of their rapid lunges inward to the corona. When observed as part of streams or bands of lumination they are either equal phase, like corrugations, obviously 'pulse waves', or unequal phase like ripples across a pond or sea waves approaching shore – presumably because they meet some kind of atmospheric resistance.

The whole auroral substorm seen as an event in time is like an unequal phase pulsation (though not repetitive within a membrane – i.e. not 'alive'). A preliminary period of generalized lumination in the sky is followed by a period of increasing excitation during the half hour before midnight, then a period of fusion for ten minutes or so from midnight, then a sudden decrease in excitation for two or three minutes, then again a variable period of diffuse lumination.

In spite of the luminations noted to North and South, the main merging streams are those from East and West. There is more lumination in the North *before* the East-West merging, and more lumination in the South *after* it. Akasofu describes the movement as 'nonexistent prior to the substorm, then away from the midnight meridian to the east, west and to the pole during the expansive phase of the substorm (T=0 to T=10-30 minutes), then equatorward and away from the midnight meridian to the east and west during the recovery phase.' Another observer writes, however, that 'there are examples of observed westward motion for several hours *before* the onset of a substorm.'

Given the primacy of two streams from east and West, and the fact that the earth rotates from West to East, it would seem logical to suppose that the West stream would, like a prevailing westerly wind near the earth's surface, have an advantage over the East stream. It would seem, however, that every few hours the East stream asserts itself against the West, that these streams then merge, release an accumulated 'charge', fuse, then discharge their energies so that the original flow, perhaps with an advantage to the West stream, continues. Then as the process begins again the East stream begins to move more strongly again toward the West and begins to luminate. There is a polarity, it seems, in all structures, whether the magnetic polarity in inert structures and the earth itself, or the head-tail polarity in organisms: even the most primitive organisms have a leading end. When organisms merge in reproduction or a non-reproductive sexual fusion, it is the tail ends which come together. Since the auroral streams seem to follow the same basic processes as living systems, even assuming they are not alive, it must be asked whether they too show signs of merging at the 'tail' ends. This may seem fanciful at first, but the idea seems to have occurred to many observers over the millenia. The ancient Chinese described the long tails of dragons in the sky, and it is thought they were referring to auroras. The familiar Yin/Yang symbol resembles the merging of the two auroral streams. Greek myth has it that the earth is a 'cosmic egg' laid by a primeval dragon or serpent, in some versions after a copulation of two serpents in empty space. It is easy, observing an aurora with intense movements of the main streams, to imagine this as the emerging of the tails of two huge serpents. The question arises: if these are the tails, where are the heads?

Put less fancifully: if there is polarity in the auroral streams, and we observe the apparent merging and discharge of radiant energy (light) from the two free ends of two streams, where are the other ends?

Since the merging of the two 'tail ends' is at midnight, which is not only an hour but a place – the point directly opposite the sun on the other side of the earth – it can be supposed that the 'head ends' are on the daylight side of the earth, at noon. The various diagrams of the auroral oval, whether it is depicted as a doughnut shaped belt around the polar region, or as intertwining spirals, do support the notion that while the substorm is occurring at midnight there is a continuum with whatever is occurring at noon. The difference though is that although measurements may be made of proton precipitation, whatever may be occurring in the noon portion of the oval is not visible. The sun's light is too bright for any such luminations as can be observed at midnight to be seen in daylight.

In the present state of knowledge it is still unclear whether the merging of the East and West streams or 'tails' takes place first in the ionosphere or in the tail of the magnetosphere. If the latter is the case, it is supposed to be the 'coupling' and uncoupling of magnetic flux tubes. But magnetic flux tubes or field lines are not supposed to have a life of their own. A random coupling, rather like the entanglement of two trailing banners in a wind would not have the apparent orderliness of what can be observed in the aurora. The observable process of increasing excitation leading to a pulsing contact then fusion or coupling of two streams is not, it seems completely explainable in mechanical, magnetic, or electrical terms. Alfven's electrical model may, like Reich's original bioelectrical model of sexual intercourse and orgasm, indicate the truth about the basic 'flows' involved. But flows of what? The 'energy source' problem may be a false one if mechanistically seen (whether by Alfven or Reich) as a question about 'where the energy comes from'. Perhaps we should ask literally: *What is the source of the energy?* The evidence from the other areas explored in this book is that 'energy' may be a result, not a cause, and 'secondary' to the primary movement of pulse-waves. (In turn, if Julian Barbour is right and there is no absolute time, this primary movement may be a *recurrent shape* in a timeless universe).

Auroral pulse waves

The source of the energy, excitation and 'orgasm' of the auroral substorm can be *observed as the pulse waves themselves*. The process of the fusion of two atmospheric streams, and the consequent excitation and production of energy, may eventually be best understood by a genuinely new physics which examines whatever processes of resonance, entrainment or resistance occur when two streams of pulse waves meet. The coupling of the two auroral streams (in the earth's slipstream, but projected onto the ionosphere) cannot help but remind us of human coupling. There is the same build up of excitation, a flare of intensity, then a fading back. It can be diagrammed like Reich's 'orgasm curve'. Does this mean the auroral streams are alive? I don't think so. They stream with pulse-waves within the earth's atmospheric 'envelope' (like a membrane) but they are not themselves pulsating. In humans, orgasm is (among other things) an intensification of the breathing pulsation. The parallel between human coupling and auroral coupling is of course far from exact. But insofar as there is a parallel, this does not require that both are 'alive' or even 'un-alive.' When we feel *moved* by the cosmos we may be recognizing that we contain the cosmos in us. But our pulsation is distinct from the pulse-waves in us and in the cosmos at large.

6

THE COSMIC OCEAN

The cosmic ocean and the Aether

Reich referred to the 'cosmic energy ocean', and I refer in this book to 'the cosmic ocean'. This implies something more active than simply 'space'. Reich discussed vortices and spirals in 'cosmic superimposition' in space, and 'spinning waves' (originally 'Kreiselwelle' or KRWs) which are visible as transient luminating spirals if you sit for a while in total darkness. These observations all suggest movement like that of currents ('streamings') in the actual ocean. The oceans on Earth are in constant movement.

Space has been considered since Newton to be 'empty' and unmoving – 'absolute space'. Actually, even in Newton's time Leibnitz postulated a relational universe in which space was not absolute, but like everything else, relative. Lee Smolin in *Time Reborn* (2013) provides a lucid summary of this difference. In Julian Barbour's minimalist physics of *The End of Time* Leibniz's view is pursued one step further and space (along with time) becomes an unnecessary concept in a universe of 'shape dynamics'. As Smolin puts it, 'In a relational world (which is what we call a world in which relationships precede space), there are no spaces without things.' And 'every property of an object in nature must be a reflection of dynamical relations between it and other things in the world'.

Reich proposed that the cosmic energy ocean, which he equated with the orgone, was in effect the 'aether' (or 'ether') which was supposedly eliminated from physics by the Michelson and Morley experiment of 1887 in which measurements with a light interferometer indicated that the speed of light was absolute and invariable – not variable as might be expected in the medium of an aether. The aether, therefore, did not exist.

This kind of 'null hypothesis' is bad science. As the saying goes, 'absence of evidence is not evidence of absence.' As I have described in *Time / No Time,* when I was a child looking out of a window during a thunderstorm I saw a fireball, an intense round light about the size of a football, drifting slowly down through the rain and suddenly disappearing with a distant 'phut' sound. I went out afterwards to look for scorch-marks but there were none. I told my parents who said something like: 'Fireballs are supposed not to exist. But now you have seen one we know they do exist.' Ghosts don't exist either, although my very sane and totally agnostic grandmother used to see one in her ancient house from time to time. So I'm ready to give the aether a chance.

A successor of Michelson and Morley at Case Western Reserve University, Dayton Miller, repeated their experiments on the top of Mount Wilson (they had worked in a basement) and came up with results supporting 'aether drift' – i.e. that the earth was 'drifting through a cosmological medium' with no absolute speed of light. If so, as Einstein himself remarked, the theory of relativity (which depends on a constant speed of light) 'would collapse like a house of cards'. Miller's experiments were duly refuted by allegations that his findings were contaminated by thermal effects (not evident in the basement apparently). Discrediting an experimenter's instruments is a typical ploy in scientific warfare. I have no way of evaluating this myself but James DeMeo does so in two extremely detailed papers, and concludes that

> 1) The cosmological ether is substantive with a slight mass, and may be blocked or reflected by dense material surroundings. 2) Earth-entrainment occurs, and the best detections are made at high-altitude locations. 3) Miller's computed axis of Earth's net motion of ether-drift is in close agreement with findings from diverse disciplines, including from biology and physics, regarding ether-like phenomena with similar sidereal-day and seasonal sidereal fluctuations. Neither an intangible static, or even a tangible entrainable but stagnant ether appear reconcilable with such results. A dynamic ether acting as cosmic "prime mover" is the alternative solution, but requires the ether to have both slight mass and specific motions in space. A solution is found in the bioenergetics research of Wilhelm Reich (1934-1957) who demonstrated an energy continuum with distinct biological and meteorological properties, existing in high vacuum, interactive with matter, reflected by metals, and with self attracting (ie., gravitational) spiral-form streaming motions.

My own difficulty with this account is that I reject the 'bioenergetic' concept of a cosmic continuum which is in some way alive. The observable universe may contain more life than we currently know about, but it is likely to be rare in the vastness of the universe. But leaving life aside, it is surely up to the physicists to revisit the evidence for the cosmological aether, given that the rejection of this since Michelson-Morleymay be on shaky grounds, and no experiment is likely to be final. So far, physicists are either not convinced or unwilling to resurrect the question of the aether. But another problem is that practical physics now lags behind theoretical physics which is now in a period of flux, in which quantum physics conflicts with classical physics, and timelessness conflicts with time. Smolin describes this as 'the crisis of physics.'

In the post-Newtonian model, where does the aether (or for that matter the orgone, or the cosmic ocean), once 'absolute space' is obsolete, fit in a relational universe? As Leibniz wrote, 'it must not be said that each portion of matter is animated, just as we do not say that a pond full of fishes is an animated body, though a fish is.' To pursue this analogy: in a relational universe all that matters is the fish – plus other inclusions such as water-beetles and protozoa and particles of weed or dirt or minerals, not to speak of billions of atoms and sub-atomic particles. The relational universe does not distinguish between life and death in distinct material objects (what Leibniz called monads). And it does not allow a background either. To a mystic or an animist, of course, there is a background and it is alive. As the writer Wyndham Lewis put it, Leibniz 'contradicts the average space-timer of post-Relativity philosophy for whom the *pond* too is virtually organic.'

Here is where Einstein's space-time universe leaves the door open to total animism, as expressed in books like Fritjof Capra's *The Tao of Physics*. This is a door that Reich's followers must go through if they identify the orgone simultaneously with the cosmic ocean/aether and with 'life energy'. But in the minimalist relational universe of Barbour, or even Smolin (who admits time where Barbour does not) this door is shut. Unless one enters an upside-down or mirror world where instead of everything being alive, everything is dead. 'Is it graveyard?' Barbour asks wistfully about the timeless and static universe he calls 'Platonia'?

Barbour and his research colleagues are working on the mathematics of this universe which eliminates all motion, including the post-Einstein theory of the continuing expansion of the universe as indicated by the 'red shift' of light from distant sources, and the theory (based on the mathematical requirements of the Big Bang) that much or even most of the universe consists of 'dark matter' or 'zero point energy' or ZPE. It remains to be seen how this intellectual battle plays out. And I have not even started to include in this discussion the 'multiverse' theory of an infinite number of parallel universes which is the only cosmological model which, so far, is consistent with quantum physics.

Given the Alice-Through the Looking Glass world of 21st century physics, perhaps Leibniz's view of the fish in the pond should be revisited in the interests of common sense. It can be translated into a view of a cosmic ocean (or aether) which is not itself alive but which includes distinct living organisms. These pulsate in a sea of pulse-waves.

Does there need to be a 'medium' for the transmission of either information or energy in the form of pulse waves? It would seem not at least a consistent or uniform medium, since radio waves can travel either through the earth's atmosphere or through space. It could be argued along minimalist lines that a medium is unnecessary: pulse waves *are* the medium – or as McLuhan put it frivolously with regard to information, 'The medium is the message'.

Similarly the earth's oceans *are* the waves and movement within them. And the cosmic ocean *is* all its pulse waves. In other words, the aether is just the sum of all its pulse waves.

If this is so, then Reich's 'cosmic' or 'atmospheric' orgone consists of equal phase pulse-waves – 'energy', yes, but *not* 'life energy'. So paradoxically the orgone is *not* alive. It does not pulsate. Reich thought it did. He might have eventually come to the definition of pulsation as 'unequal phase' which I propose: after all, I cannot claim any great originality here, since once this distinction has been noticed it is blindingly obvious. Reich, I think, fell into Freud's trap of equating the supposed 'libido' with life energy, and then he saw it in the entire universe. Indeed in *Reich Speaks of Freud* he generously acknowledged his debt to Freud's libido theory in his 'discovery of the orgone'.

As discussed earlier, I don't think 'primordial life energy' is a viable concept, and it is unnecessary given that the entire universe is full of 'energy' (secondary to movement, not causing it) in one form or another.

Furthermore, since from what we know so far over 99.9 % of the universe is empty of life, it seems unlikely that a universal energy would be alive.

It is unclear to what extent Reich thought the orgone was alive. He compared it with the aether and at times wrote as if it were a sort of substrate for life – the 'Cosmic Orgone Ocean' – which flowing into structures brought them alive. He also wrote at times of the 'Cosmic Life Energy'. Unfortunately it is easy to become bogged down in semantic discussions of whether a 'life energy' is itself alive or simply a necessity in the formation of life. It is also easy to attack Reich for the conceptual confusion implied in his various terms for life energy. But surely this is natural in exploring any new field. There is nothing wrong with trying on new words for size. But at his death his work was unfinished, and his last years were marked by a continuous battle to survive. His successors inherited his varying terminology, without his authoritative presence which might have eventually helped to clear it up. In his final year he wrote almost religiously about the Cosmic Life Energy and the Orgone Energy Ocean. Some of his successors (to my knowledge Adolph Smith and Bernard Grad) would speculate that the orgone might even be conscious. After all, it carried information... Or it might even be God. After all Reich had been accused in Norway by a newspaper columnist of 'putting God into the laboratory.' Reich was outraged by this idea.

As I have explained, I don't think the life energy concept is useful either in psychotherapy or in understanding pulsation. It is unnecessary and it introduces a hydraulic libido model of charge and discharge which is ultimately mechanistic. Reich's therapy is one of the most effective around – but not because it works with 'bioenergy': it works with movement, attention, and pulsation (although defined simply as expansion/ contraction). Similarly, although Reich, mistakenly in my view, saw 'life energy' in the atmosphere (not distinguishing pulse waves from pulsation), his observations of movement and light in the atmosphere are highly original and useful in understanding weather and climate phenomena.

My position as worked through in this book is that life can be defined in terms of pulsation without any need for 'life energy'. As for what does not pulsate – the 99% or whatever it is of the universe that is *not* alive but which consists of pulse-waves in myriads of configurations – I think it is best described as the 'cosmic ocean'. Although the terminology of pulsation and pulse-waves needs to be defined operationally, there is no need to seek for new terms. In talking with Reichian friends who use the word 'orgone' I have no objections to using the word as short-hand for the cosmic ocean. But as I have explained (Chapter 2), 'orgone' comes from the same root as 'energy' and I think it mystifies the word. 'Orgone energy' is a tautology. 'Life energy' makes no logical sense. Nor does 'Cosmic life energy': life is *not* everywhere in the cosmos. But energy (in the usual sense of physics) is. In fact it is wherever pulse-waves are.

The neatest and most logical way I can think of to express the distinction between life and the non-life of the universe at large is to distinguish pulsation from pulse-waves. And since an ocean consists of waves the term 'cosmic ocean' seems to me appropriate. This may correspond with the aether. And as Reich came to equate the orgone with the aether as well as the cosmic ocean, surely his observations of the orgone and his demonstrations and experiments with it can be included in our study of the cosmic ocean. Modern physics until very recently has rejected the aether out of hand. But if the aether becomes accepted again, then physics will have to reckon with the body of work which Reich termed 'orgonomy'.

The cosmic ocean consists of its pulse-waves. These transmit or simply *are* movement. And they become visible – in the weather, atmospheric waves of all sorts, in the lumination of the aurora, and (controversially) in such phenomena as the human aura. I have already noted my own rather startling occasional observations of auras, and my own and the biophysicist Adolph Smith's observations of at least some effects of orgone accumulators. And in *Time / No Time* I discuss the possibility (bizarre, but my experiences of this require some explanation), of some kind of 'field' in which memory and information can be transmitted.

A 'field', classically, is an area in space where energy exercises force on objects or particles within the field. Fields fade out with distance but may overlap. Perhaps the cosmic ocean can be seen as a 'field of fields.' But this is well outside my own 'field' of expertise. And again this is a model that has been formulated in terms of absolute space.

If pulsation is definitive of life, and it exists in a cosmic ocean of pulse waves, then this ocean (or field of fields) is what used to be called the 'aether'. The Michelson-Morley experiment was conducted within the now obsolete Newtonian conceptual framework of 'absolute space', and this was also the framework of Dayton Miller's work apparently demonstrating that the aether exists after all. If practical physics catches up with theoretical physics, perhaps eventually the 'aether' will be examined again with new instruments and in the theoretical context of the relational universe or whatever succeeds it. After all, in the field of biology, following the triumph of Darwin's natural selection, culminating over a century later in Dawkins's trumpeted supremacy of the 'selfish gene', for about 150 years the Lamarckian theory of the inheritance of acquired characteristics was so roundly rejected that any biologist who publicly accepted it would have lost his or her job. But in the 21st century (see the geneticist Tim Spector's *Identically Different*, 2013) Lamarck has made a come-back. Discoveries in 'epigenetics' demonstrate that, yes, various acquired characteristics can be inherited after all – and frequently.

An idea of how the aether might make a come-back in the crisis of physics emerges in *Time Reborn* where Smolin discusses the implications of Barbour's 'shape dynamics'. This is not an easy argument to follow, but it can be summarised as:

1. Before the theory of relativity with its requirement of an absolute speed of light, light was considered to propagate variably in the medium, the constant background, of the aether.
2. The aether can be seen as a 'preferred state of rest' in the universe.
3. Shape dynamics proposes relativity of size (i.e. no constancy of sizes) within a universe whose volume is unchanging (i.e. constant).
4. The unchanging volume of the universe, Smolin states, 'can be taken for a universal physical clock' (i.e. a sort of constant background against which time can be measured).
5. This constant background is, in effect, the aether.

It is worth putting together Smolin's references to the aether in this argument:

> Einstein demolished it, because his principle of the relativity of simultaneity implies that there is no aether, no state of being at rest... The elimination of the aether was a great triumph of focused reasoning over lazy habits of thought. It was so easy

to think of the world in Aristotle's terms... Only Einstein had the insight needed to demolish it altogether. And yet it seems we have reasons to go back to the idea of a preferred global notion of time. The fact that this contradicts the triumph of Einstein over the aether is a psychological barrier to taking the arguments for the reality of time seriously – or at least it was in my case... So the observations give us a mixed message. On the largest scale, there is evidence for a preferred state of rest, which must be explained by something special in the initial conditions of the universe. But on every smaller scale, the evidence is that the principle of relativity rules.

So in physics the conflict continues. The properties of this new version of the aether remain to be redefined, I suppose according to the conditions of either Barbour's shape dynamics in which it would be, in effect, the unchanging volume of the universe, or the conditions of Smolin's time reborn in which it would be the universal physical clock. The current choice in theoretical physics, as in its crisis it has to modify Einstein's general relativity in which the universe is a block of space-time, seems to reduce to:

1. A universe in which there is no time but in which shape dynamics requires a constant volume. (Barbour).
2. A universe in which there *is* time and the constant volume provides a measure of it. (Smolin).

Either way there is a possibility of a come-back in some form for the aether. Perhaps the 'something special in the initial conditions of the universe' will turn out to be, or to be related to, what Reich called the orgone. I prefer to call it the cosmic ocean, since this helps distinguish it from 'life energy'. Again, I would emphasise the distinction between the pulsation of the living and the pulse-waves of the non-living cosmic ocean.

However, as DeMeo has written to me: 'Your point about "Reich's cosmic or atmospheric orgone consists of equal phase pulse-waves – energy, yes, but not life energy", would be considered by classical physics as no less a heresy than Reich's original and "unacceptable" orgone life-energy.'

I must admit that the cosmic ocean of pulse-waves from which I distinguish pulsation does correspond in many aspects with 'orgone' as described by Reich. For the reasons stated earlier (mainly in Chapter 2 on Vitalism), I reject the concept of orgone *energy* as tautological, for one thing, since 'orgone' comes from the same Greek and Indo-European roots as 'energy', and in its failure to distinguish between life and non-life. I do not believe the cosmic ocean is alive, any more than a pond is alive, or the sea. As noted earlier, I am not sure Reich thought it was alive either – although in his view it *formed* life via 'cosmic superimposition.' And while I reject the idea of orgone as 'life energy', I do not reject it as a word for the cosmic ocean – what I called in an early poem, written at a time when I was working with Reichian therapy and thinking in terms of life energy, 'the ocean everywhere'.

So far I have described my own observations of pulse-waves at the microscopic level (typically as 'Brownian movement'), the atmospheric level (typically as so-called 'heat-waves' and in the aurora). I also take on faith the observations of main-stream physicists that sound and light waves propagate in pulses, and that atomic particles and the 'strings' of string theory vibrate and oscillate. Even a rock is oscillating and vibrating at the atomic level. Pulse-waves appear to be everywhere matter is. And electro-magnetic energy apparently travels at the speed of light, i.e. in the usual pulse-waves, even in a perfect vacuum.

Reich and his successors do not use the term 'pulse-waves', but they do claim that atmospheric orgone can be detected by various means. This involves experiments, and I am not an experimentalist. Systematic observation, e.g. of the bions, is not experimentation in which conditions are changed and controlled. In this book I describe various observations I have made, and I summarise some of those by Reich's and by others. There is no space here to describe experiments in detail or to evaluate them. What follows is a brief description of the kind of experiments that have been conducted, under headings, with a few of my own observations. Insofar as 'orgone' is a term for the cosmic ocean, experiments by 'orgonomists' like DeMeo may add to our knowledge of the cosmic ocean.

Accumulators

I had a peculiar, if banal, experience in 1974 when travelling from Boston to Montreal I stopped at White River Junction, Vermont, for fuel. I went to the fuel station men's lavatory but when I opened the door into a large room with the usual cubicles I couldn't see the light switch and the door slammed shut behind me. There were no windows. I was immediately aware of swirls of bluish light in the darkness, and a slight tingling feeling. 'This is like an accumulator', I thought. I eventually groped for the switch and turned the lights on. The entire room was lined with white painted aluminium, over brick and concrete walls (as I checked from outside), i.e. it was a room made of non-metallic materials but with a metal lining. Although Reich apparently found aluminium less consistent than iron or steel-wool as an accumulator layer, the lavatory was indeed an accumulator.

I have also mentioned my experiences building an accumulator in an unheated barn loft in November in Quebec, and becoming 'sun-tanned'. And I was once cured of a very painful boil in the backside (I don't get boils, but this one arrived after I had driven a furniture van across Canada for 3,600 miles and 5 days) by lying on my stomach for half hour sessions under a small 'orgone blanket' of alternating layers of cotton wool and steel wool. The boil shrank and disappeared after two days. (Such boils are an affliction of truck-drivers and often become dangerous).

These are of course 'anecdotal' accounts, or 'one offs'. One of the main criteria for scientific experimentation is replicability.

The most systematic experiments with accumulators, and in my estimate the most careful, have been made by James DeMeo at his Orgone Biophysical Research Laboratory in Oregon, USA, which has a dry, high altitude climate. Accumulators in particular do not work well in humid climates. All references to DeMeo's work in this and following sections can be followed up at www.orgonelab.org

DeMeo has replicated in a series and under differing conditions Reich's T-To experiment – the one Reich demonstrated to Einstein and which Einstein subsequently rejected as due to convection currents. DeMeo has scrupulously eliminated the possibility of convection in conducting experiments. His findings consistently show a small T-To difference of about 0.13 C degrees over a period of weeks. There is clearly a question here about margins of error, although his measurements are calibrated to

.002 C. For me the most striking aspect of DeMeo's findings is not so much the temperature difference as the fact that consistently there is a rise of 0.5 C degrees around solar mid-day even when the accumulators are shielded from thermal currents and light. The accumulators seem to be 'entrained' (my word, not DeMeo's) with the solar cycle. This suggests evidence of a continuum that exists between the solar cycle and changing accumulator temperature. Similar entrainment has been measured in the well-known experiments involving oysters and other marine organisms removed thousands of miles inland yet opening and closing according to the tides. In these biological experiments the question arises of how 'information' about solar and lunar cycles is transmitted from the atmosphere to organisms.

However as a neuropsychologist Stuart Derbyshire has pointed out, the concept of 'information' can only be a fiction when applied to organic cells, for example in neurotransmission, since cells have no means of receiving or transmitting 'information': they only receive and transmit chemicals and electrical currents. How can the atmosphere in an accumulator receive 'information' from the atmosphere outside? It cannot. The validity of the T-To experiments depends entirely on whether or not transmission of *heat* can occur from the outside atmosphere to the accumulator. If this is properly controlled to eliminate transmission, and the T-To difference is measurable, however small, then the difference has to be explained. According to the usual science, this can only be done via replication. But few scientists appear ready to attempt such replication.

If the T-To difference can be measured, and if the accumulator has vagotonic and healing effects, as well as in some cases even inducing a sort of 'sun-tan', does this demonstrate the existence of the orgone? Or of the cosmic ocean? What does the accumulator accumulate? When Reich first noticed various effects in the improvised Faraday cage that he developed into the accumulator, his first hypothesis was that these were somehow effects of solar radiation. He had already wondered if what he called SAPA (sand-packet) bions cultivated from sand had absorbed solar radiation. Hence DeMeo's rigorous experimental controls.

If these are not rigorous enough, then the entrainment of rising temperature within the accumulator and solar maxima can be attributed to another kind of contamination: not 'convection currents' this time, but solar radiation. I wish that experimental physicists, instead of turning their backs on Reich's work, would put some effort into evaluating it. This is unlikely in the world of research grants financed by industry. But DeMeo and a few orgonomic psychiatrists cannot do it all on their own.

Given the 'closed shop' tyranny exercised in the so-called 'peer review' process that decides what is published in scientific journals, the chances of experimental work on Reich's theories being performed and evaluated in mainstream science remain slim. Even within the mainstream, original ideas may be side-lined or drop out of sight. An example of being side-lined is the microbiologist Lyn Margulis's discovery of 'endosymbiosis' – the process in which one micro-organism engulfs another and the genetic materials of both lineages are transmitted through future generations. An exploration of how endosymbiosis might be occurring in Reich's bion observations – or even my own amateur observations of what seem to be 'T-bodies' in the cell nucleus – might be of interest. But even Margulis's original observations, less sensational than Reich's became, and made in the safe context of Harvard where Margulis was a professor in the years around 1970, were rejected by at least 15 scientific journals before they were eventually published. They may not even have been read. Her application for a research grant was rejected, with a telephone comment by an eminent colleague: 'Frankly I haven't read the proposal but let me tell you that there are some very important molecular biologists who think your work is shit.' This is the dog-eat-dog world of academic science. Forty years later Margulis's work is completely accepted.

I have, from personal experience, no doubt whatsoever that accumulators have vagotonic and other effects. Since I reject the life-energy theory, and I don't consider the atmosphere to be alive, my only hypothesis can be that these effects are properties of the cosmic ocean. Solar radiation is one such property. Are they linked? Is this why the accumulators are so difficult to demonstrate and their effects so difficult to measure in damp and relatively sunless climates? They seem to have relatively weak effects in the UK, according to the osteopath Nigel Parker who has done experiments with them here.

But even if the effects of the cosmic ocean are associated with solar radiation, the question remains of how a simple structure of alternating layers of non-metallic material and metal can exacerbate it. Further unexplained questions arise from the evidence that whatever radiation or field is involved, there is a direction of flow from outer layers of the accumulator inwards. Direction of flow also occurs in cloud-busting, although here the dynamics work in both directions: the tubes seem to both draw and 'shoot'.

'Charged' water

DeMeo has also done experiments with 'orgone charged' water, i.e. example water kept in accumulators and notes slower evaporation and higher absorption of Ultra Violet radiation during solar maxima (i.e. around mid-day) even though the accumulator is isolated from solar effects. DeMeo is able to present these findings at academic conferences on water where it seems the ideas of Reich do not cause anxiety. DeMeo's article 'Water as a Resonant Medium of Unusual External Environmental Factors' in the online *Water Journal.org* (vol.3, 2011) summarises DeMeo's work with accumulators, cloud-busting, and 'charged water'. DeMeo also cites the work of the Italian biochemist Giorgio Piccardi (1895-1972) on 'activated water' – the activation being via radio waves.

Piccardi is largely forgotten, and most of his work is in Italian. This goes much further than activated water and amounts to a striking, though neglected, theory about 'fluctuating phenomena'. He rejects replicability because at any moment conditions are different. He cites solar magnetic fields and sunspots, in particular (he also cites lunar cycles and the tides) in proposing that these affect experimental conditions and cannot be predicted. In effect, according to Piccardi, it is impossible to replicate any experiment, since even if grossly obvious local conditions can be controlled, cosmic (solar, lunar, planetary) conditions cannot.

Cloud Busters

As well as the summary cited above, DeMeo has published detailed reports of various operations with Cloud Busters, providing evidence that these can break droughts and make rain. Given the ludicrously inaccurate weather forecasts we all know from the highly financed Metereological Offices in most countries, this is an area where prediction goes wrong. And by definition a particular operation under particular conditions cannot be replicated (for what this is worth).

All I can offer here is my own observations, described in Chapter 1, of a brief and very amateurish cloud-busting experiment conducted by me and the biophysicist Adolph Smith. And all I can say is that 'something was happening.' I have also mentioned the dramatic storm which seemed to have been caused by the cloud-busting operation I observed in Ontario in 1974.

I can also add an observation of a phenomenon which readers may have observed, or may observe. In 1985 I went camping with my family on an island in British Columbia. We pitched our tent among others which were scattered in a forest mainly of firs. The night was rather humid but with no rain. I got up shortly after dawn and immediately after I stepped out of the tent there was a brief and light shower of rain, lasting only 20 seconds or so. I urinated in a bush and looked around. Through the trees I could see another tent, out of which a man emerged and began some stretching exercises. Again there was a sudden, brief shower. A few minutes later, some other people came crawling out of their tent and stood up. Immediately another shower occurred.

What is happening here? Just a coincidence… Or is there an interaction between people and the atmosphere? In a highly saturated atmosphere can we 'draw' showers upon ourselves, just as cloud-busters are supposed to 'draw' from – or 'shoot' into – the atmosphere?

The Cosmic Ocean as Continuum

DeMeo, although loyal to the orgone theory which his experiments support, relates the orgone to the aether, or a 'substrate' in the universe. Reich himself towards the end of his life, when he (understandably given his persecution and imprisonment) seemed to adopt a religious attitude towards the orgone, described it in terms of the 'cosmic energy ocean'. I have no difficulty with this – so long as the word 'energy' is omitted. As already noted, various 'Reichians' have speculated that the orgone is being rediscovered in modern theories of Zero Point Energy and of Dark Matter. If the orgone is 'mass-free', as Reich claimed, then 'Dark Matter' is by definition an unlikely candidate. Besides which, Dark Matter is now (2013) being called into question given that the extreme brightness of newly observed stars seems to contradict the dogma of the supposed expansion of the universe. This expansion may not be universal anyway. The evidence for it is in the famous 'red shift' of light, but Barbour suggests that 'red shift determinations are *local* [my italics] comparisons of galactic and laboratory wavelengths.'

Barbour's work takes off from the work of Ernst Mach whose view is summarised in quotations from it by Barbour and his colleague Niall O'Murchadha:

> The universe is not twice given, with an earth in rest and an earth in motion; but only once, with its relative motions, alone determinable.

> It is utterly beyond our power to measure the changes of things by time. Quite the contrary, time is an abstraction at which we arrive by means of the changes of things.

The Machian universe is governed by a *relational* dynamics. Everything is related to everything else.

In *Time / No Time* I propose that in the timeless universe postulated by Barbour and other modern physicists we nevertheless experience time because we are pulsating organisms in a cosmic ocean of pulse-waves. Time is experienced at the interface between pulsation and pulse-waves. I also propose:

> The earth's ocean, like its atmosphere, is a continuum. There is a bottom and a surface but no sides. This must be the case in the surface of any sphere. So the odds are that the universe contains as many continuums as it does spheres (even allowing most spheres to be barren). But it appears the whole universe is a continuum. The 'empty space' I was taught about at school is now agreed by astronomers to be dense with fields of matter / energy and greatly more with invisible or dark matter than with visible matter. In this 'set of sets', there are oceans within oceans within oceans.

In a recent *New Scientist* article on 'Quantum Weirdness', Michael Brooks writes:

> Just as quantum particles can be in two or more places at once, so seemingly can those particles be in two or more moments at once... Causal order is not apparently fundamental to quantum theory. If we accept quantum theory as the most fundamental description of reality that we have, it means that space-time itself is not fundamental, but emerges from a deeper, currently inscrutable quantum reality.

As for the constant speed of light, Brooks cites demonstrated quantum findings which are only possible if communication between particles happens at many times the speed of light – or abolishes the speed of light altogether. It seems that Einstein's house of cards has already collapsed.

In such a universe, who can be dogmatic about any cosmological theory? Surely the best strategy is to wait and see what theory prevails, while not dismissing any theory based in careful observation. Especially not on the grounds that the observation is not replicable. No instant of the universe is replicable. Perhaps each instant establishes its own conditions.

The universe as observed by Mach and Barbour is a timeless continuum of unique instants. Why not call this continuum the Cosmic Ocean?

This book invites the orgonomists and other supporters and students of Reich's work to move his work forward. DeMeo and others have moved forward in confirming many of Reich's observations, but there has been no moving forward from the equation of the cosmic orgone and 'life energy'. This equation is not demonstrable, and not consistent with mainstream science. The strategy of hostility to mainstream science, followed by some of the narrower-minded Reichians, will alienate scientists who might otherwise be ready to explore Reich's work. Reich himself was capable of questioning his own hypotheses, as when in later life he suggested a possible distinction between 'bioenergetic' pulsation and 'mechanical' pulsation. In the terms of this book, this is a distinction between the pulsation of the living and the pulse-waves of the non-living.

7

ORGASM

Human Pulsation

Human pulsation cannot be discussed fully without reference to the various ways in which people may be 'armoured', to use Reich's term, against it. Examples of this armouring, or of blocks to pulsation are the chronic tightening of the jaw and constriction of the throat to avoid yelling with pain or rage, the chronic inflation of the chest to avoid crying and sobbing, the immobilization of the abdomen and pelvis to avoid 'dirty' sensations, or the deadening of eye contact to avoid emotional contact. The repertoire is almost infinite. Armouring can involve the chronic tightening or immobilization of any muscle group to avoid the expression of any emotion. Perhaps every individual has his or her own unique pattern of armouring. But since each of these patterns blocks giving in to emotion, it will also block giving into orgasm. Orgasm is the paradigm of pulsation, and blocks to orgasm are the paradigm of blocks to emotions. Broadly speaking, a chronic block to any particular emotion will impede letting go to the pulsation – the whole body convulsion – of orgasm. Since becoming one with another person in orgasm is only possible with a complete letting go, any block to any emotion will stand in the way.

In my doctoral thesis, *Human Pulsation* (1977), I included a long chapter on 'Orgasm', as the definitive example of full human pulsation, following Reich's original description but adding details from my own experience, the experience of friends, and the experience described by people in psychotherapy. I added a discussion of blocks to orgasm and of 'orgasm anxiety'. I also discussed descriptions from the sexological research of the time, mainly by Masters and Johnston and by Seymour Fisher.

This chapter is mainly an abbreviated version of the original chapter in *Human Pulsation*. I have cut out rather than corrected most of its short-comings. In particular I have cut references to 'energy', 'charge' and 'discharge'. But I think the basic description is still valid.

Human Pulsation is something of a historical curiosity since its quite large reference base stops, of course, at 1977. We now know a lot more about neuropsychology and physiology than then. But although the references in *Human Pulsation* and perhaps its tone are dated, its argument contains points which have not been explored in subsequent research.

Even sexological research has made few advances since 1977. There are improved procedures for measurement of physiological excitation in the genitals, various aspects of sex have now been filmed, and orgasm (meaning climax from masturbation under research conditions) has been related to excitation in an increasing number of brain regions on modern brain scans – SPECT, PET, and fMRI – which can show dynamic movement of excitation in the form of oxygen perfusion or the 'lighting up' of brain areas. It was first found that the septal areas of the limbic system (a system mediating so many aspects of emotional arousal and memory that its validity as a unified system is now questioned) were aroused in climax, then other areas of the limbic system, then other subcortical and cortical areas, so that now it appears that orgasm is a whole brain event, comparable with an epileptic seizure – a 'brain-storm.' So far this research says nothing about the *function* of the orgasm. 'Discharge' from neurons following brain excitation brings us back, in fact, to Reich's hydraulic tension/release model.

For at least 40 years after Masters and Johnston's highly mechanistic research into the climax provided by stimulation of nerve-endings, their method of 'sensate focus' has dominated 'sex therapy' in clinics across the world. This focus is mainly on two processes: teaching men to prevent premature ejaculation through de-sensitising exercises, and teaching women to experience climax through a programme of mainly clitoral masturbation, first by themselves then by their partners before or during sex. The debate on 'vaginal orgasm' versus 'clitoral orgasm' which so tormented couples in the 1970s was won, on the Masters and Johnston evidence, by the clitoral side – although gradually an acknowledgment emerged that the 'female orgasm' arrived as a combination of both.

Penile-Vaginal Intercourse

The psychologist Stuart Brody has been making headlines with his research over the last decade on 'penile vaginal intercourse' or 'PVI' which he demonstrates to be associated with better health and emotional functioning than any other kind of intercourse or masturbation. Shock horror! In 2010 I attended a seminar in London on sexual functioning in which an audience of medical doctors and researchers, psychologists and sex counselors sat unflinchingly through a vivid film of gay practices and sexually transmitted diseases, which included close ups of buggery, group 'sex' in brothels, fellatio and 'fisting', then were visibly shocked and agitated by a presentation by Brody featuring various statistical graphs to illustrate the beneficial associations of PVI.

I suppose the cause of the audience's anxiety was the implication that PVI, being associated with healthiness, is here being regarded as, or promoted as, more 'natural' than other sexual practices. I should state that the following account of the orgasm pulsation, following Reich's account, does focus on PVI which is by definition between a man and a woman. This implies nothing about other forms of sexual union or even masturbation, which may involve some degree of pulsation and 'letting go' at climax. However, given that the penis and vagina and male and female bodies have evolved to 'fit' together, I think unimpeded pulsation is more likely in PVI.

Brody has summarized in a paper (2009) various studies, across many countries in Europe and the Americas, including those by himself and colleagues, which show the benefits of 'PVI' – defined as penile-vaginal intercourse without simultaneous masturbation. The following list of benefits of PVI is based on research where PVI is distinguished from other sexual activities, and where these benefits are *not* evident in oral or anal intercourse or in masturbation (even accompanying intercourse). The benefits of PVI (in approximate order of the papers that document them) are:

- Satisfaction with one's own mental health. (Masturbation is inversely correlated with this satisfaction).
- 'Marital happiness' is associated with PVI (but not with masturbation, mutual masturbation, penile-anal intercourse, and oral sex).
- 'Alexithymia', a term for lack of sensitivity to others' emotions and difficulty in expressing one's own, is less common in women who

experience regular PVI, and correlates negatively with the intensity of vaginal sensations.

- 'Immature psychological defense mechanisms' are inversely correlated with PVI.
- The beneficial associations with PVI are reduced if condoms are used.
- Depression and other mood disorder are less common in people who experience PVI but insofar as they occur this is more common as time from last experience of PVI lengthens.
- Studies of homosexuals of both sexes, even in countries such as Holland where a strongly pro-homosexual policy is promoted, show higher levels of suicidal ideation, depression, substance use and other psychiatric disorders than heterosexuals.
- Pelvic disorders including inflammation and pain are less common in people who experience regular PVI.
- Vaginal tonus, oxygenation and blood flow are better maintained across life in women who experience PVI.
- People (more conspicuously women who experience vaginal orgasm) who regularly experience PVI can be distinguished in 'blind' trials (i.e. where history is not known) by having a more fluidly moving gait and less muscular rigidity.
- Greater PVI frequency is associated with slimness. Eating disorders are inversely correlated with PVI.
- Resting heart rate variability, associated with better mood, attention, emotional responsiveness, and more robust reaction to stress, is associated with regular PVI.
- In men higher testosterone levels lead to increased coital activity, and the converse is true, in that PVI leads to increased levels of testosterone.
- The volume of the male ejaculate, sperm count, sperm mobility, and percentage of morphologically healthy sperm are all higher in men who experience regular PVI.
- Prostate cancer and breast cancer are less common in men and women who experience regular PVI.
- Various findings suggest that some of the benefits of PVI are associated with the presence of sperm in the vagina (although

findings that PVI has more beneficial effects where PVI is not accompanied by masturbation of the clitoris show that sperm-vagina contact is not the only factor in benefits).
– HIV infection is much less common in PVI than in anal or oral intercourse (most cases of HVI in Africa being due to contaminated needles, not sexual activity).
– Increased life expectancy is associated with frequency of sexual intercourse, which in most cases is PVI.

In other papers, Brody and his colleagues have demonstrated that:
– Women who experience orgasm in PVI state that they prefer their male partners to have somewhat longer than average sized penises.
– Over 80% of women have experienced vaginal orgasm during PVI, and somewhat more than half of women experience it regularly.
– Over 80% of people who practice PVI have experienced simultaneous orgasm.
– Vaginal orgasm is associated with vaginal (not clitoral) sex education, focusing mental attention on vaginal sensations, intercourse duration, and a preference for a longer penis.
– Women who rate high in 'conscientiousness' on personality scales are more likely to have vaginal orgasms (conscientiousness being correlated with the capacity for sustained attention).
– The post-orgasmic prolactin increase following PVI is greater than following masturbation and suggests greater satiety.
– Inability to attain a vaginal orgasm is associated with anxious attachment, among other indices of poorer mental health and relatedness.

In a recent paper (2011) Brody is the first to map brain activity (using fMRI) from stimulation of women's vagina, cervix, and clitoris. 'Different regions of the somatosensory cortex were activated by stimulating the three genital regions, an effect consistent with different peripheral nerves and different psychological correlates of various sexual activities. In addition to mapping a region not mapped by Penfield (he had male subjects), a secondary finding is that nipple stimulation activated both thoracic and genital regions of the somatosensory cortex.'

Again it should be noted that Brody and his colleagues do not discuss the total bodily convulsion, 'full pulsation' of orgasm. Their nearest finding to this is the association of vaginal orgasm with more fluid (i.e. less 'armoured') muscular-skeletal movement. But the research on 'PVI' states the context for orgasm between a man and a woman.

Definitions of Orgasm

A standard dictionary definition of orgasm is: 'The climax of sexual excitement, marked normally by ejaculation of semen by the male and by the release of tumescence in erectile organs of both sexes.' (American Heritage Dictionary). The word itself comes from a Greek root meaning 'to swell as with moisture' (Oxford English Dictionary). The concept of swelling with tension and subsequent release is central to even the simplest definitions, and consistent with Reich's orgasm formula: tension > charge > discharge > relaxation.

Orgasm is normally considered to occur simply as climax at the level of the genitals. One study, Seymour Fisher's *The Female Orgasm*, apparently takes this so much for granted that orgasm is not even defined anywhere in its 500 pages, and the only implication that it may consist of anything more than a feeling of climax and release in the genitals is the remark that about 5% of the women surveyed endorse the statement that 'excitement increases to a point where release is accompanied by spasms or convulsions.' The nature of these convulsions is not discussed. A standard medical definition of orgasm (Chusid) does not even mention convulsive movements but remarks that 'tonic contraction of the thigh muscles may accompany orgasm.'

Kinsey in writing of male orgasm mentions various reactions of the body: legs often become rigid with muscles knotted and toes pointed, muscles of abdomen contracted and hard, shoulders and neck stiff and often bent forward, breath held or gasping, eyes staring or tightly closed, hands grasping, mouth distorted... whole body or parts of it spasmodically twitching, sometimes synchronously with throbs or violent jerking of penis.

Lowen remarks about this description that 'one would expect such reactions from a person undergoing torture rather than the delights of an ecstatic experience.' The reactions may be seen as the activation of blocks to pulsation. But more important than whether Kinsey's description evokes a picture of pulsation or its blocking is the fact that the reactions are presented as random phenomena. Like the tonic contractions of the thigh muscles or the convulsions experienced by some women and noted by the Fisher as indications of sexual excitement, these bodily reactions are not understood as in any way functional, but presented as incidental.

Masters and Johnson, in their studies which have become the basis for most modern American sexology, also note phenomena of bodily involvement in orgasm:

> The face, for example, may be contracted into a grimace through the tightening of muscle groups. The muscles of the neck and long muscles of the arms and legs usually contract into a spasm. The muscles of the abdomen and buttocks are also often contracted. Of special interest are the reactions of hands and feet. Often a man or woman grasps his partner firmly during orgasm; the hand muscles then clench vigorously. If the hands are not used in grasping, a spastic contraction of both hands and feet known as "carpopedal spasm" can be observed. Men and women are usually quite unaware of these extreme muscular exertions during orgasm; but it is not unusual for them to experience muscle aches in the back, thighs, or elsewhere the next day as a result.

Again there is a lack of coherence in the listing of these phenomena: they are treated as unrelated side effects. And again, the description seems more like a struggle against orgasm than giving into it.

The bodily reactions which Masters and Johnson have noted as consistent accompaniments of what they call the 'plateau phase' of sexual response, are those concerned with mottling or flushing of the skin, and with erection of the woman's nipples, but these reactions do not involve movement. Masters and Johnson's detailed observations of the phenomena of excitation and release at the genital level describe the swelling or tumescence of the outer third of the vagina and of the testicles and penis, and the diminishing of this swelling after climax. One phenomenon also noted is that frequent sexual excitation in women, which is not followed by release, as happens for many prostitutes, leads to severe congestion of the pelvic organs and often subsequent pathology, a finding which supports, at least on the level of the genitals, Reich's assertions that much pathology can be caused by insufficient release of excitation. Similarly, a man may feel pain in the testicles after a period of sexual stimulation which is not followed by ejaculation. (Since I now reject this terminology of charge/discharge of life energy, I explain this evidence of 'congestion' as due to blocked pulsation.)

Masters and Johnson's contribution to the knowledge of sexuality originally came to public notice mainly through one part of this contribution, the assertion that women, especially when using electrical vibrators in masturbation, can experience 'multiple orgasms'. But here one of the problems in the normal equation of orgasm and 'climax' becomes relevant. If orgasm is by definition a release of tension and tumescence, how can one release of tension follow another in quick succession without time for an intervening build up of tension? The psychoanalyst George Frankl in *The Failure of the Sexual Revolution* writes of this problem:

> Masters and Johnson have reported that by self-stimulation of the clitoral area: 'a woman may experience five to twenty recurrent orgasm experiences with the sexual tension never allowed to drop below a plateau phase maintenance level until physical exhaustion terminates the session.' Now if a woman's sexual tension never drops below the plateau level even while she has a great number of orgasms till she drops with physical exhaustion, then we must conclude that by definition she never has arrived at an orgasm at all. If orgasm is followed by the resolution or relaxation phase then one cannot have had an orgasm if the tension never drops below the pre-orgasm tension phase. And this is precisely what does not happen in multiple clitoral orgasms. What in fact occurs is a great number of orgasm spasms without orgasm discharge.

Frankl supports this last assertion with reference to the work of Mary Jane Sherfey, which maintains that women are liberated by their capacity for these multiple orgasms, each of which tends to provoke the need for the next:

> Dr. Sherfey's observation that every instance of female orgasm leads to a further vaso-congestion in the pelvic area is quite correct if we understand that what she calls orgasm is merely an orgasm spasm.

There was a long late 20th century controversy about whether women 'should' have vaginal or clitoral orgasms, and which was 'better'. But Masters and Johnson themselves point out that the clitoris is normally involved in female orgasm, but not necessarily, since some women report orgasms as a result of stimulation of the breasts or other parts of the body. The zoologist Desmond Morris has written that orgasm can be experienced by some people as a result of stimulation of the earlobes alone, and it is known that both men and women can have sexual climaxes in their sleep without any direct sexual stimulation. Masters and Johnson conclude that it is incorrect to talk about a clitoral or a vaginal orgasm, and that orgasm is normally a phenomenon of the genitals as a whole.

But wherever orgasm 'comes from' in terms of stimulation, the problem still remains that none of the discussions of orgasm mentioned above consider it as a phenomenon which involves the whole body in a meaningful way. Reich's theory of orgasm does this, proposing that a certain kind of convulsive movement, 'the orgasm reflex,' which involves the whole body, is the meaningful (that is, not random) expression of the basic pulsation which can be found in all organisms.

Reich's research preceded that of Kinsey and of Masters and Johnson by several decades. In the 1930's, he was measuring the electrophysiological response of the human skin, and of vaginal and anal mucosa in persons experiencing sexual excitation, and expanding the frontiers of scientific investigation into sexuality. 'Discovery' has the implication of finding what is already present but unnoticed, as in the 'discovery' of America or of Mount Everest. Sex and orgasm have always been present for human beings. But just as when Freud began to listen to people's free association about childhood fantasies and dreams which previously had been considered quite irrevelant to adult human experience, he thus became a pioneer in a realm which in modern society is almost taken for granted, so when Reich began to explore not simply the fact of sexual climax but its nature, he also was a pioneer, as in their own ways Kinsey, and Masters and Johnson have been. It is not that childhood fantasies, or differences in orgasm response and pleasure have never existed. But now they are being explored 'scientifically'. The point was reached even in 1977 where a respected drug company could circulate to members of the medical profession a film of sexual activity including close-ups of the genitalia during coitus, which would until recently have been considered pornographic, as Reich's researches were considered pornographic forty years before.

It may be objected that Reich's orgasm theory implies a specialized use of the word orgasm. Since orgasm as he describes it is relatively rare, it might be proposed to consider it as some kind of variation of the 'normal' sexual response as depicted by Kinsey and by Masters and Johnson. The concept of orgasm may be legitimately extended by many researchers, just as the knowledge of America has been extended since Columbus or the meaning of a simple word such as 'bird' is extended each time a new species is found and each time a new physiological or behavioural fact is found. The facts may always have been there, but a concept is extended by taking them into account. Similarly, orgasm seems to have been present for a long time, although it is not yet clear how much it may actually be developing as a human phenomenon from its possible roots in biological pulsation. And Reich's definition of orgasm as a pulsation involving the whole body may be seen as a legitimate extension of the word, providing this pulsation can be observed.

A problem is that laboratory conditions do not necessarily provide a suitable context for the deepest kind of sexual experiences. And even statistical surveys are inevitably biased in the selection of samples, particularly in a sensitive area such as sexuality. For example, Fisher's huge study of *Female Orgasm* could be more accurately though more lengthily called: 'A study of the incidence of subjectively reported sexual climax in 300 middle-class Upper New York State women who answered an advertisement in a student newspaper offering $50 to "married women (with at least a high school education) in the 21-45 age range to participate in an experiment concerned with 'reproductive and menstrual functioning'" . Underlining the limitations of such a survey is not meant to devalue it, but to restore some proportion to the situation where a 'survey' is automatically considered to be more valid than consistent observations. Reich's description of the orgasm reflex was based on clinical experience, and the orgasm reflex is quite often observed in the context of Reichian therapy, as well as experienced in coitus and reported by many people. Reich's description of orgasm is not apparently a description of sexual climax as experienced by the majority of people, but this does not necessarily mean that it is an exotic variation of sexual experience. This chapter discusses how orgasm can be experienced and observed as a total involuntary pulsation of the human body. If this is so, the word orgasm can be legitimately extended to include this phenomenon, and the narrower phenomena of climax and ejaculation can be seen as essential parts of orgasm rather than as orgasm itself.

The Orgasm Reflex

Reich's theory and description of coitus leading to orgasm can be found in *The Function of the Orgasm*. He described coitus as beginning with a period of fore-pleasure, passing to the stage where the man needs to penetrate and the woman needs to take the man into her vagina, to when 'as a result of mutual, slow, spontaneous and effortless frictions the excitation is concentrated' in the genitals, consciousness is concentrated on the perception of pleasure sensations 'to attain a maximum of tension before orgasm occurs.' Then in a phase of 'involuntary muscle contractions', voluntary control of the course of excitation 'is no longer possible', and deep expirations of the breath occur. This results in 'involuntary contractions of the genital and of the pelvic floor. These contractions occur in waves: the crests of the waves occur with the complete penetration of the penis, the troughs with the retraction of the penis'. Both partners experience these involuntary contractions of the musculature of the pelvic floor, and Reich has previously emphasized that 'the activity of the woman normally differs in no way from that of the man'. (In a later study, Reich added that 'every friction movement... leads to a muscular contraction in healthy individuals'.)

As excitement mounts to its peak, 'more or less intense clouding of consciousness' occurs, the frictions become 'spontaneously more intensive', and 'the orgasm excitation takes hold of the whole body and results in lively contraction of the whole body musculature'. This is followed by a 'flowing back of the excitation from the genitals to the body' which constitutes gratification, and is followed by a 'pleasant bodily and psychic relaxation'. And, 'the involuntary bio-energetic contractions of the organism and the complete discharge of the excitation are the most important criteria of orgasm potency'.

Later, in *Character Analysis*, Reich explored several analogies between the orgasm convulsions and the pulsatory movements which could be observed in simple organisms, such as worms and jellyfish. He pointed out that in humans 'the largest and most important ganglion apparatus is located in the middle of the torso, close to the back', and that in orgasm the body seems to fold up from this point, with the head end and the tail end convulsing to become closer together, as if to complete a circle. 'In the orgasm, strangely enough, the organism unceasingly attempts to bring together the two embryologically important zones, the mouth and the anus'. He asked "What function does the bringing together of the two ends of the trunk have in the orgasm pulsation?' He compared this in a diagram to the movements of a jellyfish, and wrote:

> When a jellyfish moves, the ends of the body move towards each other and away from each other, in rhythmical alternation… The expressive movements in the orgasm reflex are functionally identical with those of a living and swimming jellyfish. In either case, the ends of the body, that is the torso, move towards each other, as if they tended to touch each other. When they are close, we have contraction; when they are as far apart as possible we have expansion or relaxation of the orgonotic system. It is a very primitive form of biological pulsation. If this pulsation is accelerated, so that it assumes clonic form, we have the expressive movement of the orgasm convulsions before us.

And Reich concluded: 'The expulsion of the spawn in fishes and of the semen in higher animals is bound up with the plasmatic convulsion of the entire body'.

Reich's various successors have followed his basic description. Baker, in particular, repeats it almost word for word, and also emphasizes that 'contractions… involve the entire body'. Reich had written that in extended breathing in an unarmoured person the orgasm reflex occurred (in muted form) spontaneously at the end of each exhalation. Baker refers to this as a 'spontaneous tilting forward of the pelvis at the end of complete expiration. This is the orgasm reflex.' He then corrects himself in a footnote, mentioning that this is a 'pelvic reflex', and 'the orgasm reflex implies a response in which the whole organism takes part as a unit.'

Various writers have confused the orgasm reflex and a purely pelvic movement. Martin Gardner, in an attack on Reich in *Fads and Fallacies in the Name of Science* describes the orgasm reflex as 'the usual movement of the pelvis during coitus' as if simply moving the pelvis back and forth has been mysteriously elevated by Reich into a theory. A popular book, *Total Orgasm*, by Jack Rosenberg refers approvingly to Reich but also discusses orgasm simply in terms of unblocked pelvic movement. Feldenkrais, in *Body and Mature Behavior* echoes Reich in several passages ('the release of tension in the culmination of the sexual act is essentially a vegetative phenomenon') but does not mention Reich or the orgasm reflex. He does describe an involuntary pelvic movement:

> In properly matured people, in all their functions, i.e. motor, libidinal and social, the excitement is built up to a climax at which involuntary rhythmic contractions in the muscles producing ejaculation spread to the entire pelvic floor, and the pelvis itself rhythmically oscillates in the following manner. At each expulsion of semen, all the flexors of the abdomen contract powerfully and the pubis is pulled upward and forward to its utmost capacity, while all the extensors of the lumbar and sacral region are completely relaxed. Next the pelvis withdraws so that the sacrum moves backwards and upwards again to the utmost capacity.

The concept of contractions spreading to "the entire pelvic floor" again seems to echo Reich, but Reich wrote that these contractions occurred accompanying the movements of the penis in the vagina before climax (not simply as a result of ejaculation), Feldenkrais concludes authoritatively that 'the number of involuntary movements of the pelvis varies from three to seven or eight on the average.' But his description of this movement as being produced by powerful contractions of the abdominal flexors suggest a relatively local phenomenon, a kind of 'pelvic jerk' which can be produced in many people by forced breathing which leads to an abrupt contraction of the abdominal wall. (Although Feldenkrais does not even mention the breathing).

Lowen, in *Love and Orgasm* also emphasizes the movements of the pelvis. 'Pushing the pelvis rather than swinging the pelvis will prevent the involuntary movements from occurring. The kinesthetic pleasure of sexuality depends of the quality of the pelvic movement'. Then 'as the tempo increases the pelvic movements suddenly take on an involuntary quality and induce a deeper response from the body....' And 'the body convulses as a unit in response to each involuntary swing of the pelvis.' This concept of the body convulsing in response to pelvic movement is not identical to Reich's concept of the whole body convulsing, with the pelvis a part of this. Lowen in a later work *Bioenergetics* does describe the orgasm reflex as a movement in which the head moves back as the pelvis moves forward, although his drawing representing the orgasm reflex shows a rather slight movement of the body rather than anything resembling a total convulsion.

Reich did not confuse the orgasm convulsion with a purely pelvic movement. He emphasized in a therapeutic context, the necessity for letting down the muscles of the ribs and of letting go of the head and shoulders: 'With natural deep expiration, the head moves spontaneously backward at the end of expiration.' And 'the trunk strives, with each exhalation, to fold up in the region of the upper abdomen. In other words: the neck end strives forward toward the pelvic end.' But at the same time, it may be asked why even therapeutic successors of Reich, such as Baker and Lowen, seem to have some difficulty with delineation of the orgasm reflex, at times confusing it with a movement of the pelvis alone, before correcting themselves. This may be because the involuntary movements of the pelvis, although often blocked by tension, do occur more often than the kind of involuntary movement which Reich described taking hold of the entire body.

But the problem may also come from the fact that Reich himself left out some details of the convulsion. And there is some vagueness in the very statement with which he first defines the orgasm reflex: 'The orgasm excitation takes hold of the entire body and results in lively contractions of the whole body musculature.' This can only be wrong, since not all the muscles in the body can contract at once, and for each muscle which does contract there is generally an antagonistic muscle which relaxes. It would have been more clear if Reich had emphasized that the muscle contractions were not simultaneous.

Reich also made a statement in *Character Analysis* which may cause confusion: 'The total movement of the body in vomiting is purely physiologically – though not emotionally – the same as in the orgasm reflex.' If this were exact, a person really would vomit during orgasm, and his or her emotions, which in Reich's theory are considered identical to the bodily expression, would also correspond to those in vomiting. (In the original German 'same' is 'gleiche', so there is no translator's error). The trunk does, however, fold forward in both vomiting and orgasm, and the vomiting reflex as a folding of the body is, Reich pointed out, most visible in babies where there is no muscular armouring. But the details of the gag reflex and the orgasm reflex must be substantially different, since gagging expels the stomach contents upwards, and orgasm is accompanied by contractions of the pelvic floor.

Reich himself elaborated his description of the involuntary contractions of the pelvic floor in an essay, *The Orgasm as Electrophysiological Discharge* which for a long time remained unpublished in English. It can be said that his descriptions of orgasm, taken from various works, add up to a whole description which is unique, in the view of many readers, in the excitement of discovery and of writing about what has not been written about before. At the same time there is room for further exploration of the orgasm as pulsation, and for an attempt to sort out the various minor pulsations and specific muscle contractions which the orgasm reflex includes.

The Orgasm Pulsation

What follows is a description of the sexual embrace in terms of pulsation. Where Reich's observations are not specifically referred to, the source of the observations is in the present writer's experience, descriptions by other people of their experience, and observations of pulsatory movements in people breathing and reacting in individual and group therapy. The description is in numbered sections, for ease of reference.

It should be mentioned that no attempt is made here to describe modifications of sexual experience as they may occur in different cultures or as a result of different positions for coitus. The description proposed here is in terms of pulsatory activity, such as breathing and rhythms of movement, which may occur in any sexual position, although clearly some defenses against involuntary movement and sensation, for example tightening of the legs or making abrupt or controlled movements, are easier in some positions than others. Apparently most couples in modern North American society still prefer the basic position with the woman lying prone and the man on top (Freedman, Kaplan & Sadock). By contrast, in aristocratic milieus in India and Arabia, as would appear from such handbooks as the *Kama sutra* and *The Perfumed Garden of Sheik Nefawzhi*, much energy seems to have been directed from any concentration on orgasm itself, into refining a huge variety of coital positions. Reich followed Malinowski in emphasizing that the Polynesian Trobriand islanders' practise of coitus in a semi-squatting position left both sexes free to move the pelvis whereas the prone position normal in patriarchal societies limited the woman's pelvic movements in particular. On the other hand, according to Suggs the traditional 'missionary position' was common in Polynesia even before the coming of the missionaries, although other positions were and are openly accepted. The position with the man behind the woman (entering the vagina) with both lying on their sides enables both to breathe and move freely and facilitates deep penetration. It might be proposed simply, in view of the discussion which follows here, that the more the sexual position adopted leaves both partners free to move and breathe easily, the more both are free to abandon themselves to the orgasm pulsation.

1) There may be a variety of social, habitual, or role-oriented factors which have their effect in bringing a couple together in the sexual embrace, but even these factors are perceived first through the eyes. Sexual excitement seems to begin at the eyes and progress to the genitals. As mentioned, growth is from head to tail, and Reich postulated a flow of 'energy' down the front of the body toward genital discharge. Reichian therapy normally works to dissolve armour blocks in a direction from

the head down to genitals which, though Reich did not state this, is often followed instinctively in sexual contact.

Perception through the eyes seems to come before touch, in love-making, except for those people who are blind. Even a couple who come together in bed in the dark have often made some contact through the eyes beforehand to show their desire. Although if they move blindly toward each other in the dark obviously touch comes first, and the preliminary contact through the eyes is missing. Even in this case, the movement toward contact may be accompanied by visual imagery or fantasy. In the light, the meeting of the eyes of the man and the woman can lead to melting sensations in the body. For the Trobrianders the eyes were considered sexual organs which took in a flow of excitement and channeled it down to the genitals.

2) In Western society, kissing is an important stage following eye contact, and whether kissing occurs or not, the hands and lips tend to become involved in touching and seeking the other person's body. As hands and lips touch the other person the breathing tends to deepen and melting sensations may be felt in the chest. In the woman there is feeling in the breasts and some attention may be given them in kisses and caresses, and this also has the effect of increasing excitation in the genitals. The genitals may have become almost immediately aroused through the eyes and touch, but the feeling in them builds gradually. Erection in the man, and tumescence in the woman are usually triggered, in mechanistic terms, by nerve afferents from the brain and head. Though tumescence or erection can be induced by simple touching of the genitals, through the reactions of the Autonomic Nervous System (parasympathetic branches from the sacral plexus), the Central Nervous System is involved in circuits which favour a downward progress from head to genitals. The perception in the brain of sensory inputs from the eyes, as touch and taste from lips and tongue, the sound of the voice or breathing, and the smell of the other person's body, is led downwards to contribute to genital excitation.

Most people seem instinctively to follow this downward direction of the excitation in their own bodies. Even if their passion for the other person's body leads them to caress, kiss or suck the other person's genitals with their mouth, the excitation from this moves downward to their own genitals. As the genitals become more and more the focus of sensation and excitement the penetrating nature of the man and the receptive nature of the woman become dominant. Reich wrote (some 80 years ago) that 'the activity of the woman normally differs in no way from that of the man. The widely prevalent passivity of the woman is pathological.' The man and the woman may move with the same vigour, but there is the difference that the man's movements are increasingly directed toward penetration and toward entering the woman, and the woman's movements toward receiving the man. Even if during their usual lives the penetrating and receptive roles of man and woman are quiescent, they now become the centre of excitement and pleasure.

3) Reich proposed that in the sexual embrace the ego is reduced to the function of perception. Perception and contact are first through the eyes then through the skin, with increasing focus on the skin senses. With this increasing focus the eyes become less important, although some experience of touch may provoke visual imagery. This visual imagery, for example an image of the look of the other person's genitals while caressing them, may be a natural accompaniment of the perception through touch, and is not the same as a deliberate, controlled fantasy, but part of a sense of the other person. This sense of the other person may, especially after genital contact occurs and the penis penetrates the vagina, be partly a 'plasmatic sense' of streamings. Quite apart from the tactile sensations of friction or temperature, there may be a sense of life in the other person's genitals. (Reich discussed a case where a woman's husband thought her vagina was electrocuting him). Even when the penis is motionless in the vagina, so that there is no friction, both partners may feel currents appearing to pass between them, and their breathing may deepen or quicken in unison as if an invisible communication is taking place. (Reich explained this in terms of life energy, but perhaps field effects are involved, or 'entrainment' of sensations).

Although particularly at first melting and tingling sensations may seem to pass between the genitals without the need for any movement, and excitation may build up, the urge to intensify the feeling through movement begins to dominate. At first this may be independent of the breathing, either slower or faster, but quite soon the pelvic movements forward, toward deeper penetration, become synchronized with breathing out. A long period of build-up of excitation takes place. Reich proposed (in 'life energy' terms) that each sexual movement involved a charging process on the backward swing, and a partial discharge on the forward swing. For a while the backward movement of the pelvis may be emphasized slightly more than the forward movement of full penetration. This process of charge > partial discharge > charge, seems to lead to a more intense build-up of excitation than would a consistent process of charge, as it intensifies the pulsation of the breathing and in the genitals. Again, to revert to pulsation rather than to the energy model, this is a process of intensification of sensation along with intensification of pulsation – i.e. both an acceleration and a deepening of the breathing and the circulation.

5) The genitals themselves will have become increasingly engorged. At some point during the rhythmic rocking movements of the sexual embrace, the pelvic, floor and genitals begin to rhythmically expand and contract. Sometimes even before genital contact, when a person looks with desire at another person and his or her breathing is open, there may be on exhalation an involuntary contraction of the pelvic floor. In the sexual embrace, as the pelvis is pulled back, the pelvic floor (that is the muscles of perineum and genitals) may be felt expanding and relaxing: the relaxation is like that which occurs just before urinating, as a letting go of the sphincters. It is subjectively perceived as an expanding movement of the pelvic floor. On the movement forward of the pelvis and with deeper penetration the expansion of the pelvic floor may be sustained but at the end of the forward movement a vigorous but soft contraction occurs. On the moving apart again the contraction lets go and expansion begins again. The process is felt as a pulsation of the penis and vagina synchronized with the pelvic movements.

[This genital pulsation is similar, in muscle terms, to the voluntary contraction of the pelvic floor in 'Kegel exercises', often recommended to maintain genital tonus. Towards the end of coitus it may begin to occur involuntarily.]

This pulsation is not that which occurs in ejaculation or climax. It is slower, being in time with the movements of the pelvis, although the contraction on full penetration is quite abrupt and brief. It is entirely involuntary, although it may be simulated voluntarily if the pelvic floor is not blocked. If experienced as an involuntary pulsation, accompanying the pulsatory rocking and undulating movements of the penis in the vagina, it has the effect of intensifying pleasure, and it also tends to intensify the pleasure and excitation of the partner, especially when it becomes synchronized between partners. In this case, for the man the contraction pulls the penis slightly upward, intensifying the feeling of penetration, and simultaneously the equivalent contraction in the woman grips the penis.

6) The movements of the pelvis may be accompanied by some trembling in the whole body, especially on exhalation. The pulsation in the genitals intensifies local sensation. In the man, tingling and melting feelings in the testicles may seem to unite with the same feeling all along the penis. In the woman, feeling bridges the outer sensations from the clitoris and vulva, and deep inner sensations of melting and opening. Sensations may be felt all over the body: as a tingling 'pulling' from face and head, or in legs, chest, abdomen, and back as streaming, melting feelings which pour toward the genitals.

7) Toward the moment of orgasm the movements of the body become completely involuntary. For a while they may have been in only partial control, and from the beginning, as Reich pointed out, they can have been 'effortless' and spontaneous. The pelvis is not pushed. As Lowen points out, it may swing. The movement begins to involve a flexion of the spine, but this is not entirely produced by contractions of the abdominal wall (as Feldenkrais claims). The abdominal muscles do contract in flexion of the spine, just as they do in vomiting, although the contraction may be felt as 'soft' rather than hard or abrupt. The subjective feeling in the sexual embrace is of involuntary deep movement from inside the back providing the force for the pelvic swing. This movement seems to come from the anterior flexors of the spine, the deeply hidden vertical muscles in front of the spine between the thoracic and abdominal cavities, and from the quadratus lumborum muscles, two sheet-like muscles between the lower spine and the upper edges of the pelvis. (Electromyographic tests on these muscles are impossible, and their functions are partly a mystery, but a text on kinesthesiology states that the quadratus lumborum muscles are definitely spinal flexors). The deep involuntary movements which curl the lower spine and pelvis forward with each out-breath are not dependent on the tightening of the abdominal muscles, which alone would produce a sharp pelvic jerk and suppress sensation: rather the abdominal muscles contract softly as part of a general movement whose main force comes from

the spinal flexors, and which continues slightly further after the abdominal muscles contract.

Along with flexion of the trunk as the pelvis moves forward, the head tends to fall back. But toward the climax of coitus the converse movement, of the pelvis being pulled back and the body becoming fully inflated may be quite strong, so that an oscillation takes place between extreme inflation on the in-breath and deflation on the out-breath. At the same time the build-up of sensation in the genitals and in streamings down the body becomes overwhelming. There has been throughout an increasing sense of the person's own body and of the partner's body, and this becomes transferred into an increasing sense of the genitals. Increasing sensation in the penis is at the same time a greater awareness of the vagina, and vice versa. This can become overwhelming, and when it does the whole body surrenders to the orgasm. The genital sensations of melting become so acute that consciousness clouds over.

8) With surrender to orgasm there is what Reich called a transfer of the excitement to the motor system. With each exhalation and forward movement of the pelvis, the shoulders relax forward and the neck falls easily back. The movement is very like that of a dog's back and neck in the act of mating. It may have been occurring spontaneously for some time before orgasm, on each out-breath, but it has not been quite complete. But at orgasm, the whole body surrenders to the deep flexion of the spine which involves the falling back of the neck with each exhalation and now the complete extension of the hip-joints and maximum movement forward of the pelvis. The subjective sensation is of more than the folding of the trunk which may be produced, where there is a lack of armour, by mechanical or forced exhalation. The exhalation seems to be part of a larger process of pulsation in which the convulsions of the body are felt as definite tugs which pull the genitals forward and upward and the head backward and downward, with throat and shoulders coming forward.

Simultaneously, the pulsations of the pelvic floor, previously synchronized with movement and breathing, have become a series of spasms (according to Masters and Johnson at intervals of four fifths of a second) which are somewhat faster than the spasms of the whole body. In the man the spasms accompany ejaculation, as repeated contractions of the pelvic floor which previously has been dominated by the expansive phases, with brief contractions on each forward movement and much longer expansions on the backward movement and the beginning of the next forward movement. Now contraction dominates. For the woman the process is similar but between contractions of the vagina and of the uterus, the vagina expands markedly, in a pulsatory process which can be compared to the gulping of a mouth.

Reich's description of 'lively contractions of the whole body musculature', although in fact the whole body musculature cannot contract at once, can now be examined in more detail. The relatively fast pulsatory spasms of the pelvic floor and genitals which accompany climax have been mentioned. And it can be seen that in the orgasm convulsion as described above, the main contraction involved is that of the flexors of the spine. This is the movement which Reich compared to the expansion and contraction of a jellyfish. On the in-breath the spine extends, that is arches backward in an inflated position. On the out-breath it flexes, and folds forward with pelvis and shoulders being pulled nearer to each other.

In the rest of the body, the muscular contractions which take place are not of flexor muscles, but of extensors. For example, the head falls back because of a contraction of the extensors behind the neck. At the same time the pulsation extends into the limbs: the hands will often make loose fists on the in-breath and let go by opening wide on the out-breath. And the toes may move rhythmically, flexing on the in-breath, and extending (stretching out) on the out-breath.

The general picture is of the trunk, the centre of the body, and the genitals contracting on each out-breath, but of the outer parts of the body expanding. The eyes tend to roll up and out of contact during orgasm, and they may close. But the mouth may open wide and gasp on the in-breath and close slightly on the out-breath as an involuntary sound emerges, an 'Aaah' or 'Oooh' which widens the throat and seems to express pleasure and wonder.

The thighs may be half together on the in-breath and open wider in an attitude of surrender on the out-breath and as the hip joint extends. The thighs and legs as a whole tend to rotate outward on the out-breath, and the heels kick outward and downward in another movement of extension (of the ankle joint). The movements alternately are, on the in-breath a pulling back of the pelvis, rotation slightly inward of the legs and thighs, a flexion of the knees which brings the heels outwards and is accompanied by flexion of the sole of the foot and of the toes. Then, on the out-breath a movement forward of the pelvis, rotation outward of legs and thighs, and extension of the knee joint which straightens the leg, as the ankle joint, sole of the foot, and toes extend, and the heel pushes downward and outward. This movement is rather difficult to describe, but it resembles that of the legs when doing the breast-stroke in swimming. It is quite involuntary and seems reminiscent of the swimming motions of a frog.

Again, the general picture is of flexion of the trunk, and extension of the extremities. This is consistent with a process of discharge outward from the centre of the organism.

9) This convulsion repeats itself on each succeeding outbreath, although less intensely, until after several outbreaths the breathing returns to normal. The orgasm is the most extended version of pulsation an adult experiences, but it is part of the usual series of pulsation in the breathing – intensified by 'coupling' with another.

10) After orgasm, the phase follows which Masters and Johnson have referred to as 'resolution', in which a general sense of well-being and relaxation is felt, and the body seems to glow. If both partners have experienced orgasm (and one person's orgasm will tend to trigger the other's when the whole body is involved) their bodies may convulse together for a while, more often than with Feldenkrais's suggested five to eight pelvic movements, in a process in which the convulsions diminish in intensity and become less frequent, as the breathing returns to normal, and the partners are simply lying together feeling soft, and returning to consciousness of their surroundings, although a feeling of being melted or fused together, rather than distinct and awake, may be easily followed by sleep.

In the most simple terms, the sexual embrace may be seen as a couple making contact and breathing together: the combination of contact and breathing seems to lead naturally and involuntarily to genital fusion and orgasm.

To avoid potential confusion, a working definition of the orgasm pulsation is proposed which takes into account the orgasm reflex and the other factors which are present in the complete pulsation. This definition is first set out in paragraphs and then summarized:

The orgasm reflex occurs with complete exhalation in the form of a convulsion which involves the entire body including feet and hands. It involves basically a soft, smooth contraction and folding of the trunk with the pelvis and throat being pulled forward to their utmost extent, the legs and arms falling open and extending, and the head being tugged back by a contraction at the back of the neck. The abdomen contracts abruptly as the trunk folds but the movement of the pelvis continues forward after contraction of the abdomen, indicating that the deep spinal flexors are involved. Breath is completely exhaled with a sigh or a sound, and the body may tremble. This reflex is by definition, as a reflex, out of conscious control.

There follows on the inhalation a rebound of the body in which the trunk unfolds completely, with shoulders and pelvis pulled back to their maximum extent, the legs and arms rotate inward and flex, the head comes forward, and the spine is hyperextended, as abdomen and chest inflate with the inhalation.

This reflex of extreme contraction followed by extreme expansion occurs several times, with the contraction phase increasingly predominating, so that folding forward of the body remains complete, but unfolding diminishes as the range of the convulsion diminishes into the normal breathing or into occasional local spasms or contractions with less range on each exhalation.

The orgasm reflex is accompanied throughout by repeated pulsations of the pelvic floor, including not only the muscles of ejaculation or of the vagina but of the perineum and anus. These pulsations may be somewhat faster than those of the body as a whole, but during the preceding build-up of excitation they have been synchronous with breathing and movement.

The pulsation of orgasm is an intensification of the continued pulsation of the breathing, and the convulsion of the orgasm reflex pulsation repeats itself several times, with diminishing intensity as the normal breathing pulsation is re-established.

There is subjective experience of streamings in the body and genitals, of clouding of consciousness, and of dissolving of boundaries between the self and the partner. These signs of sensory regression cannot be outwardly observed, except in the rolling of the eyeball up and out of sight, although this also is usually not visible because the eyelids are closed.

A feeling of glowing well-being and of gentle contact with the partner follows.

Simultaneous Orgasm

In other words 'coming together.' The above descriptions are inevitably clinical in tone, since they set objective, observable criteria. Even 'the sexual embrace' sounds cold. 'Coitus' is scientific. 'Having intercourse' is like something in a law case. 'Making love' is probably the most common term but 'making' introduces a purposive or artificial element. The 'act of love' sounds phoney. 'Fucking' suggests a lack of emotion, impersonality, even violence. 'Doing it' is at least neutral, but what is 'it'? 'Screwing' is worse than 'fucking'. 'Copulate' is Latin. The other languages also seem lacking: 'buileadh cracainn' in Irish is 'striking skin'; 'baiser' in French is a euphemism, although 'faire l'amour for 'make love' has a certain elegance, as does 'fare l'amore' in Italian or 'fazer amor' in Portuguese; 'ficken' in German is 'to fuck'.

It seems fair to say that the language of what we are discussing here lets us down. I think I feel best about the term 'coupling'. Yes it is associated with animals, but we are animals. And a 'couple' is a relationship.

Describing orgasm as a pulsation risks making it seem like a solo act. But in coupling both partners can 'come' and if they have experienced 'coming together' they will tend to repeat it, moving instinctively. If they have not experienced it, they can either settle for mutual servicing ('first I make you come, then you make me come'. Or 'now it's my turn'), or they 'work' on the 'problem'. Various ingenious caresses and positions may be employed – or even sex therapists may be employed. Many years ago when I had a reputation as a therapist for sexual problems I saw a young couple for several sessions in which they earnestly discussed many details, including the positions they got into in coupling. I entered into the spirit of this but when I made a suggestion about a position (I forget which), the woman said 'Oh, but that won't work because I wouldn't be able to see the

TV.' It turned out that they always watched the TV while they were, as the English would say, 'on the job'.

So lesson number one is something like: 'pay attention'. 'Be *with* your partner.

Lesson number two is: you cannot *make* another person come – although they can make themselves come with you.

There are no doubt many other lessons, but I'll stop at a third one: 'Lessons are silly. You can't teach someone how to do it. You just do it – together. You don't take turns.

Yes, it is difficult to finish being together with a sense of something missing. But if there is another time, and then others, you will attune yourselves to each other. As you feel each other's excitement there is a sort of feedback-loop in which you excite each other with your excitement, or intensify each other with your intensity. When one person comes, the other will probably not be far behind. This apparently fits with the biology, if recent research-findings are right that a woman is most likely to conceive a child if she has come and the man comes within a short time afterwards. Not that it has to be this way.

Your love life does not need to become work. But if you have some sense of what pulsation is, and then some sense of the ways in which *you* (forget your partner here) tend to block it, then you may be able, eventually, to let go of your blocks. In Chapter One I gave the example of how I realised I had been holding my belly tight, and when I let go of this (literally let go of the tendency to clamp my abdominal muscles), I let go to a full pulsation in orgasm – though not without anxiety at first.

The following sections describe blocks to pulsation in orgasm, and 'orgasm anxiety'.

Blocks to Orgasm

'Sexual dysfunction' is the term used by Masters and Johnson for the various difficulties, such as premature ejaculation, erective impotence, and female lack of climax, which are normally treated by behavioural methods in sex therapy or clinics. These methods, which involve various sensitization of desensitization procedures, may be more or less effective in achieving their goal. This goal is not orgasm as a pulsation of the body, but the ability to experience sexual climax and help the sexual partner reach climax at a socially acceptable rate.

The Masters and Johnson approach, which has become part of the general scientific/medical approach to sexuality, presents several problems when related to pulsation. For one thing it is frankly mechanistic and technologically oriented, with devices such as vibrators used to increase sensitivity to tactile stimulus. Sex as an emotional experience is not emphasized, and cannot be, within the limitations of the approach. And perhaps unintentionally the approach plays into the common emphasis on climax, and the number of climaxes, being the most important aspect of sexuality. The nature of the climax, how it is experienced, and how much of the person and the body it involves, is almost irrelevant. The effect of this is to put a particular emphasis on the sexual satisfaction of women. Men who experience premature ejaculation are worried about their inability to satisfy women. And women who do not have climaxes feel that they should have them. Both of these concerns are natural, and clinical work to alleviate them can only be beneficial. But the fact, pointed out by Reich, that erective potency in men and subsequent ejaculation are not necessarily accompanied by any pleasure at all, and indeed in some persons are accompanied by sensations of disgust and unpleasure, is not considered. In fact it is possible to imagine a situation where a man makes love to a woman, and where he has a climax (represented by ejaculation) and she has no climax, but where her sexual pleasure is much greater than his. Subjective accounts indicate that this situation is quite common. But the emphasis, in modern sex therapy, on giving the woman the capacity for climax, in particular through the stimulation of the clitoris, may be – paradoxically in view of the increased concern for women's sexuality and rights – an imposition of a male model for climax on women. [Brody's studies on 'PVI', however, redress the balance.]

What follows here is a description of the sexual embrace and of orgasm, parallel to that given earlier, in which some of the major blocks to orgasm are mentioned. A subsequent section discusses further blocks to orgasm and regression. It is hoped that the delineation of some of these blocks is helpful not merely to an understanding of how the main unitary pulsation of the body in orgasm can be blocked, but also of how other emotional pulsations may be blocked, since the orgasm pulsation can be said to contain many other basic pulsations. Conversely it may indicate how blocks to these other pulsations may become part of the blocking of the wider pulsation of orgasm.

1) Some blocks in the eyes inhibit the initial sexual contact and the expression of tenderness. Eye contact may elicit fear of pain and loneliness and therefore be avoided. A myopic person may be afraid of showing longing, or look blank to avoid showing need. A (prematurely) hyperopic person whose eyes give the basic message 'Get away from me' may feel particularly uncomfortable when close to another person's body, and intimacy may be replaced by the need to impress the partner and to dominate. Whatever the individual variation, the extent of eye-blocking can be shown by the difficulty many people have in looking at their partner in the first stages of love-making: if they look they feel anxious or whatever sensation of pleasure may be present disappears.

At a broader level, perceptual blocking through the eyes may have an adverse influence on the choice of a partner, since any severe eye blocking risks distortion of reality. Reality may be replaced by a fantasy or an expectation which does not correspond to the reality of the first stages of sexual contact and which may have to be maintained, if its absence causes anxiety, in the form of a fantasy which remains dominant throughout the sexual embrace. Some visual imagery is a natural accompaniment to touching and movement, but if the attention is primarily on voluntarily maintaining a fantasy and therefore concentrated in the brain, it is less in the body and genitals. The downward shift of attention from brain to genitals may thus be impeded from the start.

2) Kissing and caressing may be impeded by blocks in the functioning of mouth and hands which render these areas insensitive. And voluntary kissing and caressing of the partner's body as part of a wish to 'satisfy' risks becoming part of a performance if continued so long that the voluntary areas of the cerebral cortex are engaged throughout the sexual act. A continued concentration on voluntary movements will distract attention from sensation.

With kissing and caressing, the breathing normally deepens and becomes movement of the body. This may be prevented by the existence of basic blocks to breathing which may be activated in the sexual situation.

For example, breathing in a state of excitation normally takes place through the mouth, but paradoxically the instinctive reaction to a bad smell is to close the mouth, perhaps because the nose itself cannot be closed. When a person normally blocks the taking in of smells, and perhaps associates sexual smells with excremental smells and finds them obnoxious, his or her mouth closes, the nose pinches and breathing is reduced and controlled. Mouth, throat, chest and abdomen all enter into the blocking of breathing, but blocking normally starts with nose and mouth. If the person restricts the kind of sucking, nibbling and kissing actions of the lips which normally intensify sexual excitement and the breathing, the breathing may not deepen. The easy opening of the mouth may be blocked by a tight jaw or by clenching the teeth. Sounds may be suppressed and emerge as strangled groans, or uttered in a controlled manner as talking or mechanical exclamations, or grunting. Some of this blocking is simple – for example, the presence of a tight jaw – but the pressure toward increased excitation tends to provoke active blocking. And instead of deepening, the breathing may be actively held, or restricted with an effort which produces grunts and groans. Often the person will grunt with 'pleasure' but this tightening of the throat will actually impede the flow of sensation, replacing it by a more controlled 'squeezed' sensation, or one of 'pushing' (perhaps, in psychoanalytic terms, a more anally oriented pleasure in which constriction of movement becomes a kind of pleasure-substitute).

The subjective feeling in holding the breath may be that this increases excitement and concentration, as well as control of pelvic movement. But this concentration seems to be directed toward the achievement of a fantasy or the cultivation of a local excitation of the genitals (usually the tip of the penis or the clitoris) through friction alone. Holding the breath prevents any possibility of the body letting go in the orgasm pulsation, or of the build-up of excitations through pleasurable forward movements of the pelvis accompanying the out-breath.

Deepening of the breathing may produce anxiety as it threatens to trigger emotions. For example softening of the chest will be resisted in a person who is afraid to cry or seem vulnerable.

3) At the level of genital contact, the penetrative role of the penis and the receptive role of the vagina may be experienced with anxiety and so resisted by an over-emphasis on the pulling back movements, or by a

frantic acceleration of movement. If streamings are alien to a person they will not be experienced in his or her own genitals, nor will he or she feel them from the other person's genitals. A 'deadness' of genital contact often leads to forced, accelerated friction movements to provide a sensation which is largely kinetic.

4) According to *Newsweek,* in 1974, a record had become popular which reproduces the sound of human heart beats. Its manufacturers claimed that most people make love too fast, and that it is better to slow down to the rhythm of the heart-beat, thrusting with each beat. But the heart beats about 70 times a minute, and it is hard to imagine that people can make love much faster than this. For pulsatory movement and charge to build up it is necessary for breathing and movement to become synchronized, and this may happen spontaneously after an initial period of varied moving of the genitals. The movements and breathing become faster as excitation mounts, but even excited breathing rises from 12 to 18 breaths a minute to no more than 50 or 60 breaths: any faster than this is a panting which involves only the chest wall and not the whole lungs or the rest of the body – and risks hyperventilation. The rate of the final orgasm pulsations seems to vary widely, but a full pulsation of expansion/contraction cannot take place in less than about two seconds since it involves the complete inflation and reflation of the body. Actually, as sensation is lingered on in the intensity of approaching orgasm, the breathing may become more extended, and slower, with a final pulsation rate of one convulsion every 5 to 10 seconds or so.

An accelerated pace with panting breathing, or at the other extreme lying still and holding the breath – both seem to result from anxiety about feeling the body moving slowly and gently. The slow, gentle movement may threaten to become involuntary. The man may fear losing his erection, especially if he is already maintaining it by fantasy and kinetic friction. But another more mundane reason for the frantic pace of much lovemaking may be that it seems to have become the social norm. Many otherwise quite well-functioning people may be surprised to learn that it is even possible to make love in a slow gentle way in which movement and breathing are spontaneously together.

5) In many people the rhythmic pulsation of the pelvic floor does not occur at all until the moment of climax or ejaculation. Instead the pelvic

floor may be chronically tight and immobile, or without tonus. Some women, following the theories of Kegel about the necessity to squeeze with the vaginal muscles, will deliberately squeeze the penis. (This is a deliberately taught technique in some societies, such as with the Xhosa of South Africa where all girls are taught it, or learned by some women in the interests of pleasing men. Kegel exercises in which the voluntary contraction is synchronised with the breathing are useful, as noted, in maintaining genital tonus, especially in older people of both sexes). Voluntary mechanical squeezing does not have the same intensifying effect on the build-up of pleasure as when contractions occur involuntarily, although in a relatively unarmoured woman it may trigger involuntary pulsations. Women seem to find it easier to accept contractions of the pelvic floor than do men, although in both sexes it may produce anxiety about possibly breaking wind. Men feel anxious and vulnerable about involuntary contractions which tend to rebound into an expansion which dilates and opens the anus as the pelvis comes back. Sometimes the anus will be held tightly shut, the buttocks clamped tight, and the whole pelvis moved in a pushing motion of the trunk.

6) Involuntary shudders or trembling of the body may be repressed, since they make the person seem vulnerable. If repressed deliberately this is an active block, but in a simple block involving the muscles of the legs and trunk, no trembling will occur since the body is rigid. If the body is basically rigid no streaming sensations will be felt. In less rigid people they may be felt but stopped by tightening of muscles. In particular, pulling, melting sensations in the face and head may produce feelings of panic or of losing control, and can be eliminated by holding the mouth shut or contracting the back of the neck.

7) If a person is heavily armoured, movements are involuntary at no stage of the sexual embrace, and continue to be performed mechanically until the end. More usually there is less armouring and some involuntary movement, but this may become converted, because of anxiety, to active, voluntary movements which have a counter-pulsatory effect. In the man these movements may become a violent pounding. In the woman they may be side to side squirming movements of the pelvis. This side to side motion is often considered to be erotic, since it exerts mechanical friction on the penis and vagina. Functionally it is an emotional 'no' just as much as when

the head is shaken from side to side. Some women do in fact wriggle their head from side to side at the same time as the pelvis, as if carried away by passion. But 'yes' with the pelvis is a soft spontaneous reaching forward and upward, and with the head a relaxation backwards with a sigh.

Another way of blocking spontaneous movement is to clench the fists or grasp the partner tightly, which immobilizes the upper half of the body. The pelvis may be held rigid by sticking the legs out straight. Lowen maintains that the build-up of 'bioenergy' is increased by a dynamic tension in the legs which is only possible when the feet are 'grounded' by being dug into the bed or pressed against a wall. ('Grounding' – not pulsation – is the main goal of bioenergetic therapy). He repeatedly compares the functioning of the body in the sexual embrace to that of a bow, and writes: 'the greater the tension of the bow the greater the flight of the arrow,' and 'For the human body to function as a bow, the two ends of the body that correspond to the ends of the bow shaft must be sufficiently anchored to support the tension. The upper end of the body (bow) is anchored in the functions of the ego. The lower end of the body is anchored through the contact of the legs with the ground.'

This comparison contains a mechanical fallacy, and would make any archer laugh. A bow with one end stuck in the ground will not even shoot an arrow. The leverage which gives the bow its force comes from the fact that it is gripped in the middle, and both ends are free. Similarly, as Reich pointed out, in orgasm the body shows a folding movement centered on the diaphragm and the autonomic ganglia. This area corresponds to where a bow would be held. Lowen's image of the bow provides an analogy which suggests that the legs should not be grounded, but left free. They are functionally part of the pelvis and participate in the movement, closing and opening loosely. Digging the feet into the bed or pressing them against the wall keeps the legs rigid and is an active block. Lowen elsewhere notes accurately that the the pelvis 'swings' in love-making, but his 'grounding' techniques will block any such free movement. [Lowen's absurd analogy is also an example of the dangers of prescribing how to make love. My account here, following Reich's, is not a prescription but a description of possible pulsation and possible blocks to it.]Another active block which comes to play as a resistance to excitation but is considered often to be a sign of extreme passion, is to arch the back and hold it arched. Women, in particular may do this, and it does increase friction on the clitoris. The image of extreme passion may be understood, since it represents an extreme of the inflated, expanded position and extreme excitation. But it is naturally part of a pulsatory movement, and normally succeeded by movement forward in the out-breath. If inflation is held even during the out-breath it is functionally identical to the 'arc de cercle' found in hysteria and in babies with severe feeding problems. Reich called it 'the prototype of defense against sexuality'.

Some mention should be made of practices which originate in body-oriented therapies and exercise methods but which can be transformed into active blocks. The 'paradoxical breathing' taught in yoga, in which the abdominal movement is reversed so that the abdominal wall contracts on the in-breath instead of the out-breath is sometimes used instinctively by children trying to repress crying or vomiting, and its avowed purpose in yoga is to channel 'energy' upward in the body. If used in coitus it is inimical to genital feeling. The Tantric yoga practice of 'carezza' in which orgasm is deliberately blocked in favor of a highly controlled contact between penis and vagina may lead to some streaming feelings after a period of time but by definition the method prevents their resolution. Many body-oriented therapies, like yoga, seem to be aimed at more efficient control of the body. Wilfred Barlow in *The Alexander Technique* states that the normal sexual movement is to tilt the pelvis forward on the in-breath and backward on the out-breath. This is a movement diametrically opposed to the orgasm pulsation and can only be achieved by a relatively unarmoured person through painful voluntary effort. But it is a common active block, since it is controlled, the abdomen's pulsation is restricted, and excitation is kept from mounting.

Other defensive movements which are sometimes considered to be signs of pleasure are biting and scratching. These may be quite involuntary, and express other feelings but impede sexual excitation. Such active blocks tend to increase, and may become frantic toward orgasm. The feeling of approaching climax may be overwhelming and cause intense anxiety. Some people report fears and images of bursting, going on fire, splitting open, screaming, or going insane. In these cases it can be supposed that what Reich called 'orgasm anxiety' is acute. Since orgasm may be felt as a dissolution of boundaries, it may be experienced as dangerous, a 'falling apart'. And since the orgasm pulsation is the most radical spontaneous movement of the body, leading to extreme vulnerability and openness to the partner, orgasm anxiety can be seen as the most complete form of anxiety. It may sometimes be so overwhelming in itself that the person becomes paralysed and stops breathing. More often orgasm is experienced as a painful explosion which the body attempts to prevent by frantic wriggling from side to side. There may be a yell or a painful narrow "aah" sound (the sound associated with a scream of fear, rather than the soft "oh" of wonder or the broad "aah" of satisfaction). The person may pound the partner or the bed with his or her fists. Or more often the muscles of the pelvis and thighs will become rigid, the penis or vagina hurt, and much of the sensation of climax as well as the movements be blocked.

These reactions of becoming rigid to block release presuppose that tension has been built up. In a more contracted person the body is looser. In a few cases orgasm convulsions may occur throughout the sexual embrace, or at the end, without being accompanied by any sensation: here the function seems to be discharge of excitation before it can be felt deeply. More often, there are loose movements of the body but an absence of sensation, and instead the presence of feelings of despair, failure and loneliness. Ejaculation in the man is slow and not very pleasurable. Climax in the woman is not reached, or is accompanied with only slight pleasure. Or the woman may lie without moving.

When climax is reached through ejaculation in the man and a brief spasm in the woman but orgasm is blocked, there are some local contractions of the pelvic floor, and a feeling of some pleasure and relief, but the body apart from the genitals is uninvolved. The old proverb says: *post coitum omne animal triste est*— after coitus every animal is sad. This sense of sadness, loneliness, and detachment predominates if orgasm has not occurred (even if technical climax has). Instead of feelings of tenderness and thankfulness to the partner, reassurance may be sought in clinging, or detachment may be perpetuated in resentment.

Fantasy may, as suggested earlier, have a necessary exploratory function, and play some part in initiating sexual excitement, since contact through the eyes leads to imagined further contact. However, it is possible to become stuck and fixated with a fantasy. The actual experience of the partner's body is replaced by a fantasized experience. This ties up attention and seems to have to be physically maintained by rigidity of the neck: if the neck is relaxed during coitus whatever is fantasized tends to drift away and be replaced by the perception of touch and movement. A major problem in this respect is that fantasy has become a way of life. A specific kind of visual pornography is available, in which women's bodies (visual pornography is mainly oriented toward men) appear made-up, depilated of 'unaesthetic' body hair, the nipples rouged, and usually a facial expression of hard contempt, which occurs more often than inviting expressions and seems to direct the contempt toward the viewer and his interest in whatever parts of the woman's body, usually the genitals, are exposed. Whatever the psychology of this contempt, visual pornography is by definition limited to one sense. Touch and smell can enter into fantasy, but more often the visual imagery is what remains and may be required to sustain sexual excitement in an actual encounter with a flesh-and-blood woman. At the more sophisticated level of written literature, books promote a "gourmet" approach to sex in which fantasy is a major ingredient. To make sex more exciting, Alex Comfort advised in *More Joy* that a man who is in the process of sodomizing his wife should imagine that in fact he is sodomizing another man. It is as if some people are so jaded that a man has to make love to his wife imagining that in fact she is Burt Reynolds, while she is imagining that he is Jane Fonda. This is a grotesque extreme, but a fixation on fantasy throughout coitus has to be a fixation of the attention elsewhere from what is really happening. (As the novelist Erica Jong in *Fear of Flying* crudely described this: '99 percent of the people in the world were fucking phantoms').

Spontaneous bursts of visual imagery, on the other hand, occur frequently in accompaniment to movement and touching, and may in themselves be moving, as is for example a sudden image of someone loved long ago, or trees waving in the breeze. Waving, pulsating images are common, and some people at orgasm see spontaneous whirls and explosions of colour. The distinction here is in spontaneity. Spontaneous images do not fixate the attention, but the voluntary fixation on a fantasy which is in effect a deliberate substitute for the reality, without which the person would lose desire and feeling, may become an actual substitute for present sensation.

Voluntary caresses, if carried on throughout coitus in the interest of pleasing the partner or of desperately sustaining excitement, again seem to fixate attention in the voluntary control centers of the cortex. Spontaneous caressing movements of the other person intensify feeling and the flow downward of excitation to the genitals. A deliberate emphasis on friction as such, with hard, rubbing movements of the genitals, means that attention becomes fixated in kinesthetic pleasure. For streamings to intensify, soft, gentle movements seem to be necessary. Reich noted this in his electrophysiological experiments. Perhaps this is because softness is a characteristic of pulsatory movement in primitive organisms such as the protozoa.

In a therapeutic context, a mainly mechanical version of the orgasm reflex can sometimes be induced in a relatively unarmoured person through extended breathing. But this is not itself an orgasm. Because it can be induced mechanically in a suitable subject, the orgasm reflex can be observed more easily than the actual process of orgasm. But there is a difference between the induction of the orgasm reflex in the supportive atmosphere of therapy, and its occurrence in the highly charged, potentially anxiety-ridden situation of sexual contact. Some people who have experienced the orgasm reflex in a therapeutic context do not experience it outside therapy or may easily lose the capacity with time through a process of re-armouring. Another related phenomenon is that some quite armoured people can, in a situation of love and trust with a partner, let go of their blocks to the extent that some orgasm pulsation occurs, although the range may be partially limited by blocks. And conversely, in some people who are extremely contracted and so depleted of energy that no muscular armoring can be sustained (Reich noted this in working with a woman who had terminal cancer), the orgasm reflex may occur quite readily when breathing is intensified. It may even, as it was in Reich's case-example, be used as a defense against feeling.

Orgasm Anxiety

An examination of orgasm anxiety may reveal the basic dynamics of armour formation, since it specifically blocks the most intensified form of human pulsation. Orgasm anxiety may occur in the final stages of Reichian therapy, when much of the body armour has been dissolved and worked through, and the person may be overwhelmed by feelings of disintegration unless an outlet for the increased capacity for excitation is open in his or her sexual life. In coitus, orgasm anxiety is, Reich proposed, responsible for the avoidance of surrender to orgasm. Reich noted that it is frequently experienced as 'fear of dying' or 'physical destruction', and 'the fear of the overpowering orgasm genital excitation.' He later summed it up as 'fear of orgasm contact', and attributed it mainly (as a good Freudian) to 'infantile masturbation anxiety.' But at the same time he related it closely to a fear of 'psychic contact with persons and with the processes of reality.' And he described the lack of emotional contact experienced by many children with their parents, and the children's giving up 'the struggle for understanding'. He added: 'The road between vital experiencing and dying inwardly is paved with disappointments in love.'

Seymour Fisher bases a theory on his findings in *The female orgasm* which is relevant here. Although his definition of orgasm is in terms of climax alone, since climax is an essential part of orgasm his findings about inability to achieve climax can refer validly to inability to achieve any kind of orgasm. Even defined as climax, orgasm was experienced always or nearly always by only 39% of Fisher's sample. [Brody's findings are more encouraging.] Fisher considers the possibility that "an act that denoted creation of new life could, in terms of its antithetical meaning, activate and reinforce anxieties that involve concern about the death or loss of important objects." And he cites Freud's proposal that "separation anxiety (fear of object loss) represents at one level a fear of unsatisfaction, a sense of danger about the *build-up of tension* from a need that remains unsatisfied because of the absence of an important person (for example, mother) who previously took responsibility for it.... Object loss becomes identified with the danger of being over-whelmed by an excess of body excitation stemming from unsatisfied wants.'

Fisher's findings suggest that conscious anxiety which prevents orgasm is largely a separation anxiety characterized by fear of loss. Some women are so dominated by feelings of loss that full autonomy is not achieved, as if such women are clinging to lost ground, or frozen in an attitude of incipient separation. And other women so much reject feelings of loss (almost all adults have experienced loss, so most of the women who do not appear so concerned with it have either rejected it or grown out of it) that they will not 'let go' of their autonomy. But on closer examination these women too are in a relationship to loss. They may have grown out of it, but they still resist it, in an exaggerated maintenance of detachment or defiance. Here a further distinction can be proposed: those women who accept loss are dominated by the loss of 'other' and cling to a fusion with 'other'. Those women who defy loss are dominated by anxiety about the loss of self which they defy in an assertion of self.

This distinction between 'other' and 'self' is necessary because since the context of orgasm is the fusion of two beings, loss may threaten from two sides: it may be a loss of the other (the partner) in the form of rejection or detachment, or a loss of the self in the form of loss of voluntary control.

[It goes without saying that Fisher's analysis of fear of loss in women – after all, the subject of his study – also applies to men. 'Men' or 'people' can be validly substituted for 'women' in the passages quoted above.]

Why is orgasm anxiety specifically so intense and orgasm so threatening? It is not simply the loss of self or the loss of the other which give it its intensity, but a sense of dissolution of boundaries which may even be experienced as 'a fear of dying.' It is, in Reich's theory, similar to the depersonalization which is experienced in schizophrenia, and it may in some people produce a 'freezing' shock reaction. The schizophrenic split has been described by Reich as a split between perception and sensation, and by other writers in terms of various 'double binds.' What is the split and double bind in orgasm anxiety?

Neither of the two extremes defined by Fisher experiences what can be called severe orgasm anxiety: one appears to experience a fairly constant and low-charged diffuse anxiety about loss of other, and the other extreme experiences little anxiety and substitutes for it an autonomous pleasure. But each of these extremes has "cut off" one half of genital experience to some degree. What about orgasm anxiety in a woman who is excitable in both clitoris and vagina, the genitals as a whole? If orgasm anxiety occurs it can be proposed to consist of both elements: fear of loss of other, and fear of loss of self. And this, surely, presents a situation (for both men and women) of extreme double bind, an alternative as intolerable, in the presence of anxiety, as a schizophrenic double-bind between panic and pain. In acute orgasm anxiety the person may be trapped between fear of losing the self (similar to panic) and fear of losing the other (pain) – with the added element that letting go and surrendering the self may in some cases lead to rejection by the other, and rejection of the other means that letting go of the self is impossible.

Such a double bind between fear of self-loss and fear of other-loss does not have to be a conscious conflict, but part of frozen history which threatens to melt with the intensifying pre-orgasm sensations of streaming. The disappointments in love which Reich suggested 'constitute the most frequent and most potent cause of internal dying' may provide one pole of the conflict, and can be clearly seen as loss of other. There is also a precedent and the opportunity for history to become frozen, in the experience of loss of self. Even if this is defiantly rejected, it may have happened: a stifling intimacy or constant interference both threaten to rob the child of his self. Reich mentions anxiety about infantile masturbation as a root cause of the 'fear of orgasm contact'. This anxiety may come from either interference or the prospect of interference. Interference is by definition a 'striking between', an attempt to separate a person from his or her self.

The primary experience of orgasm anxiety is characterized by fear of loss of other and loss of self. Chronic contraction or chronic expansion of the breathing structure, although their individual and emotional dynamics vary, can be seen as developing in childhood in reaction to loss or threatened loss of other or of self.

A brief definition of human pulsation

The above description of the orgasm pulsation can be shortened and offered as:

> The orgasm reflex occurs on exhalation as extreme contraction of the trunk and expansion of the extremities.

> There is a rebound on inhalation into extreme expansion of the trunk and contraction of the extremities.

> The reflex and the rebound alternate several times with the reflex increasingly dominating and the rebound diminishing.

The reflex is accompanied throughout by pulsations of the pelvic floor.

This in turn can be shortened into a statement about the ordinary pulsation of the breathing (i.e. not intensified by emotional expression or orgasm):

On the in-breath the abdomen then the chest wall rise until there is a slight sensation of constriction and a turn-around when first the chest wall then the abdomen fall and at the end of the out-breath there is a slight sensation of expansion and a brief pause before the in-breath – the whole taking around 3 seconds for the in-breath and 5 seconds for the out-breath. (But breathing rates vary from person to person).

If the person pays total attention a slight feeling of anxiety (from the Latin 'angustia', meaning narrowness) may be felt in the chest at the turn-round after the in-breath, and a slight feeling of pleasure may be felt in the genitals at the pause after the out-breath.

WORKING WITH HUMAN PULSATION

Working with the Emotions

How about 'pulsation therapy'? The answer that this already exists in Reich's 'orgonomic therapy' and its various derivatives is not satisfactory, because orgonomic therapy as most strictly practiced by Reich's immediate successors still defines pulsation simply as alternating contraction and expansion, whereas, as we have seen, if it is to be distinguished from every vibration or oscillation in the non-living universe it must be defined as 'phase unequal', and this leads to new observations.

In *Human Pulsation*, although I still considered myself a Reichian I had to integrate Reich's theories and my experience of his therapeutic methods into the broad picture of psychology and psychiatry – at least the picture in 1977. This broad picture included studies of childhood development and of emotions and the autonomic nervous system (always one of the under-pinnings of Reich's own work).

At the same time, I was already moving towards applications of Reich's methods to what he called 'emotional first aid', and to self-help work. In doing so I began to establish new principles of my own.

In *Emotional First Aid,* 1984, I set out a method for simple crisis intervention in which I discussed the four main human emotional expressions, as originally identified by Charles Darwin: Fear, Anger, Grief, Joy. (Paul Ekman in the 20th century had classified these further but his distinction of Disgust from Anger is now attracting criticism, and Darwin's original scheme is turning out to be more robust.) In *EFA*, as most people have called it, I explained ways in which a friend or helper could encourage the free and safe expression of these basic emotions. I had not intended it for professional use, but it became increasingly clear that its readership was more among professional helpers than among the public at large. In the 1980s and 1990s in North America I gave various workshops on EFA to health professionals ranging from psychiatrists to ambulance paramedics, as well as to people in emergency services (police, firefighting). EFA was well received as a framework for *understanding* emotions, but it involved a more direct contact between the helper and the helped person than most people at large were comfortable with, and the book made more headway among health professionals – the very people to whom the book aimed to provide an alternative through self-help. I came to accept this, and to realize that I had been too idealistic.

The same process occurred to some extent with *Couple Dynamics* which was even more radical in its aim of returning body therapy to ordinary people, and of eliminating the various entanglements and distortions of 'transference' between therapist and client. *Couple Dynamics* was aimed at any couple who were already intimate enough to work together in exploratory exercises while remaining in emotional contact with each other. The book was *not* written as a handbook *for therapists* of Reich's methods of 'dissolving the armour' and working towards unimpeded pulsation. And although I knew the word 'dynamics' sounded mechanistic, I could think of no other word for the give-and-take interaction between sexual and emotional partners. The word, however, still implied 'energy'. I had not quite broken free of the life energy concept. I now think of dynamics, following the physicist Julian Barbour and earlier thinkers such as Leibnitz and Mach, as *relational*.

Unfortunately the publisher over-edited *Couple Dynamics* (and added an uplifting and sentimental Afterword) without my permission, and my distinction between 'Worker' and 'Helper' became rephrased, somewhat nauseatingly as I saw it, as between 'Explorer' and 'Guide.' Also, when faced with the book after publication, I realized it risked making people psychological partners rather than lovers. And like its predecessor *Emotional First Aid,* it seemed to be selling more to therapists than to ordinary people. So I was happy when the book failed to sell very well. Nevertheless, its instructions for the exploration of pulsation and the emotions through exercises and movement, best experienced in the company of another person who can give feedback but possibly done alone, may be useful as a brief primer in pulsation therapy.

Eventually, after 2000 or so, I found myself teaching in London on the 'Neuropsychology of the Emotions' in various university clinical training programmes for psychologists, neuropsychologists, and psychiatrists. Since the work of Reich is now on the radical fringe, and the courses were by definition mainstream, I left Reich mainly aside (although I did mention him) but concentrated, after an overview of Darwin and Ekman, on Jaak Panksepp's *Affective Neuroscience*. Panksepp himself, however, is well aware of the work of Reich and 'emotional first aid' measures. He has identified 'Emotional Operating Systems' in the brain and his work is shifting neuroscience from a focus on cognition to a focus on emotion.

In view of my own rejection of Reich's main paradigm of 'life energy' I have found it easier to consider his work in the context of neuroscience, neuropsychology – in which I worked for my living for 25 years – and neuropsychiatry.

Reichian therapy has a reputation for being painful with some practitioners who take an aggressive approach. (See positive accounts by Orson Bean and Myron Sharaf who both went through long therapies, and a negative account by the hostile Christopher Turner after a couple of free sample sessions.) Reich once said, 'When I see armour I want to smash it.' But in his later years he told Sharaf (who told me and others): 'It should be possible to do orgone therapy without laying a hand on the patient, just talking.'

As I have described in Chapter 1, I have limited faith in psychotherapy, even 'pulsation therapy', in which one person is the client/patient and the other is the therapist/doctor. The relationship may create a one-sided or false intimacy, and if it continues for a very long therapy it risks damage to one's 'real' relationship with a partner. However there are exceptions where the therapist is emotionally experienced and sensitive to pulsation and to the character armour which resists it, and has a clinical support network of similar colleagues. As an example of this, see a video of Daniel Schiff discussing a particular case at a 2009 conference on 'Orgone therapy: Past, Present and Future' on Schiff's website (www.dschiffphd.com).

I now support these levels of working with pulsation:

1. Emotional First Aid and self help.
2. Couples work without a therapist but using instructions as a guide.
3. Supported self help or couples work in which a clinician is a consultant to the person or couple.
4. Neurodynamic Psychotherapy in clinical health settings.

5. Neurodynamic Psychotherapy (or other Reichian, 'orgonomic' or pulsation-oriented psychotherapy) with an experienced and trustworthy clinician. I believe that such therapy, for people who are not 'mentally ill' or on psychotropic medication but who want to resolve emotional or sexual dilemmas and to live more fully, is best done on a limited term basis – say 10 to 20 sessions, with the possibility of further consultations.

Neurodynamic Psychotherapy in Clinical settings
Whether in therapy or in medicine, the observation of pulsation and its blocks may help distinguish between what is working well – is healthy or whole – and what is not. But again, I have reservations about 'treatment' – even in general medicine. After all with most of the 25% or so of people who are obese to the point that type 2 diabetes is inevitable (and often leads to brain damage) it proves impossible to persuade them to change their diet or take more exercise. Similarly it is hard to persuade many people with depression to take half an hour's walk every day – although this has been demonstrated to be more effective, even in the short term, than antidepressants. (The walking gets the breathing pulsation going, as well as the heart). I doubt if it will ever work to instruct people how to breathe more fully – let alone to undertake some form of pulsation therapy, unless they are drawn to it.

What about the psychologically or clinically disturbed people who are treated in so-called 'Mental Health' services? My view, after decades in clinical neuropsychology, is that both 'mental health' and 'mental illness' are escape hypotheses to avoid the crux of the problem: that the illnesses termed 'mental' are as much physical as mental, and are neurological and probably brain diseases, *but* they are not usually diagnosable on physiological grounds.

Clinicians treating mental or physical illness seldom pay attention to pulsation. (Exceptions include clinicians trained in Reich's methods, some old fashioned doctors, or those trained in Chinese medicine who still know how to begin diagnosis through detecting different types of pulse.) But a whole research programme is possible on the question of how much impairment of pulsation contributes to various diseases. For example, research on cancer for the past 50 years or so has focused on carcinogenic substances, and this has overshadowed the earlier work of Otto Warburg on possible systemic causes, notably a lack of oxygen in tumour cells. Warburg's work (which won a Nobel prize in 1931) implies that disturbances of the breathing pulsation may lead to cancer. This is surely true of other diseases. In memory clinics I have observed that many people with Alzheimer's Disease or other neurodegenerative diseases appear to have diminished respiration, and I wonder if this has affected oxygenation of the brain, but this is only a conjecture in the absence of research. As the word 'depression' implies, most mental illnesses involve diminution or disturbance of pulsation. The person with asthma or emphysema observably fights for breath. The person with heart arrhythmia can have it corrected by the installation of a pace-maker. The pulsation of the brain is, in contrast, unknown. Surgeons can see the brain pulsating with the heartbeat. But it is not observable in the slice-by-slice images of most brain scans, although current fMRI, SPECT and PET scans could provide successive images that might demonstrate it.

In spite of the propaganda of the drug companies, the two main categories of so-called mental illness, schizophrenia and affective disorder (e.g. bipolar disorder) do *not* arise from identifiable 'chemical imbalances' in the brain. (Such imbalances may develop after treatment with drugs, but they are not identifiable before such treatment). Nor can they be identified from investigations such as brain scans except sometimes in long-term cases where medication effects cannot be ruled out. People with long term schizophrenia or bipolar disorder will almost always have taken psychotropic drugs, and although MRI brain scans may show signs of patchy atrophy or small vessel disease, these (and the cognitive and emotional impairment that goes with them) may be due as much or more to the long-term effects of drugs than to the condition. Admittedly, correlations have been noted between depressive episodes and chronic anxiety (in otherwise healthy people) and, respectively, deterioration of the frontal lobes and the hippocampus. But these correlations are weak and inconsistent, and there are many other possible causes of these changes. To put it simply: schizophrenia and affective disorder before drug treatment have no identifiable 'signature' on MRI scan, whereas neurodegenerative diseases such as Alzheimer's or Parkinson's or Multiple Sclerosis do have 'signatures'. So called mental illness almost certainly involves changes in the brain (whether temporary or permanent is not clear), and there seems little doubt that schizophrenia is a developmental brain disease influenced by situational factors. But in the current state of neuroscience 'point to point' correlation of areas of brain damage in any brain disease (even Alzheimer's) with cognitive or emotional dysfunction is unreliable. So the concept of 'mental illness' is an understandable cop-out, especially since those who suffer from it show psychological and behavioural disturbance – but then so do people with Parkinson's disease, or MS, or Fronto-temporal dementia, or for that matter traumatic brain injuries. 'Mental Health', on the other hand is more than a cop out, it is a health industry slogan which offers something it cannot deliver and which cannot even be defined.

Most 'Mental Health' services in the early 21st century use a two pronged approach: one prong is biological psychiatry (i.e. the use of psychotropic medications), and the other is short term psychotherapy, usually Cognitive Behavioural Therapy (CBT).

CBT is neuropsychologically unsound, since the evidence is that 'emotion over-rides cognition', not the other way around as CBT claims, but it is demonstrably effective – in the short term. Just as demonstrably, it has almost no long term benefit, as public health services are discovering as the demand by people who have done courses of CBT for more and more in-depth psychological or 'psychodynamic' therapies escalates – and there is little evidence that these work at all, although some evidence that success depends on the personality and empathy of the therapist. Since the aims of 20th century psychotherapy after Freud and Reich have often grandiosely included the goal of changing people – not just helping them in their thinking or feeling – the relative modesty of CBT has at least brought psychotherapy back to earth, to the point that it can be 'manualised' and provided by therapists with very little training, or even via computer programmes. (A moment of sympathy is perhaps kind, for all those CBT therapists whose personal thoughts and feelings must be set aside in their work: they too become 'manualised'.) And, it must be emphasised, in public health services such as the British NHS, any more complex psychotherapy than the very first stages of CBT is almost always accompanied by the prescription of SSRI anti-depressants. Those messy emotions are now unable to over-ride cognition, since they are chemically suppressed. Most

21st century CBT psychologists and counsellors have made a devil's bargain with psychiatrists: 'if you diminish or eliminate the emotions, I can be free to work on the cognitions.'

A devil's bargain because so-called 'biological psychiatry' (so-called because biology is the study of life, and psychotropic drugs interfere with life) can also demonstrate some short term success, and may even be essential in emergencies, but it not only fails to achieve long term success, it damages people's brains and creates addiction and cognitive and emotional deterioration. This has most convincingly been documented by Robert Whitaker in *Anatomy of an Epidemic* (2011) and James Davies in *Cracked* (2013) but Elliot Valenstein provided similar evidence in *Blaming the Brain* (1988).

It can all be summed up in a jingle:

> Short term gain,
> Long term pain,
> Brain drugs damage the brain.

The process is simple enough: just as prolonged use of a crutch leads to muscle atrophy, so prolonged use of psychotropic drugs leads to the incapacity of the brain to produce the necessary neurotransmitters and peptides ('molecules of emotion').

Over thirty years of evidence have begun to make an impact, and conscientious psychiatrists are beginning to ratchet back their enthusiasm for medication. The eminent J Allan Hobson even stated, in *Out of its Mind – Psychiatry in Crisis* (2002), that in effect psychiatry must embrace neuroscience or die. He also mooted the possibility (following Luria) of a 'neurodynamic psychotherapy'. And neurodynamic thinking based on the research of neuroscientists like Jaak Panksepp in *Affective Neuroscience* (1998) and *The Archeology of the Brain* (2012) is coming alive.

It is ironic that what we may now jokingly call 'Big Pharma' in the form of the US Food and Drug Agency (FDA) achieved the humiliation and imprisonment of Wilhelm Reich (he died in prison in 1957) for his promotion of the 'orgone accumulator' which the FDA 'demonstrated' was a useless fraud. Whether or not the orgone accumulator worked as

Reich thought it did, it is hard to imagine that its use could have caused an epidemic of brain damage. (If it didn't work it could have caused nothing at all.)

A focus on pulsation implies a 'one size fits all' approach, in that the goal of the therapy is full pulsation. Although there are as many ways of reaching this goal as there are people in therapy, the goal remains the same. But what about pathology? Modern health services are faced with a variety of specific emotional/mood disorders, clustered under diagnostic categories such as depression, bipolar disorder, anxiety disorder, schizophrenia, and various (most often 'borderline') 'personality disorders.' As noted earlier, the main 'mental illnesses', schizophrenia and affective disorder, are almost certainly physical illness – brain diseases – although there is evidence that they can be triggered and/or exacerbated by situational stress or emotionally traumatic events. In the monistic approach of neuroscience and neuropsychology it makes no sense to distinguish the mental from the physical, the brain from the body: both share the neural network. But 'mental health' services continue a Cartesian (mind/body split) approach. Or is it just a division of the pie between rival professions?

The experience of severe and chronic illnesses like schizophrenia and bipolar disorder is horrendous for the patient, his or her family and friends, and even for the clinicians involved in treatment, whose own situational stress is considerable. (For a thoughtful blow-by-blow account from the point of view of the parent of a son with schizophrenia, see Tim Salmon's *Schizophrenia – Who Cares?*)

The capacity for full pulsation is, I think, a suitable goal in treating any disorder, and Reich himself studied such diagnostic categories as schizophrenia and borderline personality disorder (which he called the 'Impulsive' – 'Triebhafte' / 'Driven' – character). But the practical clinician in a 'mental health' service may have to put the cart before the horse and deal urgently with a specific disorder rather than the general disturbance of pulsation.

An NHS psychiatrist originally trained in neo-Reichian psychotherapy, Frank Röhricht, in his *Körperorientierte Psychotherapie Psychischer Störungen / Body-oriented Psychotherapy of Psychological Disturbances* discusses various methods of working bodily with specific 'mental health' disturbances. Orgasm is (understandably in a public health context like the NHS) set aside. But Röhricht uses and studies the efficacy of dance movement therapy and originally Reichian methods, particularly in working with schizophrenia. This in turn reduces the necessity, or at least the dosage, of damaging anti-psychotic medication which patients often hate for its side effects. The method developed by Röhricht and his colleagues draws on the work not only of Reich but of dance-movement therapists with whom Reich worked in Berlin in the 1930s. (Reich's long term companion Elsa Lindenberg belonged to this group, and dance movement seems to have made an unacknowledged contribution to his body focused orgone therapy). The NHS is funding a random controlled trial (RCT) of Röhricht's and his colleagues' methods, and since it is a requirement in the NHS that evidence based treatments should be rolled out, this may lead to more work, although indirectly, with pulsation.

Similarly my Brazilian colleague Jose Ignacio Xavier, a neuropsychiatrist and psychologist, has worked in community mental health services for people with psychosis using neurodynamic methods, as well as in private practice. Xavier trained in Reich's methods as developed by Federico Navarro (who in turn trained with Ola Raknes who had trained with Reich in the 1930s in Norway). Xavier and I have been developing what we call Neurodynamic Psychotherapy.

The central focus of this therapy is pulsation, and it could be called 'Pulsation Therapy'. But 'Neurodynamic Psychotherapy' describes better the wide focus it has to take in clinical contexts where 'psychodynamic' is already an accepted term for longer therapy than CBT and where in the coming years there is likely to be increasing integration of psychodynamic methods and neuroscience. This integration is sometimes called 'Neuropsychoanalysis' in acknowledgment of its roots in Freud's psychoanalysis. I think that Reich's methods, and the 'post-Reichian' bodily oriented psychotherapy being introduced into clinical settings by Röhricht and his colleagues are more suitable for integration with neuroscientific findings than psychoanalysis. 'Neurodynamic' is a more comprehensive term than 'neuropsychoanalysis', and it acknowledges its roots in Luria's apporach.

Röhricht's and Xavier's approaches, it can be argued, pick the cherries from Reich's pie, and avoid the risks of 'orgasm therapy' or of associating pulsation with orgasm. But they break through the self-referential approach which tends to isolate Reichian therapy and limit it to private practice. Yes, I would say the ideal psychotherapy is a 'pure' pulsation therapy, but why should elements of this not become part of public health provision? At least Röhricht, Xavier, and myself (all working independently of each other, I should emphasise, although we have at times shared our thinking) are not covering up the origins of what we do in our 'Body-oriented Psychotherapy', or 'Neurodynamic Psychotherapy'. If pulsation is, as I think on the evidence it is, definitive of life, it will find its place in the mainstream of human thought. And it will be accepted as a natural focus in all psychotherapy.

Conference Paper: A Framework for Neurodynamic Psychotherapy
Neurodynamic Psychotherapy, although proposed in theory by Luria, can only in practice be based in Reich's work. Although Reich was not a neuropsychologist his neuropsychiatric training led him to an emphasis on the Autonomic Nervous System as the main vector of pleasure and anxiety, emotional expansion and contraction. Although his life energy theory brought him eventually to biophysics, it had begun in neurology. Luria's proposed Neurodynamic Psychotherapy was in effect realised through Reich's work, and further developments in it must take 'orgonomy' into account along with 'affective neuroscience.' A more thorough conceptual framework for Neurodynamic Psychotherapy will no doubt be developed. My colleague Jose Xavier and I hope we have made a start on this. What follows in the rest of this section is an abbreviated version of a paper I gave on Neurodynamic Psychotherapy at the German Psychosomatic Medicine Conference in 2005, and which appeared in full in Portuguese in *Rivista Reichiana:*

Alexander Luria, in 1925, proposed a 'neurodynamic' approach to psychotherapy which would fulfil Freud's original but abandoned dream of integrating psychoanalysis with neurology. But when the USSR cracked down on psychoanalysis, Luria set this interest aside, concentrated on clinical work with brain trauma, and became the father of neuropsychology. Freud's dream has been revived in recent years by some psychoanalysts and neuropsychologists joining forces in 'neuropsychoanalysis'. But neuropsychoanalyisis, although acknowledging a debt to Luria, does not call itself 'neurodynamic'. Nor does it, so far, pay attention to the work of Wilhelm Reich. Surprisingly, since Reich focussed much more than Freud on the function of the nervous system. But after all not surprisingly, since a new movement attempting to release psychoanalysis from its increasingly idiosyncratic and self-referential box to claim its respectable place under the rising sun of neuroscience may not want to relate itself to *The Function of the Orgasm*, let alone to 'orgone energy'.

In this context, in early 2002, I began to correspond with Jose Ignacio Xavier whom I had heard of through Jaak Panksepp, whose *Affective Neuroscience* (1998), with its delineation of 'emotional operating systems' in the brain, had opened new directions in neuropsychology, until then over-preoccupied with the brain's cognitive systems at the expense of emotion. In November 2001 Panksepp and I had wandered together through the Freud house in Hampstead where even the distribution of furniture and ornaments in Freud's consulting room suggested to both of us a certain coldness to emotion. By contrast Reich insisted on facing the client, observing the body, feeling emotion, interacting, actively intervening. Panksepp thought neuropsychoanalysis could bridge psychoanalysis and affective neuroscience. I was not so sure, given the baleful presence of Freud and the urge of some neuropsychoanalysts to rehabilitate him as a proto-neuroscientist. But surely it was possible, given the overwhelmingly physiological and neurological base of Reich's work until he caught the vitalistic bug of 'orgone energy', to combine what I saw as his 'pulsation therapy' and neuropsychology in a new therapeutic approach.

The climate is right for a new neurodynamic psychotherapy whose approach can also become part of 'normal' psychotherapy, along with the best methods of Reich and post-Reichians. Cozolino in *The Neuroscience of Psychotherapy* (2002) cites much evidence that stress- and trauma-related damage to the neural network can be rehabilitated, and the functioning of the network's systems measurably changed, by psychotherapy as well as pharmacological intervention. The relation with the therapist and the awakening of the client's attention to neglected areas of experience lead to brain changes. According to Cozolino the intense bodily experiences and sudden emotional awareness that occur in body oriented psychotherapy and direct work with the emotions contribute more powerfully to such changes than talk therapy alone.

As a clinical neuropsychologist I had often thought of Luria's goal of a neurodynamic therapy, and wondered if it would be possible to 'close the loop' of my own experience in developing it. When I reflected on my psychotherapy training and career, I recalled my impatience with my first analyst Jean Ambrosi's emphasis on 'awareness' and his condemnation of emotional abreaction in therapy as 'exorcism'. I had preferred the more active approach of Reich – the more 'energetic' approach. But I now realised that this application of 'energy', the therapist's energy, the supposed 'energy' liberated when 'blocks' and 'armour' were worked through in attempts to change people, could often be (in a word Reich himself hated) mechanistic. This was a world away from William Blake's 'energy is delight' – the human experience of life free of interference.

Xavier and I, exchanging emails in English and Portuguese, found quickly that although we had very different clinical backgrounds and different training in Reichian methods, we agreed on one central matter. We were both indebted to Reich's work but neither of us could completely accept what Reich himself put at the centre of this work: 'life energy' ('orgone energy'). Xavier had written a doctoral dissertation on how the spontaneous movements elicited in Reichian therapy and the sudden insights which often accompanied them could be explained in terms of the neural network: there was no need for an energy concept. Since 1985 I had been working on and off on a book which discussed the Reichian concept of pulsation not as an energy event but an event in time. I had become bogged down in a large question about whether time existed at all – but in which it became more clear to me that Reich's 'orgone energy' theory, when considered rigorously, was a non-starter.

First the theory was a tautology: 'orgone' was derived from 'orgasm' which in turn is derived from the same Indo European root (*erg) as 'energy'. Second, it perpetuated the hydraulic and mechanistic libido theory of Freud. Third, although Reich claimed to have gone beyond both mechanism and mysticism, he could on the one hand define the orgone mechanistically in terms of tension/relaxation, and on the other define it mystically as the Prime Mover and origin of life – which violates the laws of physics in which energy is always secondary to movement, and Reich had not convincingly re-written the laws of physics. Finally I was personally fed up with the reductionistic 'energy talk' so rife in Reichian, as in 'New Age' circles, where everything under the sun from love and hate to the shapes of beans or of galaxies was described in terms of 'energy'.

Parallel to my correspondence with Xavier, I was corresponding with and meeting the theoretical physicist Julian Barbour whose controversial *The End of Time* proposed a universe not only without time but without action or energy, in which movement was only apparent – a succession of 'nows'. (Each now could be a moment of awareness. Perhaps the universe consists of what Thomas Hardy called 'moments of vision'.) Barbour's previous book, *The Discovery of Dynamics*, was a monumental elegy to its subject: in the classical sense there was no more dynamics. But if there is no time, no doubt we have to keep inventing it: it is a useful way of experiencing our 'nows'. Similarly with dynamics. Barbour himself, in papers exploring ideas from Leibniz and Mach, proposes a new kind of relational 'dynamics of pure shape' in which bodies do not move in the straitjacket of Newton's absolute space but relative to each other, and 'the universe is not expanding, it is changing shape.'

Panksepp states that 'affective feelings may emerge from rather primitive levels of brain organisation.' He has also demonstrated that emotion tends to over-ride cognition. But affective neuroscience has not yet reached the point where what is happening in the brain when two 'emotional operating systems' are in conflict can be described. In simple approach/avoidance conflict the neurodynamics is already clear. The conflict 'flight versus fight' is apparently regulated by the amygdala's mediating alertness to emergency, and whether norepinephrine or epinephrine is activated. The conflict 'Do I touch this person or not?' is regulated by the strength of fronto-cortical inhibition. But the internal struggles between rage and crying, or even between laughter and crying will be harder to delineate.

Furthermore, such conflicts involve what Candace Pert calls the 'molecules of emotion', neuropeptides in the fluid that surrounds the neural network. It is becoming recognised in neurology (e.g. by Richard Cytowic) that 'volume transmission' of chemical information in the brain is at least as important as transmission in the neural network itself. Pert suggests that only 2% of emotional information involves neurotransmission, i.e. the action of biogenic amine transmitters across the synapses of the neural network. The evolutionary evidence suggests that this transmission is action related. For example in chordates (slugs, the stage in the evolutionary tree of descent between the first complex multicellular organisms and vertebrates) the neurotransmitter dopamine mediates metabolic activity, and serotonin is present in the gut – as it is in that of humans. Panksepp's emotional operating systems mediate action via links from the periaqueductal grey matter (PAG) in the mid brain to the cortex and limbic system, and rely heavily, though not exclusively, on neurotransmission. But the cell receptors for neuropeptides are present in the emotional operating systems and almost everywhere else, as Pert puts it 'running every system in the body.'

In *The Expression of the Emotions in Man and the Animals*, Darwin made a clear distinction between the main emotions (he defined four: anger, fear, grief, joy) and the many possible emotional 'states' (e.g. embarrassment, guilt, shame, resentment, unease…). This is supported by the emerging distinction between the emotional expression 'channeled' via neurotransmission in the emotional operating systems (Panksepp defines seven: SEEKING, RAGE, FEAR, PANIC, PLAY, LUST, CARE) and the various emotional states mediated by the neuropeptides.

Conflict is not the clashing of two energy streams, it is the contact between two conflicting sets of emotional information mediated by neuropeptides in emotional states and by neurotransmitters in emotional expression. The cognitive neuroscientists, behaviourists and systems theorists (like Gregory Bateson and the cyberneticians of the 1970s) were quite contented with information systems without energy. But they downgraded or ignored emotion. Because, I suppose, emotion implies energy and movement. ('Emotion' is from Latin 'e-movere', 'move out'). Panksepp's affective neuroscience restores emotion to the primacy which Darwin, before the so-called behavioural revolution, took for granted. Now neurodynamics lies in the relations between the sub-cortical emotional operating systems and each other, between them and the cognitive/neo-cortical superstructure, and among emotional states and emotional or thoughtful memories – all in the dynamic continuum of our brains and indeed of our bodies, where anatomical and cellular structures channel information which also saturates the fluid in which they live – a sort of inner ocean.

Barbour has remarked that physics may have to become more like biology in its future development. Perhaps the universe at large is a 'cosmic ocean' in which the same relational dynamics operate as in the inner ocean of our bodies. We find words like 'action' and 'movement' useful, as we find 'time' useful, but neurodynamics may best develop if we think in relational, interactive terms, which means breaking free of our over-reliance on cause/effect, stimulus/response. In studying the instantaneous feed-back loops of the neural network it is impossible to draw a line between emotion and action.

That mechanism excludes the emotions is not its only problem. Emotions can in fact be treated hydraulically, as in Freud's libido dynamics or theory of repression, in Reich's armour theory, or even in common speech about anger being 'bottled up', or tears being 'held back' then 'welling over', or being 'overwhelmed' by joy. When I started sounding off about mechanism to Panksepp he stated, 'I am a mechanist' – meaning that he is systematic, logical, materialistic, and follows rigorous research procedures. Mechanistic research is a successful method. But mechanism is limited to a vocabulary of cause and effect. Many (if not all) things just occur, without cause. Most identified causes turn out to be 'necessary but not sufficient' explanations of events, and to be 'multi-factorial'. It may be that, as the philosopher A J Ayer remarked, causality is just 'one damn thing after another'. 'Lateral causality' is sometimes proposed.

Ernst Mach confirmed his credentials as a mechanistic scientist by providing a measure for the speed of sound – but this is a *relative* measure. In Mach's universe (as in Hindu cosmology, which he studied), nothing happens anywhere that does not have some effect at every other point in the universe. And quantum physics brought this line of thinking further – to 'action at a distance' in which no cause-effect relation can be discerned. Gregory Bateson pointed out that the method in psychology known as behaviourism became obsolete in 1910 when Russell's Principia Mathematica was published. It nevertheless survived for the rest of the century and is still not quite extinct. Neurodynamic Psychotherapy does not need obsolete energy concepts or a mechanistic framework. But it may find mechanistic experimental method useful. Pulsation – unlike vague concepts like 'mental health' – is observable and measurable.

Luria defined the frontal/sub-cortical loop in the brain as an *action system*.

Panksepp's sub-cortical *emotional operating systems* link in with the action system. The experience of an emotion is the experience of a possible action. The experience of conflicting emotions ('I want to tell this woman I love her – but if I do she'll reject me') is a conflict between possible actions (I tell her I love her/I talk about the weather). So as well as the known role of the frontal lobes in inhibiting excitation there is also a range of possible conflicts, emotions, thoughts, actions – all in a dynamic relationship. But not a crudely hydraulic kind of dynamics, in which an impulse to action rises from the sub-cortex to the surface, as it were, and is then pushed back down by the censorious neo-cortex.

Barbour states: 'The distinctive character of dynamics is the *interactive* nature of the motion which it describes.' He contrasts this with the mechanical 'physics of push' which existed until the 17th century. This largely ignored the fact that if one body 'A' pushes or propels body 'B', as when we kick a football, body 'B' will exert a back reaction on body 'A'. This key feature of dynamics was first explained by Newton and is the content of his Third Law.

The biophysicist Adolph Smith enjoys illustrating Reich's diagram of splitting forces (a genuinely dynamic diagram) by taking a glass jar of water and letting a single drop of ink fall on its surface. The drop splits into two descending streams, each with a 'toroid' (doughnut-shaped) leading end which becomes elliptical and stretches then splits again. One stream becomes two, two become four, four become eight and so on. The result is a sort of inverted tree of ink in the water. This is a dynamic process in which the simple impact of ink drop on water becomes much more complex than the mechanics of kicking a ball. There is a series of interactions between ink and water, between splitting and resistance, and so on. The jar of water is in an initial condition. A drop of ink falls into it, changing the condition. After which the water and the ink drop interact, neither staying the same.

This experiment demonstrates *splitting against resistance*. Reich's diagram expressed what he saw as the continuous sub-dividing into opposing directions of previously united 'orgone streams'. He even claimed this matched the processes of Hegelian dialectic which he reframed in the light of Bronislaw Malinowski's functionalism in anthropology, as the workings of a 'common functioning principle'. Here again Reich's 'energy' theory undermined his observations: he could have seen that such splitting involves resistance – and furthermore that resistance is essential to splitting. It is also, crucially, essential to pulsation. Reich's brilliant microscopic observations of the 'bions' (vesicles in cells) emphasise the importance of the cell membranes. His studies of 'The Electrophysiology of Pleasure and Anxiety' include measures of skin sensation. But his energy theory required that he think in terms of going with the flow. Resistance was the 'armour' – a defense against the flow. This seems to have blinded him to the dynamics of pulsation as something that occurs when movement meets resistance by a surrounding membrane – as occurs everywhere in any organism (but not elsewhere).

At the risk of seeming Aristotelian and 'essentialist', it may be that life *is* pulsation – a dynamic process. Measuring life by pulsation is not tautological, although it may seem so since in effect life is being measured by life: it simply means that the alternating, unequal phase expansion/ contraction that we call pulsation provides a visible measure of its presence, and perhaps of another dimension that we can call something like 'intensity'. Defining and measuring life in this way may provide a way out of the main error of the 'brute vitalism' (a phrase of Eugenio Montale's) which takes over in talk about 'life energy' or 'life space' or 'life force'. If life could be measured by sheer quantity and power then we would all be much less alive than a Rolls Royce jet engine.

As Barbour remarks in *The Discovery of Dynamics*, 'Yes, the falling apple is striking but not half as marvellous as the ripening apple.'

The dynamics of pulsation (whether as repeatedly 'changing shape' or in conventional time terms) must be the central focus of Neurodynamc Psychotherapy. Pulsation is distinct from oscillation and vibration, which involve an equal phase (sine wave) expansion and contraction, in being *unequal phase*. The breathing, or the propulsion of jellyfish, or the beat of a heart are all *unequal phase*. I propose that an essential definition of life is the presence of unequal phase pulsation. But to say this is only philosophical. The *use* of such a concept may be in its capacity to *measure* life – or 'liveliness', or possibly 'healthiness' – more directly than as usual through such proxies as temperature or changes in skin colour.

The orgasm reflex is a convulsion in which the wave-like movement of the body in breathing (like a letter S) becomes exacerbated. This, for Reich, was the index of the human organism's capacity to pulsate fully. He saw pulsation no differently from oscillation, as alternating contraction and expansion, the full capacity for which was impeded by an armour of chronic muscle tensions, based largely on the repression of painful or pleasurable but forbidden childhood experiences, which blocked full breathing in and out. But inevitably, and in spite of his protestations against 'mechanism', his attack on the armour was mechanistic. He once remarked, 'When I see armour I want to smash it', and his therapeutic method sometimes did just that. He could be his own worst enemy.

In the revised edition of *The Function of the Orgasm* he stated that 'purely physiologically the orgasm reflex is identical to vomiting.' If this was true, then during orgasm we would vomit. But this erroneous statement was a natural enough consequence of his obsession with *energy discharge* – with *getting it out.* This part of his description tends to alienate women from Reich's theory of orgasm. They do not feel they are expelling 'energy' or semen or anything else during orgasm: they just melt in ecstasy as their body convulses – as men do too.

Orgasm is a gentle convulsion, whereas vomiting is harsh. In vomiting the flexor muscles in the back of the neck and the abdominal muscles clamp and contract harshly and abruptly. In the orgasm reflex the deep flexor muscles (quadratus lumbar) of the trunk contract along with the neck flexors as at the same time the extensors of the hands and feet tend to contract – even the fingers and toes may splay open. This unified pulsation involving the whole body in an 'unarmoured' person (i.e. one who is not defended against surrendering to it) looks like an extreme version of the unified breathing of a baby (before chronic muscular defences become installed by experience) in which with every breath the whole body undulates slightly, from head to toe.

In Neurodynamic Psychotherapy the client's and the therapist's perception of pulsation is the centre of attention. This pulsation can be observed at various levels, whether as the orgasm reflex (which is not to say the client has an orgasm – the reflex without the orgasm may occur naturally on full breathing out), or in the expression of emotions, or most simply as the breathing.

So far conventional neurodynamics is simply mechanical. E.g. stimulus/ response (S/R) models of the nervous system – which we know are simply obsolete (since 1910 apparently). E.g. astronomy before Kepler and Galileo got at it. E.g. unidirectional theories of computation in the brain. E.g. crude models of excitation versus inhibition.

In a real neurodynamics, the ways in which excitation and inhibition *change each other* would be considered. We do this in psychotherapy already as we discuss conflicts, e.g. between desire and conscience, but we have not formalised it. How about the innate 'hard-wiring' of the brain as an initial condition, the 'soft-wiring' as a secondary condition – or, more simply our innate characteristics as human animals (the ethology we inherit) as an initial condition and our experiences as humans (our accumulating individual history) as subsequent conditions. The 'heredity versus environment' debate is just crudely mechanical. Dynamically, each modifies the other!

As the behavioural endocrinologists like Frank Beach were showing in the 1970s, and Panksepp now shows in much more detail, you place a male rat with female rats and the initial condition of his testosterone level becomes modified (even his brain changes shape) which affects his behaviour, which affects his testosterone etc. Biology and society interact dynamically in the brain.

Before reliable clocks were invented, Galileo in his first experiments (with falling and sliding objects, water flowing off an edge, etc.) timed the rates of falling by the units of his own pulse. Talk about the relationship between the observer and the observed! The Heisenberg 'uncertainty principle' that the presence of the observer changes the experiment can be modified in Machian terms to state that the relation between observer and observed changes both. When I mentioned to Julian Barbour the view of Karl Popper that reality is 'decided' by different observers comparing their views, as when different observers staged at various points around the edge of a field with a cow and seeing it from different angles, might come to a composite view of the reality of 'cow', Barbour remarked: 'Reality has to include not only your observation of the cow, but the cow's observation of you.'

Psychotherapy that maintains a one-sided relation in which the therapist 'interprets the material from the unconscious', or 'teaches the client to keep an ABC diary' (of Antecedents, Behaviours, Consequences), or 'debriefs' the victim of a catastrophic event, can only be an illusion – a sort of obsolete mechanics. There are two consciousnesses (or unconsciousnesses) in the room, two behaviours, two victims even – one in fact, one in imagination.

Barbour argues that Descartes and Newton incorrectly attributed to space an all-powerful mechanical guiding role that actually arises from interaction with the entire universe. It is not surprising that our perceptions of time and space cause problems in the physiology of seeing. Goethe's theory was that vision was a process of interaction between the seer and what is seen, and although this is now seen as 'not proven' it is consistent with the new physics. Gregory in his *The Intelligent Eye* takes a dynamic view of vision in demonstrating that seeing is always a process of selection – which in turn is influenced by emotional factors. 'Seeing is believing'. But 'believing is seeing'. In *Human Pulsation* I proposed a theory of 'sensory blocking' as a parallel to Reich's 'muscle blocking': our senses are also influenced by what we do *not* want to see – or hear, smell, touch, taste. This is neurodynamics.

When in an emotional relationship 'I don't want to see the truth', I may be in a dynamic conflict between (for example) loving someone and being disappointed by something she has done. I am selecting what I want to see – both literally, in my field of vision, and in 'my mind's eye'. This must, classically, involve the frontal/sub-cortical loop. People with damage in this area are 'field dependent'. They cannot select. They 'go with the flow'. Reading some of Reich's work, one would think that 'going with the flow' was the essence of a healthy life. But it is not. Being able to make choices and to resist flow is healthy. I suspect that neurodynamically a choice is a perception plus an action (or a thought of an action). I doubt if a mathematics of neurodynamics will ever be possible. But perhaps some sort of equations will be useful. E.g. Choice = Perception + Thought of Action. I think we can work out the neurodynamics of (for example) 'choice' if we pay attention to 1) the role of the emotional operating systems, 2) the excitation-inhibition in the frontal/sub-cortical loop (which can be measured on SPECT scans), 3) sensory blocking, 4) activation of muscle armour, 5) observable movement, 6) pulsation. But perhaps this is wishful thinking.

In the meantime it could be useful to identify a few simple neurodynamic processes in the form of conflictual statements: 'I don't want to see the truth.' 'I love her and I hate her' ('Odi et amo... et *excrucior*') as Catullus put it. 'I want to be friends but I can't say so.' Or perhaps in the form of observable movements or actions – e.g. in the 'spontaneous ontological movements' Navarro has categorised, or in specific activations of the armour such as the platysmus muscles contracting when a person suppresses speaking or crying out. Can we subject these processes to a neurodynamic analysis that will help us intensify awareness and attention in psychotherapy?

Bio-psycho-social aspects of Neurodyamic Psychotherapy
In bio-psycho-social terms Neurodynamic Psychotherapy may broadly be seen from the following angles:

Biological
This has been largely the theme of this book. I have set out my own methods of working with breathing and pulsation, in self-help exercises. Other methods of 'body work' (for want of a better word – although this makes me think of car-repair) exist. Some are damaging and based on false premises – such as Lowen's grotesque idea that a bow shoots an arrow further if one end of it is stuck in the ground, so a person making love should dig his or her feet into the bed or even a wall. This blocks pulsation. On the positive side, Röhricht's and his colleagues' development of expressive movement therapy with psychiatric patients can be transferred to use in individual psychotherapy. And Xavier has contributed an analysis, based on the neo-Reichian Federico Navarro's 'actings' of deliberate expressive movements, of how the spontaneous movements that occur in therapy originate in the autonomic and central nervous systems. Xavier (whose work is so far only accessible in Portuguese) has demonstrated how the concept of 'life energy' is unnecessary to explain the functions of the neural network. And Xavier and I have written on how psychiatric 'personality disorders' reflect the activation of what Reich called 'character armour' in body-oriented psychotherapy. We also emphasise *attention* – the function which neuropsychology demonstrates underlies all other cognitive functions, including memory.

The core of Neurodynamic Psychotherapy is working with breathing and pulsation using a variety of methods. The opening up of physical pulsation entails work with anxiety as well as pleasure, 'orgasm anxiety' as well as the capacity for orgasm which Reich established, convincingly in my view, as essential to full human functioning as distinct from blocked or emotionally and even cognitively blunted functioning.

In the early 21st century there is more overt discussion of sex than in Reich's time. It is impossible to ascertain whether or not this entails more widespread 'orgastic potency'. Orgastic potency was Reich's measure of health, and the goal of his therapy. But with present day clients in psychotherapy, the term seems to have no clear meaning. They will almost always report having 'orgasms' – which they equate with 'climaxes' – by one means or another. To define orgastic potency in energetic terms, as Reich did – as the capacity for full energetic discharge – is not only a mechanistic and hydraulic criterion, it is met readily with assertions that the person is 'satisfied' or 'gets their rocks off', or whatever expression is used. A form of therapy cannot be founded on logic-chopping and knife edge definitions. This is why the theme of this book, Pulsation, as Reich himself knew and originally proposed, is *the* clearest way of defining orgasm. The 'orgastic pulsation' is the criterion for health, and as has been repeatedly explained in this book, is the paradigm for pulsation as a whole – the most complete and extended version of the continual pulsation of the breathing. Clients in Neurodynamic Psychotherapy seem to find it easy to understand and work with the criterion of pulsation as identifying the fullest possible orgasm. In the presence of contact with the partner, of course, and necessarily of sustained attention. (Here Brody's findings of a correlation between the capacity for vaginal orgasm and the 'big 5' personality trait of conscientiousness is relevant: in both men and women, orgasm requires the capacity to sustain attention, to concentrate and focus on genital sensations – to *feel* the interaction of penis and vagina and not run away from it into fantasy, anxiety, calculation or distraction. In simple terms, to have a full orgasm you have to put your mind into your penis or vagina.)

In parallel to the development of Neurodynamic Psychotherapy, medical research is – without using the word 'pulsation' – increasingly finding evidence of its association with emotional and physical health. Stuart Brody's findings that resting heart variability is correlated with penile-vaginal intercourse are now being added to by research (Kok and Frederickson) into 'vagal-tone values' correlated with positive emotions and with health. This correlation was in fact pointed out by Reich in the 1920s: he emphasised the opposing functions of 'sympatheticotonia', an activation of anxiety and contraction in the autonomic nervous system, and the parasympathetic activation of pleasure and expansion via the vagal system. This prompted his emphasis on pulsation. The new research not only supports Reich's emphasis, it demonstrates that vagal function during breathing mediates a slight increase in heart rate while breathing in, and a slight decrease while breathing out. Again, pulsation!

Psychological
Reich saw the human being as a naturally pulsating biological organism whose pulsation was impeded, and 'character armour' duly installed, as the organism was subjected to the requirements of a dysfunctional society. In bio-psycho-social terms, he tended to leave the 'psycho' out. He had had enough of talk therapy. Yet in later life, as he told Sharaf and others, he came to feel that it is not necessary, after all, to intervene physically in the therapy, through pressing down or manipulating muscular 'blocks.' It is enough to make suggestions for movement, to use brief verbal interventions to help the person become aware of his or her body – in effect, to enable *attention*.

The psychological bridges the biological and the social via thinking. And thinking requires language. Body-oriented psychotherapy at worst can become a sort of narcissistic gymnastics, out of contact with thought and with other people. Or it is 'body work' as in a car repair garage. Neurodynamic Psychotherapy has to restore language to its essential place, yet not return to 'talk therapy'.

Twentieth century linguistic philosophy tends to function like a 'head on a stick' and ignore the body. This is partly remedied by Lakoff's analysis of how metaphors originate in bodily sensation and movement, and his work has become popular with neo-Reichian therapists pursuing Reich's observations that character armour expresses not only frozen emotion and action, but frozen linguistic expressions: the stiff neck stating 'I won't', the deflation of the body expressing 'I give in.' Even the most mechanistic of 'body work' therapists will often get their hapless clients to yell out 'I'll kill you!' as they strangle a twisted towel. But body-oriented therapies seem to have a mistrust of more subtle language. Again, they don't want to become 'talk therapy.'

This mistrust of language was set out in most detail by Fritz Mauthner whose massive *Beitrage zu einer Kritik der Sprache* (*Contributions to a Critique of Language*), 1902, had a huge influence on German philosophers and psychologists but has never been translated into English. Mauthner's main points as set out in an article by Linda Ben-Zui, 1980, are a useful guide to and warning about the use of language in psychotherapy (and elsewhere). They are:

1. Thinking and speaking are one activity
2. Language and memory are synonymous
3. All language is metaphor
4. There are no absolutes
5. The ego is contingent; it does not exist apart from language
6. Communication between men is impossible
7. The only language must be simple language
8. The highest forms of a critique of language are laughter and silence.

Modern neuroscience can dispose of points 1 and 2. Thinking in the sense of problem-solving at least can be non-verbal and demonstrably involve mainly nonverbal circuits in the brain. Recognition memory does not require verbal thought, visual-spatial immediate and delayed memory are demonstrable, and procedural memory is not verbal. Furthermore, the experiments of Benjamin Libert and others suggest that humans make decisions and begin to act a fraction of a second before any verbalised awareness of this occurs. As well as calling into question free will, this suggests that non-verbal thought or some equivalent of it is occurring.

In claiming (point 3) that *all* language is metaphor, Mauthner meant that any word or set of words is transferred ('metaphor' comes from the Greek word for 'transport') by the mind from language to something in the outside world which is *not* language, and so language is independent of reality. But we do not normally use the word 'metaphor' for such a huge dysjunction. Instead we use it for quite concrete meanings, either for bodily events (as in 'my heart sank') or for observable events ('Joe has dropped his girlfriend' or 'for me mathematics is a blind alley').

Points 4, 5 and 6 amount to a philosophical claim that consciousness depends on language. Again, neuroscience refutes this. Animals, and probably even micro-organisms, are conscious or at least aware. Perhaps this is why nobody now reads, or even translates Mauthner. And of course the fact that he wrote thousands of pages of language to deny that language has any meaning beyond itself can seem comic. But his ideas are a useful warning against treating language as if it is the only reality. (Mauthner was not a solipsist: he knew there was a reality out there, beyond language). Talk therapies can take off from reality into a self-referring world in which language is used by the therapist to control the language of the client in deciding what is rational. I have encountered many people who have undergone Cognitive Behavioural Therapy / CBT (and some practitioners of it) who describe it as 'brain-washing'. For example a person from a minority group may be taught that his or her fears of persecution are 'irrational' when in fact they are not. Psychoanalysis has also been guilty of similar brain-washing in providing verbal interpretations of non-verbal emotions or sensations. At the other extreme, social constructionism identifies and labels power imbalances and social control mediated by language. But both CBT and social constructionism ignore or distort biology.

The 'psychology' dimension of Neurodynamic Psychotherapy consists, I think, of relating language (whatever is said) to the physical (whatever is felt). Rather than 'explaining away' from the physical through interpretation or argument, it can 'explain towards' it. Taking Mauthner's point 3, it can relate metaphor to bodily experience. Taking point 7, it can keep language *simple*. And as for point 8, who can deny that silence and laughter have their place in any psychotherapy that aims to resolve linguistic or biological conundrums?

Conversely, Mauthner's implied warning can be heeded: psychological discourse in the psychotherapy cannot be allowed to take off and detach itself from the physical and the emotional – from pulsation.

Perhaps the role of language in Neurodynamic Psychotherapy can be, as in poetry, 'feeling thought'.

Social

This book does not discuss the social world. But it is a truism that society aims to control the biological. Reich's *The Mass Psychology of Fascism* provides as much insight into the modern phenomenon of Jihadism as it did into the phenomenon of Nazism. Society, acting through institutions and through families, becomes a kind of ideology factory in which personal desires are first thwarted as if in a dam and then diverted into big social ideas. Pulsation and its associated freedom of emotions and thoughts must be suppressed if a person is to become hardened (armoured) for the battles for social survival, social dominance, or social dominance presented as social survival. As Ferdinand Mount pointed out in his book *The Subversive Family,* personal emotions and attachments are a danger to totalitarianism or, at a less extreme level, social conformity. It is not realistic to expect the state to provide Neurodynamic Psychotherapy, any more than such things as poetry, music, and love.

A Practical View of Neurodynamic Psychotherapy

Neurodynamic Psychotherapy provides the necessary but so far unused connection between psychotherapy and neuroscience. It implements Luria's unrealised goal of a monistic psychotherapy – i.e. one that does not separate mind from body. In its body oriented work it draws on the methods of Reich and his followers, with the 'energy' concept set aside and replaced by the neural network and with a focus on pulsation as the criterion of life and of healthy functioning. Its incorporation of psychotherapeutic methods based on language (psychoanalysis, psychodrama, counselling) is less clear. How will it work in practical terms? What will the patient or client experience?

The development of Neurodynamic Psychotherapy will depend on the experience of patients/clients as well as of psychotherapists. As explained above, I think much work can be done without psychotherapists. A person working on their own or with a companion can use methods of the kind discussed in *Emotional First Aid* and *Couple Dynamics.* There are traps and dangers in signing up to psychotherapy with a professional who may, perhaps unwittingly, be part of the psychotherapy industry or the mental health industry – at their worst not even industries but rackets promising salvation at the cost of money, emotional dependence, or drug dependence. And in intensive psychotherapy the problem of positive transference – the therapist falling in love with or becoming attracted to his or her client – is difficult to resolve on both sides. Nevertheless, at times a person may arrive at a point where he or she needs help. In which case, if Neurodynamic Psychotherapy is the approach used, and since it requires knowledge across the bio-psycho-social spectrum, it will be necessary to work with a psychiatrist, medical doctor, or clinical psychologist trained in this approach. In my view, the practice of Neurodynamic Psychotherapy should also be open to properly trained practitioners of osteopathy and physiotherapy, and possibly to other clinical professions like occupational therapy and counselling. In the last analysis, it is the character and integrity of the therapist that count most – as is demonstrated in many studies of psychotherapy outcomes. However, the days of psychotherapeutic 'schools' centred around individual teachers are numbered, and inevitably in an era where increasingly 'anything goes', practitioners of Neurodynamic Psychotherapy, like other psychotherapists, will have to be regulated by their various professional bodies which impose legally enforced codes of ethics, to protect both client and therapist.

It is sometimes said that psychotherapy is 'a relationship about relationships' – a kind of meta-relationship in which 'transference' and emotional issues can be explored in partnership. (Cognitive-behavioural therapy plays it safe by eliminating any aspect of a 'relationship' from the therapy, but this artificial limit can seem inhuman, the therapy which is already mechanistic, becomes more so, and the client feels ignored.) The expression of emotion and the opening up of intimate stories can swiftly turn the 'meta-relationship' into a real one. Paradoxically, the more open emotionally the client and therapist are, and the more effective the therapy, the more likely it will crash into a tormented personal relationship. Sometimes an effective therapy must be terminated by either client or therapist to avoid this dénouement.

It can be argued that properly trained psychotherapists in the analytic tradition and its derivatives can work through any problems that arise through 'transference', and indeed turn this transference (in which the client sees the therapist as a mother or father or lover) to positive ends. Having supervised dozens of psychotherapists who have been analytically trained, I think this is wishful thinking. Therapists and clients fall in love, or are sexually attracted to each other, or at a gut level dislike each other. Being super-aware of possible transference may even backfire. On a rather superficial level, admittedly, the educationalist A S Neill left anecdotes about the psychoanalyst Wilhelm Stekel who had a practice in London in the 1930s. One day Neill arrived at Stekel's door as a woman was coming out. He asked Stekel if this had been Stekel's wife. Stekel replied: 'So you want to sleep with my wife!' On another occasion, Neill asked to go to the lavatory and Stekel said: 'So you want to sit on the master's throne!'

Reich's methods introduced a new risk of transference problems by including touch. But it is worth emphasising in this age when unregulated 'therapists' offer so-called 'tantric therapy', 'yoni massage', and 'lingam massage', along with straightforward prostitution, that even in the early days of character analysis and orgone therapy, although the work involved manipulation of muscles, this never included touching the patient's genitals. Reich remarked that this was one taboo which his therapy respected.

Nevertheless, the accusation emerged that because Reichian therapy aimed to elicit the orgasm reflex, the therapist 'gave the patient orgasms' – either in the therapy itself, or in the orgone accumulator. This accusation became a stick to beat Reich with, wielded often by political enemies who felt threatened by the possibilities of personal and sexual freedom which Reich's work encouraged. After all, he had demonstrated in *The Mass Psychology of Fascism* that totalitarianism flourished under conditions of sexual repression. His books were banned and burned by the Nazis in 1931, along with Freud's. And in the 1950s the main attackers of Reich on account of his orgone theory were closet members of the Communist Party and controlled from Moscow. (Reich was accused of a paranoid delusion in thinking this, but it turns out to be true, as documented even by Chrisopher Turner's hostile *Adventures in the Orgasmotron*).

As mentioned in Chapter 1, Reich told Myron Sharaf that it should be possible to do orgone therapy without touching the patient. However for most of his therapeutic career he used used various hands-on methods of applying pressure selectively to tense muscles to work through various blocks to the breathing pulsation. This was *not*, as some accounts assert, 'massage', with its connotations of giving people pleasure or relaxation, and it could be painful. Reich once said, 'When I see amour I want to smash it.' However, one result of these methods, often applied quite aggressively by Reich and his successors (and I have used them myself), was that they opened up sensations of pleasurable 'streamings' and tender emotions. Undoubtedly this introduced another level of transference, an intimacy of sorts, which had eventually to be worked through. In *Emotional First Aid*, I proposed a very limited set of procedures including touch (for example, massaging the back of the neck so that the head could fall backwards in giving into crying). And in *Couple Dynamics* I proposed a method where the couple, who were already intimate, could apply touch.

In Neurodynamic Psychotherapy, I follow Reich's own late idea that touch is not necessary. I do, however, in some cases where the client has chronic muscular blocks which would benefit from some mechanical releasing, refer the client for a session or two with an osteopath colleague who has trained in Reichian methods. This kind of working partnership between a psychotherapist and a physically oriented therapist (osteopath, physiotherapist) can be useful, especially in Brief Neurodyamic Psychotherapy.

My current prospectus for 'Brief Neurodynamic Psychotherapy' includes the following summary:

> My approach in psychotherapy is 'neurodynamic'. The 'neuro' part of this word refers to the nervous system – not only the brain but the entire 'neural network' that governs both voluntary and involuntary attention and movement. 'Dynamic' refers traditionally to action and reaction, but neuroscience increasingly sees dynamics as relational interaction – between ourselves and others, as well as within ourselves between conflicting emotions and thoughts.

> The key functions in neurodynamic psychotherapy are attention, contact, and pulsation – all of which can become impaired when we are under stress in emotional and relational dilemmas, or when our spirits are low.

> Attention underlies all neuropsychological functioning.

(When it is impaired, so is memory, awareness of sensation, and sustained emotion or thought.) The neurodynamic approach encourages the client to pay attention to every moment, as in 'mindfulness', but also intensifies it through work with the breathing and bodily movement.

Contact with others, as in sustained eye contact, perception and responsiveness, is attention turned outwards to the other, and again it can be impaired by emotional 'blocks'. Neurodynamic Psychotherapy focuses on contact in terms of relational dynamics.

The pulsation of the breathing is what keeps us alive, but it is impaired by blocks to contact and to free movement, in the form of chronically immobilised muscles which prevent the lively expression of emotion, and in turn awareness of feelings and of 'forbidden' or self-censored thoughts.

This psychotherapy offers the client a free and open space and time in which to pay attention, to enter into contact with self and other, mind and body, and to allow a more open breathing pulsation.

The most intense human pulsation can be experienced in orgasm. Neurodynamic Psychotherapy does not involve sexual experience or exploration, but it does include discussion of sexual experience, and its direct work to dissolve blocks to the breathing pulsation and to the expression of emotions can lead to a more full pulsation in orgasm.

The goal of the therapy is to advance the client to as full an experience of pulsation as possible for him or her. Pulsation is the observable measure of a more intense emotional, thinking, and relational life.

It is useful to attend wearing loose-fitting clothes, since

working with pulsation is body-oriented and you will be asked in most sessions to spend some time lying on a couch paying attention to breathing and movement. This is not a hands-on therapy, and there is no massage or touching, but you may be asked to make voluntary movements or to tighten muscles, as well as to let go to involuntary movement while staying on the couch.

The course of attendance is limited to from 10 to 20 weekly one hour sessions. These can be followed by one-off consultations, but this method encourages independence and a guided Do It Yourself / DIY approach, with the client doing much of the work outside the sessions. This 'home-work' can be done alone or with a partner, using reminder notes which are provided.

The course of psychotherapy can itself be undergone either individually or as a couple. If you attend as a couple, each of you will be encouraged to observe and comment on the other's breathing and movements, and in some cases to encourage these through touch.

This brief and time-limited psychotherapy does not offer a cure for 'mental illness'. The client is expected to be in fair health, and not to be currently taking psychotropic medications (e.g. anti-depressants, anxiolytics) that can restrict emotion. However the work may help the client deal with depressed or anxious mood, whether situational or long-term.

APPENDIX

Pulsation 'Home-work' in Brief Neurodynamic Psychotherapy

The word 'therapy' is from the ancient Greek word for an attendant, and it can be achieved through a careful attention to oneself. Ideally a person – or perhaps a couple, or a group of friends – can work towards a full experience of life's core function, pulsation, using books, talks or videos as a guide. It is not necessary to hand oneself over to the power of another. Where an outside perspective is needed, clinical specialists or therapists can offer their services as coaches – giving occasional advice, pointing to resources, but not becoming part of the person's life. These explorations can also be the 'home-work' part of neurodynamic psychotherapy with a clinician.

Here I am referring to healthy people or perhaps the 'worried well'. The capacity to pay attention is dependent on neurological intactness. And Reich, referring to a tall story by Baron Munchausen, joked that self-therapy was like pulling oneself out of a swamp by one's own hair.

The couples exercises given given below involve a laying on of hands, but not a painful or aggressive one. Self-therapy can benefit from input from an outside observer. The texts provided below are used as hand-outs in my own practice of Brief Neurodynamic Psychotherapy. They are set out for couples. They can be easily adapted to work on one's own, but in this case they may be less effective unless the person attends also for individual brief psychotherapy.

These explorations originate in the therapeutic methods of Wilhelm Reich. For a detailed explanation of his concepts of 'character armour' and his ways of working through it in therapy, see the chapter section 'The Expressive Language of the Living in Orgone Therapy', in his *Selected Writings*. Neurodynamic Psychotherapy does not use Reich's language of 'life energy', but Reich's own summary of his method in this 40 page chapter is the original text which lies behind subsequent developments such as Neurodynamic Psychotherapy.

The explorations are set out here as four sessions, but these sessions may be broken down into shorter ones. There are no 'rules' beyond these basic considerations:

1. Only do these explorations with someone who already knows you intimately, preferably someone with whom you already have a sexual relationship. (Otherwise you will give too much of yourself to someone you may not trust).
2. If you do the explorations, over a number of sessions, it is best to complete the series of sessions as 'worker' before switching roles to 'helper.'
3. The worker is in control – not the helper. He/she can stop the proceedings at any time, without explanation.
4. The worker decides what to reveal. He/she does *not* need to provide the *content/information* behind any emotional expression. (One of the most helpful interventions of my first training therapist Jean Ambrosi was to say 'pas de commentaires!' 'No need for commentary!' You can simultaneously feel and think without having to report on it.)
5. If you decide to do these explorations alone (which is easily possible, although obviously interventions that require touch from another person are not feasible) it is a good idea to have another trusted person in the same house in case you find yourself emotionally fragile and need support.
6. Some people may show signs of hyperventilation during deep breathing: speeding of the breath, panting – and in extreme cases so-called 'tetany' of the hands in which they gradually become fixed in a clench. The standard first aid remedy for hyperventilation is to have the person breathe into a paper bag (NOT a plastic one, which can suffocate them) so as to reduce oxygen intake. But this is unlikely to be necessary: it is almost always effective to ask the person to make eye contact, to hold their hands, and encourage them to SLOW their breathing down. [If working on your own it is also

effective to SLOW your breathing down. Another remedy is to hold your breath for as long as you can at the end of the OUT-BREATH, then to breathe in very slowly several times and AVOID GASPING for breath. Then discontinue the session until your breathing has returned completely to 'normal'.]

7. If the worker feels 'electric shock' type of sensations in your hands or elsewhere, STOP the exercise. (Soft tingling sensations are different and can be allowed to happen.) If the worker feels any muscles beginning to cramp, they should STOP the exercise, get up and stretch, then resume or postpone to another occasion.

To do these explorations all you need is a quiet setting and a mattress to lie on, preferably on the floor (you might otherwise risk falling out of bed). Wear loose clothes (no belt or tight buttons) or underclothes.

The instructions below are written to the helper. They can be adapted for use alone.

When mentioning the worker I avoid the clumsiness of 'he/she' and 'his /hers' by using 'they' or 'them'.

These instructions are written as for a right-handed helper but can of course be modified for left-handers.

SESSION A: MAKING CONTACT

1:1   Ask the worker to **lie on their back, knees up, feet flat.** Sit on their right side on a cushion or low chair.

1:2   Ask **how they feel.**

1:3   **Observe their eyes.**

1:4   Ask the worker to **look at you** for a few seconds, then **look away.** Alternate a few times.

1:5   **Share your impressions** of the worker's eyes: what you see and sense in them.

1:6 Observe the position of the head.

1:7 Observe the face: Shape? Mask? Expression?

1:8 Share impressions.

1:9 Observe the body: Inflated? (chest high, back arched) Deflated? (chest low, body folded forward). Shape? Complexion? Disparities.

1:10 Share impressions.

1:11 Observe breathing: Chest moving? **Abdomen** moving? **Depth, speed, pauses.**

1:13 Observe pelvis and legs: Pulled back? Pulled forward? Loose? Tight? Still? Moving?

1:14 Share impressions.

2:1 Position as in 1:1 above. Ask the worker to **close the eyes** and keep them closed, **breathe in through the mouth, breathe out immediately** and fully with an **Aaaaah** sound, and to **pause** before breathing in again.

2:2 Put **one hand** on the worker's **forehead,** the **other hand under the neck. Tilt the worker's head slightly back.**

2:3 **Squeeze cheeks gently** to open mouth wide. Press chin gently downward without changing to back tilt of the head.

2:4 **Press gently down on chest** with each outbreath, using one hand clasped over the other and pressing down on the sternum, and without pushing past resistance encourage the worker to **let their chest down.**

2:5   **After 12 or so presses, pause** and ask the worker to keep on breathing fully out. **Observe.** Ask them to open their eyes. **Make eye contact.** Briefly, how do they feel? Ask them to close the eyes again.

2:6   Slide your left **hand under the small of the back,** put right **hand on abdomen between the ribs and the navel.** Ask the worker to breathe in fully under your right hand. Ask them to **relax into** your **hand under the back** every time they beathe out. Make sure they breathe out fully making an **Aaaaah** sound. Continue for about ten breaths.

2:7   Withdraw hand from under the back. Move right **hand to lower abdomen** between navel and pubis. Ask the worker to **breathe in fully** under this hand.

2:8   **Observe the breathing** and encourage the worker to **fill with breath from the abdomen up** and to **empty the breath from the chest down.**

2:9   Ask the explorer **keep breathing in this extended way** and to **move the knees in and out** slowly: open to the widest extent, close until the knees touch. Ask them to synchronise this movement with their breathing, **opening as they breathe in, closing as they breathe out.** Ask them to **find** the position **where the legs are most shaky** (approx. 45 degree angle), to **keep the legs in this position** and **not to stop the vibration: let go to it.**

2:10   Ask the worker to open their eyes and **look at you while breathing fully out.**

2:11   Ask them to **describe** their emotions and **bodily sensations.**

2:12   Share impressions. **Be in contact** before stopping.

FEAR

1:1 Ask the worker to **breathe out with an audible sigh,** establish a breathing rhythm with the **emphasis on the out-breath.**

1:2 Ask them to **track your finger.** Move it freely, about twelve inches above the eyes, in wide circles or zigzags for about a minute. If the worker moves their head with the eyes, ask them to follow the finger with their nose for a few seconds, but then to keep their head still and continue to track with their eyes only. If they cannot do this, DISCONTINUE the fear exercise.

[Problems with free eye movement suggest anxiety and the person may find it useful to consult a specialist in EMDR – Eye Movement Desensitization and Reprocessing – a therapy – or a neurodynamic psychotherapist.]

1:3 Ask the explorer while still tracking your finger to **imitate fear by opening the eyes wide.**

1:4 Ask them to relax again and stop the tracking exercise.

1:5 Have them imitate **freezing fear:** open the eyes **wide while looking at the ceiling, breathe in sharply,** raise the eyebrows, breathe into the upper chest with a gasp, look at the ceiling, and **hold the breath for a moment** then let go.

1:6 Ask them to **repeat this exercise** and in the phase of holding their breath to **either press** their **hands back into the mat by their sides or to raise their hands with fingers open and palms outward,** as if warding you off.

1:7 Ask them to make a **sound,** but **not to force it.**

1:8   Ask them to **show you fear, to look at your eyes. Open your own eyes wide as if in fear.**

1:9   Ask them to **push both palms upward** against one of your hands, to **look at you** and to breathe in and out **exaggeratedly.**

1:10   If this produces feelings of panic, have the worker **show it in their eyes, first looking at the ceiling, then looking at you.**

[To sum up: you ask the worker to open their eyes wide – raise the eyebrows – open the mouth wide – gasp sharply into the upper chest – freeze – push against your hand – make a sound – breathe fast and high – show fear in their eyes looking at the ceiling – show fear in their eyes looking at you.]

1:11   Ask the worker to **relax** after nine or ten of these fear breaths. **Be reassuring. Hold their hand** if this feels right.

1:12   **Discuss** if the worker 'flashed' on any particular incident.

1:13   **Discuss** this exploration in general.

ANGER

2:1   Ask the worker to **imitate anger,** as if acting it, without any special breathing.

2:2   Emphasise that no-one is going to get carried away. Emphasise two basic rules: **worker stays on the mat at all times,** and **worker does not touch the guide.**

2:3   Ask the worker to **close their eyes tight** and **breathe out sharply, clenching their fists** each time they **breathe out** and **making a sharp sound.**

2:4   Ask them to **relax** this action each time they **breathe in.** Continue for some minutes.

2:5   **Take a break,** without discussion.

2:6   Give the worker a **towel to hold in both hands,** hands close together and touching, twisting from opposite directions. Tell them to **twist hard.**

2:7   At the same time, ask the worker to **breathe out** and **make a sound.**

2:8   Ask them to **frown** and **focus their eyes on the towel,** and to knot their brows.

2:9   Ask them to **stick their jaw forward** while still making a sound.

        [To sum up: on each out-breath the worker will narrowly focus their eyes – knot the brow in a frown – stick the jaw forward – make a loud sound (growl or roar) – twist hard on the towel.]

2:10   After nine or ten breaths, **take a break.**

2:10a   Variation: ask the worker to put the towel aside and **make fists,** then to **breathe in fully while raising fists high** in the air and to **hold the breath while clenching the fists tightly – for 10 seconds or so.** Then **release the breath, thump both fists down** on the mat by their sides and **yell: 'No!'** Make sure the worker keeps their **eyes focused on a single point on the ceiling.**

2:11   Ask the worker to **show anger in their eyes,** directed **to your eyes,** and to **shout: 'I hate this!'** or **'I've had enough!'**

2:12   **Pause.**

2:13   Ask the worker to **stick their jaw forward** and with your **thumb, press firmly against their chin.** Ask them to **keep pushing against your thumb** and to say **'I won't!',** with you replying, **'You will!'**

2:14   Take a break. Discuss.

LONGING

3:1   With the worker in the usual position, knees up and feet flat, small of back relaxed into the mat, head tilted slightly back (as if freeing the airway in CPR), **encourage them to breathe for a while in an extended way, being sure to emphasise the OUT-breath.** Instruct the worker to: '**BREATHE OUT counting to yourself 1, 2, 3, 4, 5, then HOLD for a second, then BREATHE IN (don't gasp) counting 1, 2, 3 then turn the breath around immediately and breathe OUT.'** Or count out loud for them.

[NOTE: The breathing pulsation at rest in all animals and in babies is longer phase on the outbreath, then a slight pause, then a shorter inbreath and an immediate turn-around to the outbreath. The ratio is approximately 3 out to 2 in. In adult humans this is often disturbed because of chronic 'armouring' against emotions which have either caused distress or been suppressed by other people. This armouring is in its own way natural, and even useful, but needs to be 'disposable.']

3:2   **Now, as the worker breathes out, ask them to fix a point on the ceiling and try to reach it with their hands. The palms should be turned inwards and reach up as far as the worker can on each OUTBREATH.** Encourage the worker to **Let the chest-wall collapse downwards as they reach up.**

3:3   Encourage the worker to **Make a sound while doing this: Aaaah, or Ooooh! BREATHE OUT ALL THE WAY, then gently in, then turn the breath around instantly and again BREATHE OUT ALL THE WAY MAKING A SOUND AND REACHING.**

3:4   After ten or so breaths, the worker can **PAUSE. Take stock.**

GRIEF

4:1   Ask the worker to **imitate grief.**

4:2   Ask them to **look around** the walls **longingly** and **slowly, allowing their head to move as if they are following their eyes with their nose,** stretching their vision to the edge of its range, **changing direction** occasionally, searching slowly.

4:3   Ask them to **sigh out on each out-breath,** making an **Ooooh** sound, keeping the head back.

4:4   Ask them to **squeeze their eyes tight** on each **out-breath.**

4:5   Give them a pillow to hold and tell them to **squeeze the pillow gently** on each out-breath.

4:6   Ask them to **roll over** on their side and **draw up their knees.**

4:7   Encourage them to **breathe out** fully. Say 'Don't breathe in' at the end of each outbreath, so that they linger before breathing in.

4:8   **Massage the back of their neck gently.**

4:9   **Press** gently **along the sides of their spine** each time the worker breathes out.

       [To sum up: ask the worker to sigh out with an Ooooh sound – to squeeze the eyes tight – to squeeze a pillow – to pause at the end of each out-breath – let the body fold forward – let the head fall back.]

4:10   Ask the worker to **imitate sobbing** from the chest with an **'aho-aho-aho-aho'** sound. **Imitate with them.**

4:11   Take their shoulders and **gently rock them** back and forth.

4:12   Make sure the worker's **mouth is open,** press the cheeks in gently.

4:13   Make sure the **neck 'gives',** head coming back.

4:14   **Comfort** the worker gently but let them 'hide' if they feel like it.

4:15   Ask them to 'come back' when ready, **make eye contact,** discuss.

JOY

5:1   Ask the worker to **stand** and find a path for **walking around the room.**

5:2   Ask them to **walk slowly** and **go with gravity.**

5:3   Ask them to do the following, progressively: let the **head hang forward** – let **the mouth hang open** – keep **sighing out, audibly** – let the **shoulders droop forward** – let the **arms hang down** – let the **chest collapse** inward – let the **pelvis come forward** – walk **more and more slowly.**

Ask them to walk like this for a few minutes.

5:5   Ask them to do the following, progressively: begin to put a **spring into their step** – begin to **bounce slightly** as they walk – begin to **straighten up the pelvis and lower trunk** – begin to **breathe in more** – bring the **shoulders back** – pull up to **full height** – begin to **swing arms** and **open hands** – bring **head up** – **smile** – **look around** the room with **wide open eyes** – breathe fully in and out and say 'Ha!' **on each out-breath** – do **anything else** that comes to mind – **tell you how they are feeling.**

5:6   **Discuss.**

1:1   Ask the worker to **find a position** on the mat, **following their first instincts** – whatever they want.

1:2   Ask them to **take stock:** what are they aware of **in their body?** Any tension or pain?

1:3   Ask them to **describe** what they are most aware of and to **focus** in **on one particularly prominent area.**

1:4   Ask the worker to **intensify tension in the area,** to follow whatever urge they have, so long as the tension is increased.

1:5   Ask them to **maintain the tension** just short of intolerable discomfort. (Do not let them push into severe pain, ask them to back off from it). Tension may be maintained for up to twenty minutes or so.

1:6   Tell them, if they feel another tension developing elsewhere, to wait until it is as severe as the first and then **shift the attention to this new area, intensify it, and maintain it.**

1:7   Tell them, if they feel the **urge to spontaneous movement** to **pay attention** to it, and when it begins to be irresistible, to **go with it.**

1:8   If the **movement is continual, do not interfere** except in the interests of safety. Encourage the worker to stay on the mat.

1:9   If the **movement is frantic** and seems potentially dangerous, **call the worker by name, make eye contact,** and ask them to **slow down.**

1:10   If the **movement is very rapid** or seems potentially **exhausting,** suggest the worker **slows down.**

[Insist that they stop if the session goes over an hour.]

1:11   While the worker is maintaining tension **watch for signs of slackening** and **encourage them to persist** (short of pain).

1:12   **Discourage continued reportage** but every few minutes ask if they want to **make a brief statement of feeling.**

1:13   If nothing happens within twenty minutes or so, suggest that the worker **moves slowly into a position** which seems to them **opposite** to the one they have been in.

1:14   After a few minutes in the new position, ask them to **move slowly back to the original position.** After a few minutes, suggest they **move slowly to the opposite position again.** If nothing happens in the way of spontaneous movement, suggest they finish the exploration, stopping in the more extreme position.

1:15   If spontaneous movement is toward an opposite position to the one the worker has been in, **encourage exploration of the second position** or of the **alternation between both.**

1:16   If spontaneous movement is toward a **new intensification** position, **do not interfere,** do **observe.**

1:17   After the session, **make eye contact** and **hold hands** for a while.

SESSION D: WORKING THROUGH BLOCKS.

[This can be done in one long session, provided a particular phase does not become absorbing. Alternatively one or two 'segments' can be taken in a session. However later (lower) segments should not be undertaken before the early segments have been gone through at least once. In particular make sure the eyes ('ocular segment') are free and the worker not prone to undue anxiety: the worker must be capable of making and sustaining eye contact with you, the helper.]

OCULAR SEGMENT

1:1   Ask the worker to **roll their eyes around, stretch** their gaze out to the sides, breathing out audibly with an 'Aaaaah' for a few minutes.

1:2   Ask them to **look at you** and **tell them what emotion you see** in their eyes.

1:3   Kneel behind the worker's head and move your finger (or a pencil or pen) around about twelve inches above their face, asking them to **track it with the eyes only,** not moving the head. **Make sure they continue breathing fully, without gasping on the in-breath, and prolonging the out-breath with a slight pause before the in-breath.** Continue for about five minutes.

1:4   Ask the worker to **let the head move with the eyes and to track as if with the end of the nose.** Provided this is not painful, continue for a further five minutes or so.

1:5   Ask them to move their **hands and feet** as if running on the spot, **making continuous sound while tracking.**

1:6   Urge them to **give in to any involuntary movement** so long as you judge it safe.

1:7   Ask the worker to return to **lying quietly** on their back, and make a few slow passes around for them to **track with their eyes only.**

1:8   Ask the worker to **look at you** and **tell you how they feel.**

ORAL SEGMENT

2:1   Ask the worker to **make faces:** to open the mouth as wide as possible, close it tight, press lips together, stick lips forward, draw lips back, pull jaw back, and stick jaw forward – while **keeping breathing** – and to **exaggerate** any expression you notice coming through and can identify to them.

2:2 **Press down gently on the jaw,** ask the worker to **push their jaw forward against your hand.**

2:3 Ask the worker to **bite** down hard on a **towel, while breathing out through clenched teeth,** vigorously, while **squeezing their eyes shut** and **clenching their fists on each out-breath.** Then as they **breathe in, let go** of squeezing and biting, then resume each time they breathe out.

2:4 Ask the worker to breathe quietly, look around while **gently moving lips, mouth and jaw,** making a soft sound 'wawawawa....'

2:5 Ask the worker to **scream,** while **squeezing the eyes shut** [this prevents accidental damage to blood vessels while screaming] **raising open hands in the air and shaking them,** and with head tilted back to **open the mouth** in a big square shape.

2:6 **Make eye contact. Discuss.**

THROAT SEGMENT

3:1 Ask the worker to **make an open sound while breathing out,** and to find the position of the tongue that makes the sound most open.

3:2 Ask them to **mobilize their tongue** while making sounds – licking their lips, sticking their tongue out, stretching it, curling it, then to adopt the **optimum position:** tongue tip against palate just above upper front teeth, and maintain this while **sighing out, Aaaah…**

3:3 An alternative, or further exploration to mobilize the tongue is to have the worker **curl the tongue down over the lower lip while making a sound.**

3:4 Ask the worker to **choke a towel,** holding **both hands close and twisting from opposite directions** and to **make the sound**

louder and as open as possible.

3:5   If attempts to make a loud sound produce strangled or forced noises, ask the worker to back off from the sound and make the **loudest sound they can do easily.** Make sure they **continue the sound,** even quietly, **to the end of each out-breath.** If making the sound is difficult try having them **breathe under your hand resting gently on their diaphragm area** and to **drive the sound from that point** while **breathing out.**

3:6   **Pause. Discuss.**

3:7   Ask the worker to **gag,** to let the **head tilt back,** to **breathe out** with a sigh; then toward the end of the out-breath to **stick their middle finger down their mouth** and **touch the back of the throat gently** until the gag reflex comes without coughing and without swallowing. [They will not actually vomit].

3:8   **Make eye contact.**

CHEST SEGMENT

4:1   Ask the worker to lie **face down, their face turned to one side.**

4:2   Ask them to **sigh out audibly.**

4:3   Ask them to **keep their neck loose.**

4:4   **Press down with the heels of your hand on the muscles beside the spine** each time the worker **breathes out.** [Do not push on the kidney area or on the spine itself.] Encourage the worker to **make an open sound** as you do this and to **prolong the out-breath.**

4:5   Encourage the worker to **kick for a while,** banging the front of each leg down alternately, moving them **from the hip-joint,** keeping the **knees straight.**

4:6   Ask the worker to turn over and **lie with their knees up and to keep the chest moving** with the breathing, and to put the emphasis on **breathing out all the way.** Keep encouraging the worker to **let the chest down,** to breathe **out** more than usual, and to **pause at the end of each out-breath.**

4:7   After one or two minutes, ask the worker to keep breathing while they **wriggle the shoulders** up and down, then **wriggle the pelvis** up and down, then **roll the head back and up again**, and finally wriggle all over in random way.

4:8   Stop all movement and ask the worker to concentrate again on letting the **chest down** all the way **with the out-breath**, and to **give into anything that happens.** Caution them **not to make** anything happen, and **not to stop** anything happening. Encourage them to keep **breathing out** and to 'follow through' You may help the chest movement downward by pressing with the heels of your hands on the upper chest with each out-breath.

4:9   *For inflated chest:* Straddle the worker on your knees, take their hands, and **lift their upper body toward you each time they breathe out,** asking them to **let their head hang back.** Have them **breathe out fully** as you do this.

4:10   Altenatively, ask them to **reach** up high toward the ceiling, **with hands, mouth and eye-gaze** on each out-breath, retracting them on the in-breath.

4:11   *For deflated chest:* Ask the worker to **stand up and swing the arms** and to **keep breathing.**

4:12   With the worker lying on their back, have them **breathe into the upper chest,** moving the **shoulders back on the in-breath, forward on the out-breath.** If they show signs of anger, encourage the anger exploration.

DIAPHRAGM SEGMENT

5:1   The diaphragm muscle cannot be directly reached by hand, but can be best mobilized by gagging. It can also be mobilized by work with the muscles around the waist area. Ask the worker to **lie face down**, and look for a 'belt' of raised muscle around their back. **Put pressure with your knuckles on this 'belt'** while the worker **breathes out.**

5:2   With the worker lying on their back, **massage gently along the line of the lower ribs** (if this hurts, stop). **Press down gently** on upper abdomen **with each out-breath.**

ABDOMINAL SEGMENT

6:1   **Press down gently** with fingertips **along base of diaphragm** just above navel or just inside the hip bones. **Span the abdomen** at a level just below the navel **with your thumb and fingers and press down gently massaging each time the worker breathes out.**

6:2   Try **tickling the flanks** and along the base of the ribs, while the worker keeps breathing. [Pre-arrange a stop signal: e.g. 'Enough!']

6:3   Make sure the worker is **breathing down into the abdomen** before stopping. [Of course respiration takes place in the lungs, not the abdomen, but as the diaphragm moves down on the in-breath, the intestines are pushed down and the belly comes out. The belly has to be soft for this to work fully.]

PELVIC SEGMENT

7:1   Ask the worker to **pull the pelvis back when breathing in,** and let it come **up and forward while breathing out.** The **lower back**, behind the waist, **should stay down.** You can slide your hand palm upwards under the back and ask the worker to press down against it. There is no need for the worker to push on the feet.

7:2   Ask the worker to do the **same movements,** but with the feet pushed down and the **pelvis hanging** several inches above the mat.

7:3 With the pelvis still above the mat, ask the worker to **breathe fully down into the abdomen,** and without deliberate pushing, let the breathing move the pelvis as much as possible. Make sure they **breathe in from the bottom up, breathe out from the top down.**

7:4 Ask the worker to **thump the pelvis** up and down on the mat, to bang the buttocks down hard then thrust the pelvis up as high as possible, to keep breathing with the feet firmly planted on the mat and the mouth wide open, letting out a **continuous sound.**

7:5 Ask the worker to **roll over on to their stomach. Press down with the heels of both hands on the upper buttocks,** holding the hip joints down on the mat while the worker **kicks vigorously** up and down, slamming the front of the legs and knees into the mat, **keeping the legs straight.** As they kick, remind them to make a **loud sound and keep breathing.** Ask them to shout out anything that comes to mind.

7:6 [Take a brief break]. Ask the worker to **roll over onto their back,** knees up, and **breathe easily into the abdomen.**

7:7 Ask the worker to **open their knees wide** and **join the soles of their feet,** heels lightly pressing together, balls of the feet together. Encourage a light, constant pressure between the feet. Keep **upper body relaxed,** back let down into the mat (not arched), head falling easily back, neck loose, **breathing low in the abdomen,** easily, without forcing.

7:8 Have the worker **breathe along** in this way for about three to five minutes. Make sure breathing is steady, but not intensified.

7:9 Ask the worker to **raise the knees slowly,** and to **let the feet roll**

flat onto the mat but still touching at the sides, knees held at about a 20 degree angle.

7:10 Tell the worker **not to stop any trembling** or vibration of the legs. (If the worker becomes anxious, tell them to stretch their legs straight and push away with their heels). Encourage them to accept involuntary movements.

7:11 **Take a break.**

7:12 *For the inflated (tucked back) pelvis:* **Put one hand under the worker's back** and ask them to **push down hard on your hand as they breathe out,** then to **release the back upward** and away from your hand as they **breathe in.**

7:13 Ask the worker to **bang the pelvis hard on the mat, pushing it upward vigorously in between bangs, making angry sounds.**

7:14 Ask the worker to **turn over on their stomach and pound their genital area against a pillow.**

7:15 Reverse this and have them **thrust the pelvis upward, hard,** toward the ceiling, **on each out-breath,** making sounds.

7:16 *For the deflated (held forward) pelvis:* ask the worker to **breathe against your hand under their back, and emphasise the pulling back of the pelvis** as the abdomen fills **on the in-breath.**

7:17 Pelvic banging as in **7:13,** emphasis on the **movement backward** of the pelvis.

7:18 *Pelvic floor:* Ask the worker to **concentrate their attention on the pelvic floor without moving** and to describe what they feel. [The pelvic floor is the ring of muscle around the genitals and anus which you tighten in 'Kegel exercises'.]

7:19   Ask them to **tighten** and **hold the pelvic floor. Oserve abdomen and pelvic for surrounding tension. Communicate what you see.** Ask the worker to **tighten and to let go of the pelvic floor without visibly tightening abdomen or buttocks.**

7:20   Ask the worker to **breathe out fully and just before the end of the out-breath, tighten the pelvic floor. Hold** this for a few seconds each time until the end of the breath, then **release it, breathing in.** Continue for several minutes.

A note on the orgasm reflex:

If you are emotionally and physically open to pulsation, when you emphasise the OUT- breath – continuing it to the very end, making an open sound in the position described where you are able to let the small of your back sink into the mat and your pelvis tilt upward – you will feel an involuntary reflexive folding of your body. In this, there is a tugging from inside your pelvis in an involuntary contraction of the deep quadratus lumbar muscles. Your head falls back and your throat comes up at the same time as your pelvis – as if the two ends of your trunk are trying to meet. This is the 'orgasm reflex'.

It is not accompanied by an orgasm, although you may recognize it as part of what you experience during orgasm. It is similar to the whole body convulsion that occurs in vomiting (although it is not accompanied by vomiting), or in deep sobbing. It is a reflexive whole body pulsation. You may find it provokes anxiety, since it is powerful and involuntary, and it is a 'letting go' which the Elizabethans called 'the little death'.

But it is characteristic of life, not death. It can be seen as a woman in child-birth allows the baby to be born on an outbreath. When you experience it with your sexual partner, two pulsations become one.

The above explorations may in themselves release various emotions and feelings of anxiety or of pleasure. If these spill over into the relationship with the partner after the exploration, then well and good. More likely they will help future emotions come out more easily, and with more contact. It may be useful to re-read chapter 7, on orgasm and orgasm anxiety, to make the connections between these explorations and human pulsation and its blocks.

BIBLIOGRAPHY

Akasofu, S.I., 1981. 'The Aurora'. *American Scientist,* 69, 5.

Ambrosi, J., 1979. L'Analyse Pyschoenergetique, Retz, Paris

Bak, P., 1996. How Nature Works. Springer.

Baker, J.W. & Allen, G.E., 1975. Matter, Energy and Life. Addison & Wesley, New York.

Barbour, J.B., 2000. The End of Time. OUP, New York, London.

    2001. The Discovery of Dynamics. OUP, New York.

    2010 with Niall O'Murchadha. 'Conformal Superspace'.

Proceedings of the Royal Society A382, London.

Ben Zui, L, 1980. 'Samuel Beckett, Fritz Mauthner, and the Limits of Language. PMLA, vol.95, no.2, New York.

Bergson, H., 1959. Oeuvres. (Works). Presses Universitaires de France. Paris.

Brody, S., 2010. 'The Relative Health Benefits of Different Sexual Activities', Journal of Sexual Medicine, 7. London

Brooks, Michael, 2013. 'Quantum Weirdness'. *The New Scientist* 2928, 3 August. London

Buck, C.D., 1949. A Dictionary of Selected Synonyms in the Principal Indo-European Languages. University of Chicago Press.

Burr, H.S., 1972. Blueprint for Immortality. Spearman, London.

Buvat, R., 1969. Plant Cells. World University Library, New York.

Capra, F., 1975. The Tao of Physics. Random House, New York

Chamberlain, J.W., 1961. Physics of the Aurora and Airglow. Academic Press, New York.

Chargaff, E., 1978. Heraclitean Fire. Rockefeller University Press, New York.

Correia, P.N. and Correia, A.N, 2010. Wilhelm Reich's Claim of the Heterogenesis of Eukryotic Amoebae. *J Biophys Hematol Oncol,* 1, 1: 1-17.

Corrington, R.S., 2003. Wilhelm Reich, Psychoanalyst and Medical Naturalist, FSG, New York.

Cozolino, L., 2002. The Neuroscience of Psychotherapy. Norton, New York.

Cytowic, R., 1996.   The Neurological Side of Neuropsychology. MIT Press, Cambridge, Mass.

Damasio, A., 2000. The Feeling of What Happens. Vintage Books, New York.

Davies, J., 2013. Cracked. Why Psychiatry is Doing More Harm than Good. Icon, London.

DeMeo, J., 1999. The Orgone Accumulator Handbook. Natural Energy Workshop, Ashland, Oregon.

2011. Water as a Resonant Medium of Unusual External Environmental Factors, *Water Journal.org,* Vol.a

Dick, S.J. & Strick, J. 2004. The Living Universe – NASA and the Development of Astrobiology. Rutgers University Press, New Brunswick, NJ.

Dixon, B., Microbe of the Month, in *The Independent,* 15 October 2013, London.

Ferenczi, S., 1968. Thalassa. Norton, New York.

Fisher, S., 1973. The Female Orgasm. Basic Books, New York.

Fodor, J & Piatelli-Palmarini, M., 2010. What Darwin Got Wrong. Profile Books, London.

Grad, B., in *International Journal of Parapsychology* 3, 1961; 5, 1963; 6, 1964.
in *Journal of the American Society for Psychic Research 59,* 1965; *61,* 1967.

Gregory, R.L., 1973. Eye and Brain. OUP, London

Grote, M., 2011. Jeewanu, or the 'particles of life'. Journal of Biosciences, Bangalore, India.

Haldane, S., 1977. Human Pulsation, PhD dissertation, Saybrook Institute, San Francisco.

1984. Emotional First Aid. Station Hill Press, New York.

2004. Uma abordagem relacional para a psicoterapia neurodinamica, in Revista Reichiana, n.13. Rio de Janeiro.

2011. with José Ignacio Tavares Xavier, Transtornos de Personalidade na Psicoterapia Corporal, in Intercambio das Psicoterapias. Roca. Rio de Janeiro.

2013. Time / No Time. Parmenides Books, Cork.

Hall, T., 1969. Ideas of Life and Matter. Chicago and London.

Harvey, W., 197- (orig. 160-). The Circulation of the Blood (De Motu Sangui), trans.

Hobson, J. Allen., 2001. Out of its Mind: Psychiatry in Crisis. Basic Books, NewYork

Internet Encyclopedia of Physics, 2006

Jacob, F., 1973. The Logic of Living Systems. Allen Lane, London.

Jezzard, P., Matthews, P.M., Smith, S.M. Functional Magnetic Resonance Imaging: An Introduction to Methods. Oxford University Press, 2001.

Jones, P., 2013. Artificers of Fraud. The Origin of Life and Scientific Deception. Orgonomy, UK. Preston.

Kammerer, P., 1919. Das Gesetz der Serie. Deutsche Verlags-Anstalt, Berlin.

Kammerer, P., 1922. Allgemeine Biologie. Berlin.

Kaplan-Solms, K & Solms, M – *Clinical Studies in Neuropsychoanalysis*, London, Karnac, 2000

Kok, B & Frederickson, B., 2010. Upward Spirals of the Heart. *Biological Psychology*, 85 (3)

Kilner, W.J., 1911. The Human Atmosphere. London.

Kraus, F., 1926. Allgemeine und Spezielle Pathologie der Person. Leipzig.

Krippner, S & Rubin, D., 1974. The Kirlian Aura. Anchor/Doubleday, New York.

La Mettrie, O., 1960. Man the Machine, ed. Vartanian. Princeton, N.J.

Luce, G.G., 1971. Biological Rhythms in Human and Animal Physiology. Dover,

Luria, A. 1967. The Working Brain. Penguin Books, London.

1925. 'Psychoanalysis as a System of Monistic Psychology'. Moscow.

Manwell, R.T., 1968. Introduction to Protozoology. Dover, New York.

McCormac, B. (ed.) Aurora and Airglow. Reinhold, 1967.

Medawar, P., 1967. The Art of the Soluble. Methuen, London.

Monod, J., 1970. Le Hazard et La Nécessité (Chance and Necessity). Ed. Seuil, Paris.

Moss, T., 1979. The Body Electric. Tarcher, Los Angeles.

New York

Panksepp, J., 1998. Affective Neuroscience. OUP, New York and London.

2002. Biological Psychiatry. Wiley, Chichester.

Pert, C., 1997. The Molecules of Emotion. Touchstone, New York.

Pierrakos, J., 1971. The Energy Field in Man and Nature. New York.

Pribram, K., 1991. Brain and Perception. Lawrence Erlbaum, New Jersey.

Reich, W., 1964. Cosmic Superimposition. Farrar Straus & Giroux. New York.

1960. Selected Writings. Farrar Straus & Giroux, New York.

1961. The Function of the Orgasm. Farrar Straus & Giroux, New York.

1973. Ether God and Devil. Farrar Straus & Giroux, New York.

1979. The Bions. Farrar Straus & Giroux, New York.

1987. The Bioelectrical Investigation of Sexuality and Anxiety. Farrar Straus and Giroux, New York.

1994. Beyond Psychology. Farrar Straus & Giroux, New York.

1999. American Odyssey.Farrar Straus & Giroux, New York.

2012. Where's the Truth? Farrar Straus & Giroux, New York.

Reichenbach, K von, 1977. The Mysterious Odic Force. Aquarian Press, London.

Röhricht, F., 2000. Die Koerperorientierte Psychotherapie Psychiser Stoerungen, Goettingen

Salmon, T., 2010. Schizophrenia: Who Cares? Artaxerxes Press, London

Seymour-Smith, M. 1975. Sex and Society.

Sheldrake, R., 1981. A New Science of Life. Blond & Braggs, London.

Smith, A. & Kenyon, D. Is Life Originating De Novo? (in Perspectives in Biology and Medicine, 15, 1972)

Smith, A., 'The Origin of Viruses' (in *Enzymologia*, 43, 1972)

Smolin, L., 2013. Time Reborn. Allen Lane, London

Spector, P., 2013. Identically Different. Phoenix, London.

Strick, J., 'Swimming Against the Tide – Adrianus Pijper and the Debate over Bacterial Flagellae, 1946-1956'

   2000. Sparks of Life – Darwinism and the Victorian Debates over Spontaneous Generation. Harvard University Press, Cambridge, Mass.

Thompson, D., 1942. On Growth and Form. Cambridge University Press.

Tomatis, A.A., 1963. L'Oreille et le Langage. Seuil, Paris.

Turner, Christopher., 2011 Adventures in the Orgasmotron. Farrar Straus and Giroux, NewYork.

Varenholt, F. 2013. The Neglected Sun. Stacey International, London.

Warburg, O., 1965. Nobel Lectures. Elsevier, Amsterdam.

Xavier, José Ignacio Tavares., 2004. Atencao a Si e Psicoterapia Corporal, Rio de Janeiro.